FROM SHANTIES TO SCHOOL

FROM SHANTIES TO SCHOOL

A SILENT MOVEMENT

Manimala Roy

KONARK

Konark Publishers Pvt Ltd
New Delhi • Seattle

Konark Publishers Pvt. Ltd
206, First Floor,
Peacock Lane, Shahpur Jat,
New Delhi 110 049
Phone: +91-11-41055065
e-mail: india@konarkpublishers.com
website: www.konarkpublishers.com

Konark Publishers International
8615, 13th Ave SW,
Seattle WA 98106
Phone: (415) 409-9988
e-mail: us@konarkpublishers.com

Cataloging in Publication Data--DK
Courtesy: D.K. Agencies (P) Ltd. <docinfo@dkagencies.com>

Roy, Manimala, author.
From shanties to school: a silent movement / Manimala Roy.
pages cm
Includes bibliographical references and index.
ISBN 9788194201816

1. Children of migrant laborers--Education--India--Delhi. 2. Education and state--India--Delhi. I. Title.

LCC LC5153.I42D45 2020 | DDC 371.82624 23

Edited by Padma Alva
Typeset by Saanvi Graphics, Noida
Printed and bound at Thomson Press (India) Ltd

For all those children who live in shantytowns against all odds and aspire to a better future through learning

Contents

List of Tables xi

List of Figures xvii

Acronyms xxi

1. INTRODUCTION 1

- Education and Human Development 3
- Economic Reforms in India and the New Economic Policy, 1991 8
- How Did the NEP Influence Education? 10
- Migration and Free Movement of Labour Encouraged by Economic Reforms 13
- Migration and Education 14
- Why Do People Move Within the Same Country? 16
- Need for the Study 18

2. BACKGROUND OF THE STUDY 22

- EFA: Who are 'All'? 22
- Access to Education 24
- How Economic Reforms impacted India's National Education Policy 29

- Educational Planning in Post-Reform Period 35
- Quality Concern in Education 37
- Millennium Development Goals: Can it be achieved for poor migrant children in Delhi? 39

3. DELHI – A CASE STUDY 43

- Delhi and its Vital Statistics 45
- Delhi and its Population 46
- Linguistic Division of Delhi 49
- Economics of Delhi 51
- Indices of Development 53
- Delhi's Human Development Index (HDI) 61
- Political Patronage and Media Support to Slums 62
- Role of Delhi Development Authority 62
- Industrial Policy Reforms in Delhi since 1991 63
- Post-Reform Trends in Migration and Delhi's Slum Population 64
- Out-of-School Children and Non-Formal Education 65
- How Much Ownership has been Taken by the Government in Delhi? 68
- Educational Responsibilities Shared by the Non-Governmental Organisations 72

4. FROM ANCESTRAL VILLAGE TO SHANTYTOWN 82

- Life of a Migrant Child in a Slum 82
- The Why and How of this Narrative 87
- The Terms – Their Meanings and Subtexts 88
- The Methodology 91

5. ANALYSES OF DATA 100

- From Ancestral Village to Shantytown: Why did they Migrate? 100

- Testing of Null Hypotheses 104
- Qualitative Analysis: Descriptive Statistical Analyses of Survey Questions 106
- Contribution of the NGOs 116
- Rising Enrolment and Academic Success Rate of Delhi's Migrant Children 120
- Economic Reforms Opened More Opportunities for the Skilled and Educated Migrants 147
- Fruits of Labour 158
- March from Shantytown to School – A Silent Revolution 161

6. INTERPRETING THE DATA 163

7. THE FUTURE ROADMAP 176

- Challenges of Inclusion 176
- A Dual Life 181
- The Task Ahead 182

8. CONCLUSION 185

Annexure A: Questionnaires used for the survey 189

Annexure B: Scale of educational aspiration 202

Annexure C: List of Educational NGOs in Delhi 204

Annexure D: Lists of vocational subjects offered by CBSE for 2013 and 2018-19 206

Bibliography 217

Acknowledgements 229

Index 232

List of Tables

TABLE NO.	TITLE	PAGE NO.
1.1	Per capita income for Delhi vis-à-vis India	12
1.2	Distribution of JJ Colonies with respect to landowning authorities	15
2.1	Types of schools in Delhi	25
3.1	Vital statistics of Delhi	45
3.2	Exponential annual growth rate of Delhi's population	47
3.3	Main languages spoken in Delhi	50
3.4	Development indices: Delhi vis-à-vis India	53
3.5	HDI for Delhi and migrants' states of origin	61
3.6	School connect: DISE data for Delhi	61
3.7	Countries with more than a million children out of school in 2010	66
3.8	Reduction in drop-out	67
3.9	Out-of-school children to be covered in 2011-12	69
4.1	Migrants in Delhi: Population classified by place of birth	91

TABLE NO.	TITLE	PAGE NO.
4.2	Composition of the sample	94
4.3	List of slums from where data related to migrants have been collected	95
5.1	Causes of migration	100
5.2	Occupational status of the parents of migrant children	102
5.3	Desired occupations of migrant children surveyed	103
5.4	Educational aspirations of the interviewees	104
5.5	Occupational aspirations of the interviewees	104
5.6	Estimated chi-square values	105
5.7	Desire of parents for same type of occupation for their children	106
5.8	Sharing of ambition among migrant parents and their children	108
5.9	Considerations for choosing the child's school	109
5.10	Level of education as desired by migrant parents for their children	110
5.11	Parents' opinion on part-time odd jobs for their children	111
5.12	Reasons behind the desired occupation and educational aspirations	112
5.13	Confirmation by teachers of migrants' rising aspirations	113
5.14	Bigger flow of migrant children to school in post-reform years	114

TABLE NO.	TITLE	PAGE NO.
5.15	Increased occupational aspirations of the migrants for their children (Teachers' observations)	114
5.16	Migrants' awareness of new job opportunities in post-reform era (Teachers' view)	115
5.17	List of NGOs assisting Delhi Government in running Special Training Centres for out-of-school children	119
5.18	Academic performance of the migrant children surveyed	123
5.19	Time series analysis of enrolment and success rates in Class X in government schools in Delhi	124
5.20	Slum literacy in Delhi	127
5.21	Slum vs. non-slum literacy in Delhi – A comparative analysis	128
5.22	Migrants' support for their children's education	129
5.23	Monthly average expenditure on stationery by migrant children	130
5.24	Medium of instruction in school	132
5.25	Instructions followed in class	133
5.26	Vocational courses in school	135
5.27	Teachers' observations regarding course preference by children	136
5.28	Non-conventional career choice by the migrants for their children	137

TABLE NO.	TITLE	PAGE NO.
5.29	Non-conventional areas parents would like their children to pursue	138
5.30	Reason for choosing non-conventional careers	138
5.31	Idea about the cost of pursuing a non-conventional career	138
5.32	Support received from teachers	140
5.33	Teachers' help to students	141
5.34	PTMs: Meetings of migrant parents with teachers	142
5.35	Meeting of migrant parents with Principal (as informed by migrant children)	142
5.36	Migrants' reasons for sending their children to school	143
5.37	Social gaps between migrant and non-migrant students	145
5.38	Special steps taken by schools for migrant students	146
5.39	Income of the migrant households interviewed	149
5.40	Increased work participation in post-reform Delhi	150
5.41	Migration data for Delhi	151
5.42	Job creation in Delhi after reforms	152
5.43	Distribution of employed people	153
5.44	Minimum National Floor Level Wages	154
5.45	Average daily wages in 2010 – An inter-state comparison	155

TABLE NO.	TITLE	PAGE NO.
5.46	Monthly per capita consumption expenditure for Delhi and some other states	156
5.47	Human Development Index for Delhi	157
5.48	Household possessions in Delhi slums	158
5.49	Family's benefits from the child's achievements	159
5.50	Fruits of labour if not reaped	160
7.1	Children's expectations from their school	177
7.2	Migrant children's requirement for extra help in studies	178
7.3	Sources of academic help for migrant children	179
7.4	Psychological stress for migrant children	181

List of Figures

FIGURE NO.	TITLE	PAGE NO.
3.1	Wage differentials: Delhi and other states in 2009-10	51
3.2	Census highlights for Delhi, 2011	55
3.3	Annual average growth rate of population	55
3.4	Rate of urbanisation	56
3.5	Literacy rate	56
3.6	GER: Delhi vis-à-vis India	57
3.7	Total Fertility Rate	57
3.8	Per capita consumption	58
3.9	Labour force	58
3.10	Growth in annual employment	59
3.11	Sex ratio	60
4.1	Zone wise sample for migrant children and parents	96
5.1	Causes of migration	101

FIGURE NO.	TITLE	PAGE NO.
5.2	Migrant parents' occupations	102
5.3	Do the migrants want their children to follow the same occupations as theirs?	107
5.4	Do your parents share your ambition?	108
5.5	Considerations for choosing the child's school	109
5.6	How far do you want your child to study?	110
5.7	Reasons behind the desired occupation for the migrant children	112
5.8	Teachers' observations on migrants' rising aspirations	113
5.9	More requests from migrants for admissions in post-reform periods?	114
5.10	Teachers' view: Rise in migrant children's occupational aspirations	115
5.11	Migrants' awareness of new types of jobs (Teachers' observations)	116
5.12	Academic performance of the migrant children surveyed	124
5.13	Enrolment in government schools in Delhi (Class X)	125
5.14	Pass percentage in government schools in Delhi (Class X)	126
5.15	Government vs. Public schools – A comparative result analysis for Class XII	126
5.16	Government vs. Public schools – A comparative result analysis for Class X	127

FIGURE NO.	TITLE	PAGE NO.
5.17	Slum literacy	128
5.18	Slum vs. non-slum literacy in Delhi	129
5.19	Parental support to children's education	130
5.20	Monthly expenses on stationery by migrant children	131
5.21	Medium of instruction for migrant children	132
5.22	Hello, are you with the class?	133
5.23	Course preference of students	136
5.24	Non-conventional career?	137
5.25	Support from teachers?	140
5.26	Help from teachers	141
5.27	PTMs	142
5.28	Meeting with the Principal	143
5.29	Why schooling is essential?	144
5.30	Get cooperation from school?	144
5.31	If yes, how does the school help you?	145
5.32	Any problem arising from the social gap between migrant and non-migrant children? (Teachers' responses)	146
5.33	Steps taken by schools to cater to migrant students	147
5.34	Income of the migrant households	149
5.35	Comparative wages: Delhi and other states	155
5.36	Benefits to the family	159

FIGURE NO.	TITLE	PAGE NO.
5.37	If returns of labour is nil?	160
7.1	Children's expectations from school	177
7.2	Need extra help in studies?	178
7.3	And HOW?	179
7.4	Inferiority complex or humiliation?	181

Acronyms

BRC	Block Resource Centre
CBSE	Central Board of Secondary Education
CCE	Continuous and Comprehensive Evaluation
CGDR	Centre for Global Development Research
CII	Confederation of Indian Industry
CPWD	Central Public Works Department
CRC	Cluster Resource Centre
DDA	Delhi Development Authority
DDE	Delhi Directorate of Education
DISE	District Information System for Education
DJB	Delhi Jal Board
DPEP	District Primary Education Programme
EFA	Education for All
EFAGMR	Education for All Global Monitoring Report

EWS	Economically Weaker Section
GER	Gross Enrollment Ratio
HDI	Human Development Index
HDR	Human Development Report
HOS	Head of the School
ICT	Information and Communication Technology
IER	India Education Report
IMF	International Monetary Fund
IT	Information Technology
ITC	Industrial Training Centre
ITI	Industrial Training Institute
L&DO	Land & Development Office
MCD	Municipality Corporation of Delhi
MDMS	Mid Day Meal Scheme
MHRD	Ministry of Human Resource Development
NCF	National Curriculum Framework
NCR	National Capital Region
NCRL	National Commission of Rural Labour
NCT	National Capital Territory (of Delhi)
NDMC	New Delhi Municipal Corporation
NEP	New Economic Policy
NFE	Non Formal Education
NHDR	National Human Development Report
NPE	National Policy on Education
NSS	National Sample Survey
PSUs	Public Sector Undertakings

PTM	Parent Teacher Meeting
RMSA	Rashtriya Madhyamik Shiksha Abhiyan
SSA	Sarva Shiksha Abhiyaan
SES	Selected Educational Statistics
UIS	UNESCO Institute for Statistics
UEE	Universalisation of Elementary Education
UN	United Nations
UNDP	United Nations Development Programme
UNESCO	United Nations Educational, Scientific and Cultural Organisation
UNICEF	United Nations Children's Fund

1

INTRODUCTION

A devastating famine took in its grip large parts of Bihar in 1966-67, following two successive years of drought. In the predominantly agrarian state, where repeated crop failures had left the marginalised rural segment with no choice but to move to the distant cities, the famine was the ultimate trigger. Many people, traditional farm hands or share-croppers, took the train out of the gloomy landscape of death and starvation. They went to Calcutta, Delhi and Bombay to swell the ranks of the unorganised labour, working as daily wage earners. Ram Ratan was one of them. A stout young man from the rural hinterland of Purnia, he landed in Delhi hoping the national capital would give him a little space. With the help of a few acquaintances—those who had come here from his village years ago—he met a local politician in East Delhi. Pledging his support to the councillor's party, he moved into an unauthorised slum. Though the *jhuggi-jhopdi* (JJ) cluster had people from many parts of the country, those from Bihar were clearly the dominant group. So, for Ram Ratan, it was almost like an extension of the village community he had left behind. He started earning a living by doing odd jobs—as a painter's assistant, working with a welder, pasting posters on walls, canvassing support for the councillor during municipal elections.

On a bright winter morning in 2010, I met Deepak Kumar, a well-behaved, smooth-talking 20-year-old at the approach to the slum from National Highway 24, near the Mother Dairy chilling plant. In a cheap jacket and jeans, he was talking on his cell phone. I told him about my research project to assess the aspirations of the migrant workers for education, for a better tomorrow for their children. I showed him the questionnaire I had prepared for the survey and asked if he would help me collect data from the slum. Deepak, a commerce graduate from Delhi University, an aspiring political activist, was Ram Ratan's son. He was of the age, I guessed, when his father had come to the city fleeing the spectre of famine haunting large swathes of rural Bihar.

The question of education for children from homes like Ram Ratan's, was first raised and answered by the country's first Prime Minister Jawaharlal Nehru. 'We have to build the noble mansion of free India where all her children may dwell,' Nehru said addressing the Constituent Assembly on the midnight of August 14-15, 1947.

The first Prime Minister's assurance of a just, humane and equitable social order to a nation waking up to freedom, provided an unambiguous roadmap right at the outset. As numerous government documents subsequently testified, policy planners increasingly recognised the crucial role of education in human development. More than any other interventions it is education that softens the rough edges of life for the marginalised, and raises the living standards of the underprivileged.

It is not just that a skilled or educated man earns better wages, but education changes his life in a comprehensive manner along with impacting his milieu. This transformation has a cascading effect. The process that begins with learning the three R's actually empowers the powerless and gives them total control over their lives. The silent upheaval with its epicentre in the bare primary school enables a vulnerable villager to take decisions for himself. The alphabet and a little arithmetic turn into a new avenue of self-assurance and empowerment. The learner begins to look at themselves as an individual. The yearning for illumination of the self at the touch of education has been at the core of India's civilisational journey and nothing recaptures this aspiration more succinctly than the *Mundaka Upanishad*:

> *Tameva bhanti anubhanti sarvam*
> (Everything shines only after that shining light)

Education and Human Development

The United Nations Development Programme (UNDP) coined the term Human Development Index (HDI) in 1990 with educational attainment of a country's population as one of its main components to assess the level of development of different countries better. As early as 1996 when the process of economic reforms in India was still at an incipient stage, the Human Development Report of the UNDP cautioned: 'Human development is the end—economic growth a means... the recent decades show all too clearly that there is no automatic link between growth and human development. And even when links are established, they may gradually be eroded—unless regularly fortified by skilful and intelligent policy management,' (Human Development Report [HDR], 1996).

The report also pointed out that while some 15 countries had achieved spectacular economic growth with a remarkable rise in income for most of their 1.5 billion people since 1980, during the same period, economic decline and stagnation severely affected the life of the common man in some other parts of the world. For 1.6 billion people, income actually went down (HDR, 1996). The rise and fall in incomes, and also the decline in prosperity across the world point to the overwhelming role of education in determining the economic conditions of people. It is not for nothing that education is counted among the three crucial components that together form the human development index. It is now widely acknowledged that without a high literacy rate no country can achieve affluence or an impressive and sustainable growth (HDR, 1996).

In 1993, well-known economist Jagdish Bhagwati in his book, *India in Transition – Freeing the Economy*, lamented that the planners of India had underestimated the productive role of education and health and allocated funds much less than the sectors required.

Similarly, Jean Drèze and Amartya Sen in their book, *India – Economic Development and Social Opportunity* (1995), observed that 'somehow the educational aspects of economic development have continued to be out of the main focus, and this relative neglect has persisted despite the recent radical changes in economic policy'. The book insisted that besides its intrinsic importance, education plays a vital role in a man's life enabling him to make use of economic opportunities, to acquire the power of decision making, perform his social role in a better capacity and empower him to resist oppression of any kind. 'Greater literacy and educational achievements of disadvantaged groups can increase their ability to resist oppression, to organise politically and to get a fairer deal.'

The two eminent economists argue that 'if we see economic development in the perspective of social opportunities in general, both for their intrinsic importance and for their instrumental value, we cannot afford to miss this crucial linkage'.

An interesting point to be noted here is that this new focus on the interlinking of education and economic prosperity came in the years after the government initiated economic reforms in 1991 fundamentally changing the direction and dimensions of its policy. For the first time India admitted the inadequacies of the socialist model and the big-government concept. And for the first time, market acquired a whole lot of new meaning both as an ideology and a strategy. As the subsequent parts of this book will seek to explain and establish, the economic liberalisation of 1991 reinvented education as a tool for the people on the margins of the social canvas to strive for better standards of life, and in the process, social respect and empowerment. With new capital coming into the market, suddenly there were a large number of white-collar jobs available. The migrant community which had long settled down in the outlying city slums to eke out a living as labourers or semi-skilled workers, sensed a new opportunity. With some education, they reckoned, their children could be candidates for the new jobs.

Drèze and Sen argued that the government could afford to neglect basic education denying the sector the priority it deserved primarily because the poor, silent masses did not have the requisite political clout (Drèze & Sen, 1995: p.137). As a constituency they were unorganised and therefore, unheard.

The Tenth Plan recognised the role of education, particularly primary education, in transforming society and took steps to provide free and compulsory elementary education to all children in the 6-14 age group. The Plan laid a big emphasis on Universalisation of Elementary Education (UEE) guided by five parameters: (i) Universal Access, (ii) Universal Enrollment, (iii) Universal Retention, (iv) Universal Achievement and (v) Equity. The major schemes of the elementary education sector during the Tenth Plan included Sarva Siksha Abhiyaan (SSA), District Primary Education Programme (DPEP), National Programme of Nutritional Support to Primary Education, commonly known as Mid-Day Meal Scheme (MDMS), Teacher Education Scheme, Kasturba Gandhi Balika Vidyalaya Scheme, Lok Jumbish and Shiksha Karmi (The Planning Commission, GoI, Eleventh Five Year Plan, Vol. 2. 2008: p.1).

Although the Tenth Plan saw some progress in various segments of the programme, an impressive enrolment rate did not signify much in the face of high dropout rates among the disadvantaged children particularly in classes I and II—22 per cent at the end of the Plan period (Planning Commission, GoI, Eleventh Five Year Plan, Vol. 2, 2008: p.3). It was observed that retaining the children in school was a bigger challenge than enrolling them initially. Retention was a tough task if the 'opportunity cost' for their parents in sending them to school was taken into consideration. It was not easy for the poor families to overlook the extra couple of rupees the children would fetch selling their labour. Besides, two major issues under UEE, namely quality and equity, remained almost unaddressed (Planning Commission, GoI, Eleventh Five Year Plan, Vol. 2. 2008: p.5). The target to achieve education for all by 2000, therefore, remained an illusion by the end of the Plan period. The condition of the deprived and underprivileged in rural as well as urban areas continued to be as bleak as before with a significantly large percentage of children from poor households remaining out of school and many more becoming 'nowhere children'.

National Human Development Report (NHDR), 2001 comes out with startling revelations about these children analysing the statistics contained in the 1981 census. The census data painted a depressing picture: 52.9 per cent of the children in the 5-14 age group were 'nowhere children'—they were neither enrolled in school nor were they counted as child workers due to the narrowness of the term's definition although they were found to be working either on their own or with their parents. The figure marginally decreased to 45.2% by the 1991 census (National Human Development Report [NHDR], 2001: p.95). Although SSA interventions have brought down the number of out-of-school children from 32 million in 2001-02 to 7.0 million in 2006-07, an independent study in 2005 by Social and Rural Institutes in Delhi estimated that about 6.9 per cent of the total children in the 6-13 age group were out of school, and of them 2.1 per cent accounted for dropouts and 4.8 per cent for the never-enrolled category. A bulk of them undoubtedly belonged to the poorer segments of rural society (Planning Commission, GoI, Eleventh Five Year Plan, Vol. 2, 2008: p. 4).

The Tenth Plan target and achievement analysis reflects that the Plan had an ambitious goal of putting 'all children in school by 2003' whereas in 2004-05 a huge number—0.95 crore—were still out of school. The plan for five years of schooling for all children by 2007, too, was a failure with a 29 per cent dropout rate in primary and

50.8 per cent in middle schools in 2004-05 (MHRD, GoI, Selected Educational Statistics, 2004-05).

The approach paper to the Eleventh Five Year Plan stressed the importance of education in empowering the deprived, socially disadvantaged and economically marginalised. The document recommended that six per cent of the GDP be spent on education (Approach Paper to Eleventh Five Year Plan). Consequently, the Eleventh Plan decided to put a big focus on 'inclusive growth' for all programmes and recognised the crucial role of education to achieve this.

The role of education is important in facilitating social and economic progress. It opens up opportunities for individuals as well as social groups. 'Education, in its broadest sense of development of youth, is the most crucial input for empowering people with skills and knowledge and giving them access to productive employment in future. Improvements in education are not only expected to enhance efficiency but also improve the overall quality of life. The Eleventh Plan places the highest priority on education as a central instrument for achieving rapid and inclusive growth' (Planning Commission, GoI, Eleventh Five Year Plan, Vol.1, 2008: p. 1).

Primarily concerned with the economy and infrastructure, the World Bank began to shift its focus in the 1970s for the first time from developing physical capital to human capital. Admitting that education and economic growth are intertwined, the World Bank started diversifying its priority promoting the literacy campaign.

Addressing the Commonwealth education conference at Edinburgh in 2003, the Nobel Laureate Amartya Sen said, 'H. G. Wells was not exaggerating when he said in his *Outline of History*: 'Human history becomes more and more a race between education and catastrophe.' If we continue to leave vast sections of the people of the world outside the orbit of education, we make the world not only less just, but also less secure' (Sen, 2003).

He dwelled on the theme of human insecurity manifested by the 9/11 tragedy and argued that 'widening the coverage and effectiveness of basic education can have a powerfully preventive role in reducing human insecurity of nearly every kind.'

He referred to the studies conducted by the Pratichi Trust—set up with his Nobel Prize money in India and Bangladesh—pointing out that the most deprived people have an aspiration to give their children basic education. 'The first and most immediate contribution of successful school education is a direct reduction of this basic deprivation which continues to ruin the lives of a large part of the global population' (Sen, 2008).

The National Human Development Report, 2001 saw development as a process that widens an individual's choices in society. 'Education, in the context of such an approach, has a critical dimension of building an individual's capability and ultimately his/her well-being' (NHDR, 2001: p. 95).

Economic Reforms in India and the New Economic Policy, 1991

The economic reforms introduced in India in 1991 was perhaps the most radical policy shift effected by the government marking a serious departure from the direction of a controlled economy lorded over by an oversized and unwieldy public sector. *The Economist* likened the momentous decision to the daring act of 'unleashing the caged tiger'.

The trend the world over was to open up and reduce control over the private sector. The dismal growth rate of the domestic economy controlled by the government through the instrument of a notorious 'license-permit raj', huge deficit financing pushing the inflation rate to double digits and dwindling foreign exchange reserves that could support only a few weeks' imports, left the government with no option other than opening up. In one stroke it brought about structural changes to tide over the immediate crises and boost growth in the long run. Piloted by Dr Manmohan Singh, a distinguished economist holding the finance portfolio in the government, the New Economic Policy (NEP) was tabled in Parliament on 24 July 1991 leading the country towards the path of liberalisation, privatisation, and globalisation (Economic Survey, 1991-92, pp. 80-82). Abolition of the license regime for setting up a new business venture (except for strategic and environmentally hazardous industries), reducing the number of PSUs through disinvestment (keeping only five strategic areas under government control), modification of the MRTP Act and allowing a higher share of equity to foreigners for investing in India put the country immediately on a high growth path (Budget Documents, 1991; Economic Survey, 1991-92).

Revisiting the historical moment after 20 years, *The Economist* in its July 21, 2011 issue commented:

> On July 24, 1991 Manmohan Singh, then India's finance minister, presented a budget to India's parliament that would change his country and the world. It was an unlikely triumph wrested from a moment of national humiliation. Thanks to political turmoil, high oil prices and fiscal profligacy, India was left with barely enough foreign exchange to last a fortnight. Like an indigent household pawning the family jewels, its central bank was forced to airlift 47 tonnes of gold to the Bank of England as collateral for a loan, while it waited for more help from the IMF.
>
> In that fraught summer, Mr. Singh devalued the rupee, abolished most of the quotas and licences that dictated who could produce what, and opened some industries to foreign capital. His reforms ripped pages out of the Red Book of regulations with which customs inspectors tormented Indian businessmen.
>
> (*The Economist*, July 21, 2011)

The freeing of the entrepreneurial impulses of the Indian industry and infusion of competition ending monopolies in key sectors had a profound impact on the country. For the perennially sluggish economy it was the magic moment.

The country's trajectory of growth registered an unusual movement—from a conservative *Hindu growth rate* of less than four per cent to one of the highest in the world. India which in the sixties evoked images of backwardness such as bullock carts and famished villages in the Western imagination (Myrdal, Gunnar, 1968) today is recognised as a major IT power (Friedman, Thomas, 2005).

The foreign exchange reserves swelled so remarkably within a year that the country could repay the IMF loan ahead of schedule, and the economists started worrying about the crisis of plenty and cautioned the government to manage the foreign exchange funds intelligently which otherwise might lead to domestic price rise.

Growth led to employment. Incomes rose faster for poorer households than ever before. Augmented production and import brought prices of commodities down and the next decade was the success story of India. Global recession in the late 1990s could not affect the one-billion strong nation in any significant way; rather consumers were happy to get more goods at cheaper prices and allowing them to realise their dreams of a holiday abroad. In fact, experts at one point cautioned against *overheating* of the economy.

The phenomenal growth has created more job opportunities and a huge demand for skilled workers.

How did the NEP Influence Education?

There is no automatic link between the two, HDR cautions all the countries (HDR, 1996). Did the Government of India take adequate steps to train and develop its human capital? Was the government conscious enough to allocate sufficient funds to spread education among the masses, particularly the disadvantaged children like those of the migrant workers? Did it consider more allocations for training and skill development of the future workforce of the country, of people who started moving out of their villages chasing the new jobs in the big cities?

Realising the need for trained and skilled workforce in 2001-02 the government introduced Sarva Shiksha Abhiyan (SSA) to provide free and compulsory quality education to all children in the 6-14 age group. The budget allocation to education rose from 7.68 per cent in the Tenth Plan to 19.29 per cent in the Eleventh Plan (Eleventh Five Year Plan Document). The budget allocation for education increased by 18 per cent for the year 2012-13. Out of ₹61,427 crore allocated for the education sector, 22 per cent would go to SSA and 29 per cent to RMSA. A Credit Guarantee Fund has been proposed to boost skill development for the young people (retrieved from http://www.indiaeducationreview.com). But various statistics so far reveal poor implementation of policies in the field of education, particularly elementary education, even two decades after the reforms began.

However, an interesting aspect of the impact made by India's New Economic Policy (Bhalla, Surjeet S., 2000) on school education has so far gone almost unnoticed by the social scientists. For the first time the relatively better-off among the marginalised in urban areas have begun to see education as a vehicle to ride to new opportunities, a key to access higher-paying jobs. This trend is quite strong in the capital city of Delhi. Those segments among the slum-dwellers which have risen above the grim struggle to meet the basic needs, now aspire to give their children better education—more than the ability to sign one's name and count the wages (retrieved from http://www.chintan-india.org).

Unnoticed by any major survey or study, this significant social trend can be traced to the rise in wages for the skilled and semi-skilled workers in the years following economic liberalisation of 1991. A comparison of per capita income between 1991 and 2010 shows a rising trend for Delhi. Just as Delhi's per capita income is higher than the national average so too is its minimum wage levels (retrieved from www.paycheck.in). The national floor-level minimum wage was ₹100 in 2010 raised from ₹80 in 2007 (it was ₹35 in 1996, ₹45 in 1999). The minimum daily wage in Delhi in 2010 was more than double the national average—₹203 for unskilled, ₹225 for semi-skilled and ₹248 for skilled workers.

Table 1.1
Per Capita Income for Delhi vis-à-vis India

Year	Per Capita Income (at constant 1980-81 prices) (₹)	
	Delhi	India
1991-92	5,972	2,213
1997-98	6,478	2,840
	Per Capita Income at current prices (₹)	
1999-2000	38,682	15,839
2000-2001	41,436	16,648
2005-2006	61,676	25,716

Source: Economic Survey 2007-08, p. A-13 & National Human Development Report (NHDR), 2001, p. 146. Data compiled by the author.

Globalisation, an important element of the NEP, in the Indian context has meant greater integration of the country's economy with that of the world, doing away with government control and heralding large-scale entry of foreign capital and technology into the domestic market. This economic process has impacted the social landscape ushering in new values. After fulfilling the basic needs of life, people become more aspirational, wanting better health care facilities and education for their children. With a significant rise in wages, even those without proper education have now ambition for their children. As a result, there is pressure on schools to admit the first-generation literates (Right to Education Bill, No. LXV, 2008, GoI, as cited in the *Financial Express*, 1 November 2008).

The marginalised, migrant communities living on the fringes of the cities are now willing to spend a significant part of their earnings on their children's schooling. A pilot study showed that such people living either in slums or rural clusters within the city boundaries, themselves barely educated, often put their children in English-medium public schools (*Deepalaya News*, Vol. xvii, retrieved from www.deepalaya.org on 8 September 2011). Without any support from the state, major social, political or religious organisations, such communities have seen education as an investment in the future.

Migration and Free Movement of Labour Encouraged by Economic Reforms

Opening up of the economy encouraged movement of labour. Even before 1991 the flow of workers from rural or semi-urban areas to the major cities and industrial towns was a common feature. But expansion of industries and job opportunities combined with an improved and faster mode of transport and communications, resulting from the economic reforms of the 1990s and new technological breakthroughs, gave a big push to the movement of labour predominantly from the rural hinterland to the urban sprawls. The trend of rural-urban migration got stronger in the post-reform years with the new jobs beckoning the landless and marginalised farmers to the big cities.

The 2001 census brought home the truth that India's population would continue to grow without any sign of decline for the first half of the twenty-first century triggering stronger trends of urbanisation. The cities which have attracted greater capital investment and become the epicentres of growth offering economic opportunities and diverse employment possibilities, attract migrant workers from the other parts of the country (Census of India, 2001). Despite efforts at the state level to resist the inflow, the rural poor have continued to arrive at the big cities to eke out a living. This has strained the facilities and infrastructure of a city on the one hand and on the other, pushed the poor rural migrants to the outskirts giving rise to slums and informal settlements.

Migration and Education

Earlier only the head of a household or the male wage earner of a family would take the night train out of the distressed countryside for the big city. Other family members would have stayed behind and received money orders. But the recent studies point to a change in the migration patterns. The trend over the years has been of entire households relocating to the cities and settling in shantytowns. This has raised the question of education for young children of the migrant families.

Interestingly, a large number of women, particularly from Uttar Pradesh and Bihar, have migrated to the capital city on their own. In fact, a recent study by ASSOCHAM, one of the apex trade associations, has found that 70 per cent of migrant women in Delhi hail from these two states (*The Hindu*, 17 December 2010). The majority of migrant women work in unorganised sectors, particularly as domestic helps. This might have been one reason for heightened educational aspirations for their children. As housemaids they come in regular contact with the educated urban women working as professionals, their outlook towards life in general and children's education in particular get very much influenced by them.

This study concentrated on migrants in and around Delhi existing at the subsistence level with an annual income of less than ₹1 lakh. Officially this community has been defined as the economically weaker section (EWS). Most of them live on the fringes of the city, in slums or JJ clusters. Some of these slums and clusters are recognised by the authorities but many remain unauthorised. According to the Delhi Urban Shelter Improvement Board, the capital city has 685 JJ clusters or colonies with 4,18,282 *jhuggis*, covering 70,00,562 square metres of area (retrieved from www.delhishelterboard.in). The distribution of these *jhuggis* with respect to landowning authorities tells an interesting tale.

Table 1.2
Distribution of JJ Colonies with respect to Landowning Authorities

Landowning authority	Number of *Jhuggi Jhopdi* clusters
Delhi Jal Board (DJB)	3
DUSIB	99
DDA	352
CPWD	19
MCD	58
NDMC	8
L & DO	27
Cantonment Board	11
Flood Control	12
Agricultural Institute	1
Total	685

Source: www.delhishelterboard.in, compiled by the author

The slum population in Delhi in 2001 was 1.85 million which rose to 2.15 million in 2011 (retrieved from http://planningcommission.nic.in/reports/sereport/ser/ser_slum.pdf). A Report on Access and Opening of Schools in Delhi on the SSA website claims that in October 2011 out of 1812 total habitations in Delhi, 1810 have schooling facilities (retrieved from www.edudel.nic.in). It also mentions that Delhi was ranked first in the country by NUEPA with respect to availability and infrastructural facilities for the universal access programme under UEE up to the upper primary level (retrieved from www.edudel.nic.in).

Given the greater accessibility to school, the author found that in the post-reform period there was a marked appreciation in the attitude of the migrant community to the issue of quality education for their children. Earlier they would either take their children along to work with them or send them to work elsewhere. The older ones, particularly the girls, would have been left at home to look after the younger siblings. But empirical observations revealed an opposite trend in the recent years, and an in-depth analysis found an interesting correlation between availability of jobs in the post-reform era and educational aspirations of migrants. They have realised that education will open up new avenues of white-collar jobs for their children and raise their income levels. A study conducted by the Centre for Global Development Research (CGDR) commissioned by the Planning Commission, corroborated this trend. It found that 'about 91 per cent of the estimated households responded in the positive when asked about the value of education in terms of prospect for employment'.

It is significant that in their responses the migrants unknowingly confirmed the outcome of a major survey conducted by the UNDP and published in the HDR, 2009 which concluded that 'most migrants, internal and international, reap gains in the form of higher incomes, better access to education and health, and improved prospects for their children. Surveys of migrants report that most are happy in their destination, despite the range of adjustments and obstacles typically involved in moving' (HDR, 2009: p. 2). Unaware of the study carried out at the global level, the uprooted people in the shanties of Delhi corroborated its findings through their own experiences and gut feelings.

Why Do People Move Within the Same Country?

Like Ram Ratan, thousands of people leave their villages for the cities every day for work and opportunities. The question is: Who can be identified as a migrant? Anyone who permanently moves out of his place of origin and settles in another location? Should we include the seasonal migrants travelling in search of work for a few months in a year and returning to their places of origin at the end of the working season? What should be the duration of such an outing as to qualify for the seasonal migrant's definition? Should the children of a migrant born in another place be called a migrant?

The term 'migrant' covers a wide spectrum of people. The migrant, whether international or internal, is one individual or household that permanently moves out of his place of origin and settles down in another place. There are instances of seasonal migration among farm workers. They relocate to other places in lean periods only to move back to their villages for the busy seasons of sowing and harvesting. This study will solely concentrate on the educational aspirations of the poor internal migrant population in and around Delhi.

HDR 2009 came out with a study about the impact of migration on human development. It observed that the number of people moving internally from one part of the country to another is much larger than the movement across international borders. It also pointed out that contrary to the notion of an overwhelming majority of migrant footfalls in the direction of the developed world from the developing countries, actually a significantly large number of people move within the arc of the developing countries. To answer 'How and why people move' the HDR stated, 'Discussions about migration typically start from the perspective of flows from developing countries into the rich countries of Europe, North America and Australasia. Yet most movement in the world does not take place between the developing and developed countries; it does not even take place between countries. The overwhelming majority of people who move do so inside their own country' (HDR, 2009: pp. 1-2).

It is estimated that approximately 740 million people are internal migrants—almost four times as many as those who have moved internationally (HDR, 2009: pp. 1-2).

The phenomenon of migration can be explained in terms of factors like demand pull and supply push. On the demand side, more and better paying jobs created by the expansion of the private sector after economic liberalisation can be identified as the most significant factor contributing to migration. The communications revolution has removed the imperfection of the labour market, and combined with easy transport, reduced the barriers to movement from one place to another. On the supply side we find a surplus work force in the less developed states or areas who want to try their luck in a big city.

Need for the study

The open economy boosted the job market by creating new and diverse openings. Education and training for the masses no longer remained confined to the paradigm of social responsibility of the government but created a demand-driven pull for itself. Education, thus demanded by the people, has come out of the control of the government and decentralisation has taken place automatically with participation of a large number of private schools and NGOs on the supply side. Market has acted on its own and the invisible hands of demand and supply started working in the field of education for the poor as well. This startling development, however, has received practically no attention so far.

The trend visible to a keen observer in the preliminary survey was interesting enough for a deeper and closer examination of the issue. Initially average students from the lower middle-class homes opted out of studies after completing the Class XII Board examination to take up a job at a McDonald's outlet or with a cell-phone service provider. For those with a better ability to communicate in English joining a call centre seemed to be a natural choice.

But the survey conducted for this book has revealed that those migrants from rural areas who work as auto-rickshaw drivers, mechanics, painters, masons or vegetable vendors, now are keen to send their children to school so that in a few years they, too, can eye such higher-paying, seemingly more respectable jobs. Very often schools are approached by such people for admission of their children. With a little money to spare, the more ambitious among them succeed in putting their children in the so-called public schools despite the inevitable culture clash over their ability to speak English.

Besides, the post-reform, economically liberalised economy of India has begun to erase the cultural barrier between the socially advantaged and the historically deprived as far as school education is concerned. For the first time there is a tangible incentive for the marginalised to look at education as an important tool to change their economic situation (*Deepalaya News*, Vol. XVII). And English has become the language of aspiration. In an interaction at a book event with Justice Leila Seth, the first woman Chief Justice of a High Court, the issue came under sharp focus. She illustrated the point with the story of her chauffeur. The man took his son out of a government school where education was free and put him in a public school and started paying his fees. When questioned by Justice Seth, he candidly talked about his ambition. If the child studied in a Hindi-medium government school, he feared, the boy would grow up to become a driver like him. 'If the boy goes to a public school, who knows, maybe one day he will be a judge like you, madam,' the simple man said about his parental dream (Seth, Leila, personal communication, 24 April 2011).

This was the common refrain of the poor migrants living in slums. They want their children to do better, landing white-collar jobs and earning more. And they aspire for a better life for their sons and daughters. They are willing to work harder, earn more to support their children's education. And 'English', as Justice Seth succinctly pointed out, 'has become the language of aspiration'.

How the New Economic Policy, with the entry of the multinational companies (MNCs), big brands, their retail chains, call centres, cell-phone networks and the Internet has raised the aspiration levels of the community of migrant workers in the soft underbelly of a metropolis, was an engrossing subject for research. Though primarily conducted from the viewpoint of Education this study will surely have implications for the disciplines of Economics and Social Sciences. Of the many shades and levels of migration, this inquiry leaves out the high-end movement of professionals from one city to another and entirely focuses on the rural-urban migration of the marginalised.

Delhi has been chosen as the area of study and inquiry, for the city has attracted migrant crowds from different parts of the country and even from outside its borders—Nepal and Bangladesh. The picture here has all the elements that are pertinent to the study. This interesting socio-economic trend is distinctly visible in all its manifestations in the national capital making it an obvious choice for a study of the migrant community's aspirations for education and through it higher standards of living in the post-reform period when the New Economic Policy of Liberalisation, Privatisation and Globalisation was adopted by the Indian government to bring about a structural change and consequently, push the economy into a higher trajectory of growth.

References

- Bhagwati, Jagdish. *India in Transition: Freeing the Economy*, p. 36. Oxford: Claredon Press, 1993.
- Bhalla, Surjit S., ed. *New Economic Policies for a New India*. New Delhi: Har-Anand Publications, 2000.
- Census of India, 2001. New Delhi: GoI, 2000
- Deepalaya News, Vol. XVII. Delhi: Deepalaya Human Resource Centre.
- Drèze, Jean and Amartya Sen. *India: Economic Development and Social Opportunity*, Ch. 2, pp. 13-16, 137. New Delhi: Oxford University Press, 1995.
- Economic Survey 1989-90, 1991-92.
- Friedman, Thomas. *The World Is Flat*. USA: Farrar, Straus & Giroux, 2005.
- GOI (2008). 'Right to Education Bill (Bill No. LXV, 2008).' As cited in the *Financial Express*, 1 November 2008.
- Government of India. National Human Development Report, 2001, p. 95. New Delhi: OUP, 2001.
- http://planningcommission.nic.in/reports/sereport/ser/ser_slum.pdf

- http://www.chintan-india.org
- http://www.indiaeducationreview.com
- Ministry of Finance, GoI (1991). 'Budget document, 1991.' Delhi: GoI.
- Ministry of Human Resource Development, Government of India (2004–05). 'Selected Educational Statistics.' New Delhi: GoI.
- Myrdal, Gunnar. *Asian Drama – An Inquiry into the Poverty of Nations*. New York: Pantheon Books, 1968.
- Planning Commission, Government of India (2008). 'Eleventh Five Year Plan, 2007-2012, Social Sector' (Vol. II, pp. 1-5). New Delhi: Planning Commission.
- Planning Commission, Government of India. 'Approach paper to Eleventh Five Year Plan.' New Delhi: OUP.
- *The Economist*, 21 July 2011.
- UNDP. Human Development Report. New Delhi: Oxford University Press, 1996.
- UNDP. HDR, 2009, pp. 1-2. New Delhi: OUP, 2009.
- www.deepalaya.org
- www.delhishelterboard.in
- www.edudel.nic.in
- www.ncrpb.nic.in
- www.paycheck.in

2

BACKGROUND OF THE STUDY

EFA: Who are 'All'?

More than half a century ago, the UNESCO at its eleventh General Conference adopted a Convention against discrimination in education. Held on 14 December 1960, the meet, attended by the representatives of the member States, seen in perspective, was a turning point in the movement for spreading education across all social strata. Recalling the declaration of Human Rights by the UN on 10 December 1948 which 'asserts the principle of non-discrimination and proclaims that every person has the right to education' (UNESCO, The State of the World's Children, 2000), the gathering suggested that the Convention they had adopted be of equal import.

The convention considered discrimination in education a violation of those rights (UNESCO, Convention Agenda paper, 2003: p.3). Regrettably, more than 50 years after the adoption of that policy and active supervision of the UNESCO, almost 130 million children of the world are still out of school. Almost two decades into the twenty-first century, still the unschooled children have a unique status—either they have never enrolled or dropped out (UNESCO, The State of the World's Children, 2000). India, a country of more than a billion people, has the largest share of those children. The World Bank reports indicate that in 1998 India had 35 million children in the school-going age who were out of school whereas it was only 1.4 million for China (www.unesco.org visited on 4 June 2012). The figure was 32 million in 2001-02. Although it had come down significantly, still 7 million children in the 6-14 age group in India were out of school in 2006-07 (World Bank, World Development Indicators, retrieved from www.data.worldbank.org & Eleventh Plan, Volume II, p.2). When we consider the children from poor migrant households living in the slums of the metro cities, the gap in educational achievements of children in India appears all the more glaring.

The marginalised population from villages and small towns migrate to the large cities in search of a better life—jobs, more income, education for children and a higher standard of living. Eventually they land up in festering slums and JJ colonies as a decent home in a big city remains unaffordable for them. A study conducted in 2009 revealed that about 500,000 people every year migrate to Delhi from the other states seeking a better life, employment and education for their children (Chauhan, Chetan, 2009 as cited in the *Hindustan Times*,19 March 2011. Retrieved from www.OneWorld.net).

Delhi, the capital of India, has the second largest slum population, preceded only by Mumbai. An estimated 1.9 million people in Delhi lived in slums in 2001 (Census of India, 2001). A news report on *Zee News*, a popular television channel, mentioned that 52 per cent of Delhi lives in slums (www.zeenews.india.com on 17 December 2009). However, the census data for 2011 mentions 24 per cent of population of Delhi living in slums. Although on the periphery of the national capital, the migrants somehow manage to get one or the other job raising the level of their income and living standards. However, for them survival remains difficult. The first-generation migrants are those who themselves left their place of birth to settle at another place. In the 1990s, the existence of a large number of second-generation migrants, born and brought up in the city itself, lent a new layer to the migration picture. Their parents had mostly migrated from Bihar, Uttar Pradesh, Orissa and West Bengal and settled down in the slums of Delhi about 10-15 years ago.

Migrant children, whether global or internal, face high academic challenges. The survey conducted by Samajik Suvidha Sangam Society under the aegis of the Delhi Government in 2008-09, pointed out that in Delhi, a city with 1.38 lakh millionaires, the stark rich-poor divide is alarming. Out of 25 lakh slum-dwellers surveyed by the organisation, 2.48 lakh children did not go to school. That makes Delhi's Gross Enrolment Ratio (GER) 71 per cent as against the national average of 94.5 per cent. The survey found out that among all the major cities Delhi had the highest level of slum illiteracy (25.4 per cent). Amod Kant, a well-known retired Police Commissioner, who was the Chairperson of the Delhi Commission of Protection of Child Rights, pointed out the failure of the state in providing alternative education to the out-of-school children, particularly the ones living in slums (*Hindustan Times*, 15 January 2009).

But a parallel trend is also visible. While collecting primary data, the author observed an interesting development. For well over a decade now the migrant community has reappraised their attitude towards education. The slum-dwellers no longer send their children to work to earn a little extra for the family kitty. Asked about their plans for the children, each respondent talked about their ambition of sending them to school. 'I don't want my children to live my life; they should do better,' was the refrain in the rabbit warrens along the slum clusters. The migrants stuck in lowly-paid jobs, had high hopes for their children. They saw education as the vehicle to ride on to a better future.

Access to Education

Delhi has over 5000 schools catering to various segments of its population. The state government has covered the migrant pupils under the Universalisation of Elementary Education (UEE) programme and accommodate the children from the disadvantaged homes in its primary, middle, secondary and senior secondary schools. Though there has been no special government drive to do anything in particular for the migrant population, their children have benefited from subsidised education. The strategy behind the Sarva Shiksha Abhiyan (SSA) is to accommodate the marginalised urban children, but not specifically the migrants in the slums. The term 'Focus on Special Groups' in SSA literatures insists that 'there will be a focus on the inclusion and participation of children from the SC/ST, minority groups, urban deprived children, disadvantaged groups and the children with special needs, in the educational process' (SSA documents retrieved from www.edudel.nic.in), but it says nothing specific about the migrant children.

Table 2.1
Types of Schools in Delhi

Types of school	No. of schools
Govt. schools	937
MCD schools	1780
NDMC schools	77
Govt. aided schools	214
MCD aided schools	44
Public unaided schools recognised by Directorate of Education	1240
Public unaided schools recognised by MCD	770
Kendriya Vidyalayas	41
DCB schools	6
Total	5109
ECCE centres	300
CRC centres	136
Jawahar Navodaya Vidyalayas	2
NDMC aided schools	3
NDMC recognised unaided schools	4

Source: www.edudel.nic.in, the official website of the Delhi Directorate of Education and compiled by the author.

In the Eleventh Plan, the SSA has eventually added a special dimension to its endeavours by introducing NPEGEL for covering the education of slum children which is a component of its drive to take care of out-of-school children in urban areas and improve the status of SSA in 35 cities with population over one million (SSA and Girls Education for the Eleventh Plan—Working Committee Report: p. 57).

It is natural for the migrants living in the city slums to send their children to government schools where education is completely free. But the post-reform era has seen a paradigm shift in their approach to schooling of their children. They now prefer private schools, where they have to pay tuition fees, to free education in government schools. They, too, are aware that the standards of the government schools are quite low. Absentee teachers, inadequate infrastructure, poor facilities and lack of accountability on the part of the administration were the main reasons for the substandard quality of education in government schools. In fact, 'Elementary Education in India: Analytical Report, 2004-05' (Mehta, Arun C., NUEPA, 2004-05) mentioned a decline in enrolment in primary schools in 236 districts run by the state governments as a possible reason for the transfer of students from the government to private schools.

In order to reap the benefits of schooling, the poor migrants now want to send their children to English medium private schools, which they feel, maintain higher standards. They cannot afford the reputed public schools although the Delhi government had directed all recognised, private unaided schools in the capital to reserve 15 per cent of seats for the economically weaker sections (EWS). This quota was revised upward to 25 per cent from 2010-11 onward. A report on the website of the Delhi Directorate of Education shows that only 7,797 EWS children got enrolled in 394 private unaided English medium schools against the available reserved seats of 48,304 in 2009-10. Reservations for such disadvantaged children in all schools remained only on papers. The reputed public schools were reluctant to enroll children from the slums anticipating a culture clash between them and those from middle-class homes. They were also apprehensive of emotional issues to be accentuated with the entry of the slum children. They themselves were likely to undergo psychological trauma and create a distressing situation for others when they mix up with the children from educated, well-off homes. Many reputed public schools in Delhi ran a separate wing in the evening using their existing infrastructure exclusively for the children from nearby slums and poor households and gradually integrated them into the school mainstream. In fact, this system worked better in providing training and education to the disadvantaged children.

On the other hand, a large number of middle-level, un-recognised English medium schools mushroomed in Delhi and NCR around this time tapping the potential market. In a blog post titled 'Southasiamasala', author Manu Sundaram claims that even the most underprivileged people in urban areas are more interested in putting their children in the unrecognised low-cost private schools rather than free, low performing government schools. 'The poorest parents are finding ways to access quality education of their choice. The urban poor are increasingly favouring the 'affordable private schools' that are mushrooming in slums and lower class neighbourhoods'(Sundaram, Manu, 2009, retrieved from www.southasiamasala.com). The article referred to the survey findings by James Tooley and Pauline Dixon in the Shahdara slums of East Delhi as supporting documents.

The Oxfam Education Report (2000) points out that 'the role of government as a basic provider of education is under constant review in almost all countries' (Watkin, Kavin, 2000). While referring to India, the report says, 'State power in India has often been captured by elites who, in many cases, have little interest in the needs of the poor' (Watkin, Kavin, 2000). Taking the example of Brazil in this context the report shows that the level of expenditure per pupil in municipal schools in North-eastern Brazil is almost 1/6 of that in urban State schools and in south Brazil the gap is even wider – 1/20 (Watkin, Kavin, 2000).

A similar study was conducted by the Centre for Civil Society, a social think tank in Delhi, covering 238 government schools in various parts of the capital city. The findings reported in the *Business Standard* in September 2008 revealed that there are wide disparities in per capita funding of children in different government schools in Delhi. In 2006-07 'in some schools it was as meagre as ₹75 per month whereas in some schools it was ₹7,220—higher than even the most expensive, elite public schools in the city' (Samuel, John Raja D., *Business Standard*, 8 April 2008, retrieved from www.businessstandard.com).

This has encouraged the processes of privatisation and consequently decentralisation of education in most of the developing countries. But the marginalised and the underprivileged hardly get the benefit of social changes. The private cost of education on the parts of parents who put their children in the Delhi government schools is nil or negligible whereas the amount is almost ₹3,500 per month or more in a recognised public school in this city. The public schools in the capital, therefore, are out of bound for the distressed migrant workers. Although the low-cost unrecognised English-medium schools have caught the fancy of the migrant community as they are affordable, after the primary level they gradually realise the limitations involved in sending the children there. As these schools are not recognised by any of the Education Boards or the Directorate of Education they cannot contribute to the building of their students' career. No student from an unrecognised school can write the Board examinations conducted by the CBSE or any other Education Board. Although they can appear in the examinations conducted by the National Open School or as a private candidate in CBSE examinations, that is not what they aspired to. So willingly or unwillingly the migrants are left with the option of sending their children to nearby government schools only.

The Municipal Corporation of Delhi (MCD) and NDMC are responsible for providing primary and pre-primary education to children in the city. Primary schools, commonly known as MCD schools, are run as independent units. Children from some of the MCD schools go to the nearby secondary or senior secondary schools run by the Delhi Directorate of Education (DDE). However, the Directorate of Education recently introduced the concept of composite schools by adding a primary section to its existing secondary or higher secondary schools. 'The Government of Delhi has converted 326 of its schools into composite schools now known as Sarvodaya Vidyalayas with classes from I to XII' (Gupta, Soumya as cited in the journal *Centre for Civil Society*). Similarly, NDMC, though mainly concerned with primary education, also runs a select number of middle, secondary and senior secondary schools in the city. The government efforts are complemented by a number of private schools engaged in imparting education at all levels of schooling. Some of them receive grant-in-aid from the Government of Delhi and are called government-aided schools. The ones which do not take government grants and are self-sustaining, mainly through their earnings from tuition fees, are the private un-aided schools—commonly called 'public schools'.

For the disadvantaged migrant children access to these schools is a big hurdle.

How Economic Reforms impacted India's National Education Policy

As mentioned in Chapter 1, the economic reforms of 1991 liberated the economy from the dreaded license-permit raj and boosted the growth of the private sector. The Hindu rate of growth was soon replaced by a vibrant industrial progress and fast development of tertiary services.

To maintain the tempo of progress the country needed to manage its manpower which so far had only counted as a huge number at the centre of all economic problems. The time to reap the benefit of demographic dividend was ripe. The Ministry of Human Resource Development (MHRD) had to plan and link manpower progress with industrial growth. Here came the need to educate and train the workforce to create socially and economically useful manpower who can boost the progress of the country.

An analysis of the National Policies on Education over time will clearly reflect this change in focus.

The National Policy on Education, 1968

NPE 1968 saw education as a tool to promote greater cohesion and integration of the country by providing a feeling of common citizenship and culture. Consequently, a big emphasis was put on 'a radical reconstruction of the education system' and 'a closer relationship between education and life of the people' (NPE 1968, retrieved from www.mhrd.gov.in). NPE 1968 set an ambitious goal of making schools more accessible—within one km of every home. Its thrust areas were: Common School System, introduction of the 10+2+3 system and making Mathematics and Science compulsory for school children (NPE 1968 retrieved from www.mhrd.gov.in). But it failed to achieve its targets due to ineffective implementation of the programmes.

If we observe the subsequent education policies the change in objectives becomes very clear.

NPE 1986

It aimed to use education as a catalyst to the complex and dynamic growth process of the individual who is a positive asset for the country. Here the policy recognised a child as a resource to be developed through education and used in the process of national growth. It put a big focus on using the instrument of education to reduce rural-urban disparities, create employment opportunities, control population growth and inculcate right values in young people to adapt to the new challenges before the nation (NPE 1986 retrieved from www.mhrd.gov.in). NPE 1986 talks about education for 'all' but does not elaborate it further.

NPE 1992

It is actually a modified version of NPE 1986. It views education as an investment. 'In sum education is a unique investment in the present and in the future. This cardinal principle is the key to National Policy on Education' (MHRD, GoI, NPE 1986, modified in 1996, Part II: p. 5). In Section 3.2 the policy recommends access to education for 'all students, irrespective of caste, creed, location or sex'. It envisioned the 'nation as a whole' with the responsibility of providing resources for implementation of the programmes required to reduce disparities, and to ensure universalisation of elementary education, adult literacy, scientific and technological research etc (NPE 1986, modified in 1996).

Clearly NPE 1992 made sure that the issues of providing education to the underprivileged were handled carefully and provisions were made for bridging the gaps. But the gaps have remained till date.

Right to Education Act, 2009

The Right of Children to Free and Compulsory Education Act, 2009, passed in Parliament on 26 August 2009 and commonly known as the RTE Act, declares education as a fundamental right to the children of India. The major thrusts of the RTE Act as mentioned in the Gazette of India are:

- *Every child of the age of six to fourteen years shall have a right to free and compulsory education in a neighbourhood school till completion of elementary education. [RTE Act, Ch II, Section 3(1)].*
- *No child shall be liable to pay any kind of fee or charges which may prevent him or her from pursuing and completing the elementary education [RTE Act, Section 3(2)].*
- *Where a child above six years of age has not been admitted to any school or though admitted could not complete his or her elementary education then, shall be admitted to a class*

appropriate to his or her age and in order to be at par with others will have a right to receive special training. A child so admitted shall be entitled to free education till completion of elementary education even after fourteen years (RTE Act, Section 4).

- *Where a child is required to move from one school to another, either within a state or outside, for any reason whatsoever, shall have a right to seek transfer to any other school, [excluding the school specified in sub-clauses (iii) and (iv) of clauses (n) of Section 2 i.e. a school belonging to a specified category and an unaided private school] for completing his or her elementary education. The head teacher of the first school should immediately issue the transfer certificate. Delay in producing transfer certificate shall not be a ground for either delaying or denying admission in the other school where the child is seeking admission. The Head teacher or in-charge of the school delaying issuance of transfer certificate shall be liable to disciplinary action under the service rules applicable to him or her [RTE Act, Section 5(2 & 3)].*

While describing the responsibilities of the Central and State Governments, Local authorities and parents and guardians of the children, the RTE Act is very clear and specific:

- *For carrying out the provisions of this Act, the appropriate Government and local authority shall establish, within such area or limits of neighbourhood, as may be prescribed, a school, where it is not so established, within a period of three years from the commencement of this Act (RTE Act, Ch.III, Section 6).*
- *The Central government and the state governments shall have concurrent responsibility for providing funds for carrying out the provisions of this Act [RTE, Act, Section 7(1)].*

- *The Central Government shall: (a) develop a framework of national curriculum; (b) develop and enforce standards of training of teachers; and (c) provide technical support and resources to the state governments for promoting innovations, researches, planning and capacity building [RTE Act, Section 7(6)].*
- *The appropriate government shall: (a) provide free and compulsory elementary education to every child of the age of 6-14 years and ensure their compulsory admission, attendance and completion of elementary education; (b) ensure availability of a neighbourhood school; (c) ensure that a child belonging to weaker section and the child belonging to disadvantaged group are not discriminated against and prevented from pursuing and completing elementary education on any ground; (d) provide infrastructure including school building, teaching staff and learning equipment; (e) provide special training facilities ; (f) ensure and monitor admission, attendance and completion of elementary education by every child; (g) ensure good quality elementary education conforming to the standards and norms specified in the schedule (RTE Act, Section 8).*
- *Every local authority will also be responsible in ensuring the above steps as mentioned in section 8, for children under its jurisdiction. Additionally, local authorities shall ensure admission of children of migrant families* [RTE Act, Section 9(k)].
- *It shall be the duty of every parent or guardian to admit or cause to be admitted his or her child or ward to an elementary education in the neighbourhood school [RTE Act, Section 10].*
- *With a view to prepare children aged between 3 and 6 for admission to elementary schools at the age of six, the appropriate government should make necessary arrangements for providing free pre-school education to them (RTE Act, Section 10).*

Very clearly Section 9(k) indicates the responsibility of MCD schools to ensure education for the migrants' children. Besides, in conformity with this Right to Education Act, the Delhi Government directs all schools, including unaided private schools, to ensure a minimum of 25 per cent reservation for EWS category of students at entry levels. Whether this will enable the slum-dwellers to enter the big good public schools is still not known. The income limit for EWS category is rupees one lakh per annum. Many in the lower middle-class segment coming under that bracket will qualify for the elite public schools ahead of the children coming from the slums. As corruption is rampant in the city and laws leave loopholes, there are unscrupulous agents in the capital city who can somehow tweak norms to obtain a certificate for EWS category. They act as middlemen facilitating school admission for children from those families who otherwise would not qualify for the free reserved seats in a public school. A principal of a reputed public school in Delhi, on condition of anonymity, revealed that at the time of disbursal of grants to EWS students, a particular parent did not turn up. In order to wind up the work the school sent someone to the residence of that EWS student to handover the cheque. To their surprise, it was a well-off family with visible signs of a high standard of living. The Directorate of Education has specified the distance from home as an important condition for admission of EWS children giving the first preference to people within one km radius of the school, then up to three km. An observer appointed by the government has to be present at the time of draw of lots and the whole process to be video-recorded. There are no doubts about the good intention of the government to promote inclusive education and accelerate Education For All (EFA) but adoption and implementation of policies without taking into consideration the ground realities do not yield desired results.

Educational Planning in Post-Reform Period

✣ Five Year Plans

The Tenth Plan emphasised the enrolment of underprivileged children in neighbourhood schools and curriculum changes with more orientation towards vocationalisaton of secondary education.

The Tenth Plan insisted on improving access to education and reducing disparities by emphasising the Common School System in which 'it is mandatory for schools in a particular area to take students from low-income families in the neighbourhood' (Planning Commission, GoI, Tenth Five Year Plan). The Tenth Plan also focused on revision of curricula with a focus on 'vocationalisation and employment-oriented courses, expansion and diversification of the open learning system, reorganisation of teacher training, and greater use of Information and Communication Technologies (ICTs)' (Planning Commission, GoI, Tenth Five Year Plan).

Although the stress on universalisation of secondary and senior secondary education was observed in the Tenth Five Year Plan statistics show that only 37 million children in India in the 14-18 age group attended school out of 121.1 million children in this age group in 2011 (Planning Commission, GoI, Eleventh Five Year Plan, Vol. 2. 2008: p. 14).

The largest segments of these children are in rural India and in urban slums. There is considerable concern among the policy planners about ways of bringing them under the literacy programme. The special focus area for the Eleventh Plan does not say anything in particular for the education of the migrant children although it puts a special emphasis on promoting literacy among target groups such as SCs, STs, minorities, women, low literacy states, tribal areas, other disadvantaged groups and adolescents.

❖ National Curriculum Framework (NCF)

Teaching-learning process is at the centre of all other processes in an educational institution. The National Curriculum Framework provides schools the necessary guidelines for curriculum planning and transactions. NCF 2000 insists that curriculum development be seen as a 'permanent search for qualitative improvement of education in response to various changes in society' (NCF 2000: p.1).

It suggests that the curriculum rest on the 'three pillars of relevance, equity and excellence' (NCF, 2000: p.5). It very categorically points out the importance of education in reducing social discrimination and benefitting the disadvantaged children. While talking about the education of the disadvantaged groups it says, 'Even the problem of educating the migrating population shall have to be handled through specific condensed educational programmes based on the main ingredients of the national curriculum' (NCF, 2000: p.6).

National Curriculum Framework, 2005 reiterates this and insists, 'We need to affirm our commitment to the concept of equality within the landscape of cultural and socio-economic diversity from which children enter into the portals of the school' (NCF 2005: p. 2). In Section 1.6 it points out the inadequacy of the educational planning in India to cater to the aspirations of the urban poor (NCF 2005: pp.2-9).

Quality Concern in Education

The quality dimension of education has remained almost unaddressed in India. In fact, the quality of education in general and quality of classroom teaching in particular has remained a major drawback for the success of India's educational initiatives. NCF 2005 points out the quality constraints in the Indian education system ranging from non-availability of proper physical infrastructure in government schools to neglecting the children's mother tongue in elite private schools (NCF, 2005, p.8).

A working paper, presented by the UNICEF at the meeting of the International Working Group on Education in Florence, Italy, in June 2000, pointed out the requirements of quality education. First of all it requires a welcoming, non-discriminatory climate within the school and classrooms (UNICEF, 2000; retrieved from http://www.unicef.org/education/files/QualityEducation.PDF). Quality is essential in all dimensions of education to ensure lifelong learning of a child. The document points out that only when a physically and mentally healthy learner, is studying in a safe, gender-sensitive, secure environment, with respect to relevant curricula executed by trained teachers by child-centric approaches will that experience be called quality learning. And when a learner receiving quality education is assessed skilfully the learning outcome will encompass knowledge, skills and attitudes, and will be linked to national goals for education and positive participation in society (UNICEF, 2000. *Defining Quality in Education*: p. 3). And hence quality in education is required to ensure all this.

The basic needs of a child can be seen under four broad heads:

- Physical: Safety, good health, food, exercise, shelter, hygiene
- Social-emotional: Acceptance, kindness, friendship, desire to love and to be loved
- Mental: Intellectual growth, creativity, stimulating challenges
- Spiritual: Contribution, meaning and uniqueness

The presence or absence of them in the lives of the children gets reflected in their academic achievements and behaviour (Covey, Stephen, R., 2008). The education system, if quality conscious, will keep all this in mind in planning and execution of the programmes.

But we observe their stark absence in education. The government is so overwhelmed by the quantitative dimension of literacy that no strong steps have yet been taken to keep a check on quality in educational institutions. Very recently CBSE has introduced the concept of accreditation for schools as a measure of quality check.

SSA, the flagship project for UEE, could not fulfil the quality dimension till the end of the Tenth Plan. 'Two major issues yet to be addressed satisfactorily under UEE are quality and equity,' lamented the educational planners at the end of the Tenth Plan (Planning Commission, GoI, Eleventh Five Year Plan).

Although the Eleventh Plan had put a lot of emphasis on quality, the approach paper to Twelfth Plan states:

> 'Despite improvements in access and retention, the learning outcomes for a majority of children continue to be an area of serious concern. Several studies suggest that nearly half the children in grade 5 are unable to read a grade 2 text. Concerted efforts are required to ensure that a minimum set of cognitive skills are acquired by all children during eight years of elementary education. Thus, quality issues and determinants thereof such as ensuring availability of trained teachers, good curriculum and innovative pedagogy that impact upon learning outcomes of the children must be addressed on priority basis' (Planning Commission, GoI, 2011; the approach paper to the Twelfth Five Year Plan retrieved from www.planningcommission.gov.in).

It also suggests greater community involvement in monitoring quality in schools. Unless the quality issue is addressed on a war footing, going to school for the disadvantaged migrant children will not help fulfilling their dreams. Even after graduating from school they will not be ready to work in the industries.

Millennium Development Goals: Can it be achieved for poor migrant children in Delhi?

Millennium Development Goals set by the United Nations are:

- End of Poverty and Hunger
- Universal Education
- Gender Equality
- Child Health
- Maternal Health
- Combat HIV/AIDS
- Environmental Sustainability
- Global Partnership

All the member countries were expected to achieve these goals by 2015 (www.un.org/millenniumgoals).

'The State of the World's Children, 2012: Children in an Urban World', the UNICEF report, released on 28 February 2012 in Mexico City, lays bare the miserable conditions of the children living in urban slums all over the world. It has estimated that of the one billion minors in distressed city hovels, many do not have access to education and health facilities even when they live very close to them. It talks about lack of data with respect to children living in slums and blames the political leaders for hushing up the problems to gain advantage. The report shows that the involvement of stakeholders in planning and implementations of programmes ultimately benefits all. It significantly notes, 'Where the excluded have been included in urban planning and decision-making, advancements have followed—in literacy, infrastructure and safety, for example.' (http://www.unicef.org/sowc/index_61804.html).

In Delhi, we come across instances of slum dwellers' involvement in planning and implementation of education and health-related programmes for their children and themselves, particularly with NGO initiatives, where the living conditions and literacy levels of the slum children have really improved. Some of them have been cited in the research findings in subsequent chapters.

As rightly pointed out by the UNICEF report, the absence of relevant data is a problem in understanding the educational facilities accessed by the marginalised migrant children in Delhi as well. No specific information related to the academic achievements of poor migrant children in Delhi has yet been recorded in any study so far. The achievements of these children can be guessed from the performance of the EWS category but as mentioned earlier, a child from an economically weaker section is not necessarily someone from an indigent migrant household living in a slum. Besides, the data collected so far by the Delhi Directorate of Education from schools or collected through DISE by NUEPA in recent years provide information about only enrolment of EWS students, not their performances or success rates. An all-India study conducted by Jyotsna Jha and Dhir Jhingan deplores the absence of an initiative to carry out a survey with respect to the academic achievements of the migrant children as a separate target group (Jha and Jhingan, 2005).

Conclusion

It was, therefore, appropriate to conduct this study at this point of time when the share of the youth in India's population is about 52 per cent but the country is not yet well prepared to provide training and education to develop their skills and knowledge to convert them into human assets in order to reap the demographic dividends. This study looks into the educational aspirations of one of the disadvantaged groups of children i.e. the children of the needy migrants living in the slums of Delhi. The research wants to highlight the recent trends reflected in the rising educational aspirations of the migrants and how it has been possible. No studies have yet been done in this specific area. Although a few researchers have conducted studies among the slum children highlighting their inaccessibility to education, no one has yet focussed on the gradual rise in their aspirations for education in post-reform period.

References

- Census of India, 2001.
- Chauhan, Chetan. 'The have-nots of Delhi.' *Hindustan Times*, 14 January 2009. Accessed 19 March 2011. https://www.hindustantimes.com/delhi/the-have-nots-of-delhi/story-Gg4SRHPq2Zm2E8gcHt8L6M.html
- Covey, Stephen R. *The Leader in Me*, p.38. UK: Simon & Schuster, 2008.
- Gupta, Soumya. 'Overview of School Education in Delhi'. *Centre for Civil Society Journal*, New Delhi. Retrieved from https://ccs.in/internship_papers/2003/chap27.pdf
- Jha, Jyotsna and Dhir Jhingran. *Elementary Education for the Poorest and Other Deprived Groups: The Real Challenge of Universalization*. New Delhi: Manohar, 2005.
- MHRD, GoI. 'National Policy on Education,' 1968. Retrieved from www.mhrd.gov.in
- MHRD, GoI. 'National Policy on Education, 1986 (Modified in 1992),' Part II, p. 5. Retrieved from www.mhrd.nic.in.
- MHRD, GoI. 'National Policy on Education, 1986.' Retrieved from www.mhrd.nic.in
- NCERT. 'National Curriculum Framework, 2000,' Ch. 1, pp. 1, 5, 6. New Delhi: NCERT, 2000.
- NCERT. 'National Curriculum Framework, 2005,' pp.2-9. New Delhi: NCERT, 2005
- NUEPA. 'Elementary Education in India: Analytical Report, 2004-05.' New Delhi: NUEPA, 2005
- Planning Commission, GoI (2011): 'Approach Paper to 12th Five Year Plan.' Retrieved from www.planningcommission.gov.in
- Samuel, John Raja D. (2008, 8 April). *The Business Standard*. Retrieved from www.businessstandard.com.

- SSA and Girls' Education for the XI Plan — Working Committee Report, Chapter on Elementary Education, p. 57. Retrieved from www.edudel.nic.in.
- SSA documents; retrieved from www.edudel.nic.in
- Sundaram, Manu. 'Education policies for the most disadvantaged: Lessons from the Indian urban poor.' *South Asia Masala*, 13 August 2009. Retrieved from http://asiapacific.anu.edu.au/blogs/southasiamasala/2009/08/13/education-policies-for-the-most-disadvantaged-lessons-from-the-indian-urban-poor/
- The Gazette of India.
- The Planning Commission, Government of India. 'Eleventh Five Year Plan 2007-2012,' Vol. II. New Delhi: Oxford University Press, pp. 2, 14.
- The Planning Commission, Government of India. 'Tenth Five Year Plan 2002-2007.' New Delhi: GoI.
- UNESCO (1990): 'Convention Against Discrimination in Education,' Agenda paper ED/2003/CONV/H/1, p. 3. Retrieved from www.unesco.org
- UNICEF. 'Defining Quality in Education.' A UNICEF paper presented at the meeting of The International Working Group on Education, Florence, Italy, June 2000, pp. 3, 7. Retrieved from http://www.unicef.org/education/files/QualityEducation.PDF
- UNICEF. The State of the World's Children, 2000. New York, NY: 2000.
- UNICEF: 'The State of the World's Children, 2012: Children in an Urban World.' UNICEF report released on 28 February 2012 in Mexico City. Retrieved from http://www.unicef.org/sowc/index_61804.html
- Watkins, Kevin. *The Oxfam Education Report*, pp. 224-25, 229. Oxford: Oxfam GB, 2001.
- World Bank. 'World Development Indicators.' Retrieved from www.data.worldbank.org
- www.un.org/millenniumgoals
- www.unesco.org
- www.zeenews.com. 17 December 2009.

3

DELHI – A CASE STUDY

Introduction

Nestling in the lap of the Aravalli Range, Delhi is a landmass of 1483 square kilometre positioned at 28°38' North and 77°12' East. The capital of India earned its status as a full-fledged state in 1993. With the statehood the city and its adjoining areas came to be known as the National Capital Territory of Delhi.

Although it has its own legislature and administrative structure headed by the Chief Minister, Delhi—unlike the other states—comes under the control of the Union Government in some important ways. The Centre asserts its authority in certain key areas. For example, the issue of land allotment is controlled by the Delhi Development Authority (DDA) which is an arm of the Union Urban Development Ministry. Besides, Delhi Police, too, comes under the direct control of the Centre as the Police Commissioner reports to the Lieutenant Governor, a nominee of the Union Government. The uncertainties and incoherence resulting from this dichotomous arrangement have

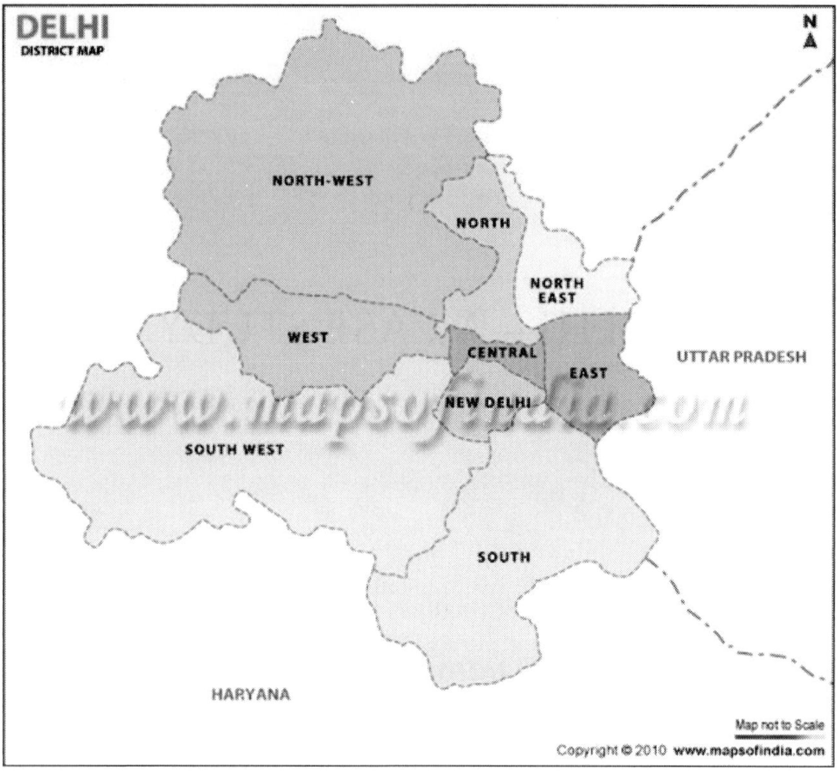

Source: www.mapsofindia.com

been reflected in the administration and development programme of the state. For example, on the crucial question of acquiring land for new projects, the Government of Delhi has no choice but to depend on the Centre. The inability to allocate land for its projects has hurt the growth impulses of Delhi's education programme.

Keeping in view the land scarcity in the Capital, satellite townships have come up in the adjoining areas of Uttar Pradesh and Haryana. Cities like Gurgaon and Noida have absorbed the excess population of Delhi and provided land for the new education hubs to come up. In fact, a large number of people commute between Delhi and the urban agglomeration of Gurgaon, Noida, Faridabad and Ghaziabad. At present Delhi's urban agglomeration is the third largest in the country after those of Mumbai and Kolkata.

For administrative purposes Delhi is divided into five zones: North, East, Central, South and West. They are further subdivided into nine revenue districts: North West, North, North East, East, Central, New Delhi, South, South West and West. North West District is the biggest having the maximum share of Delhi's population with a density of 8298 people per square kilometre (Census of India, 2011).

Delhi and its Vital Statistics

Table 3.1

Vital Statistics of Delhi

Economic Indicators	1991	2001	2011-12
Per capita Income[1]	₹5,972 (1980-81 prices)	₹41,436 (current prices)	₹1,75,812[2] (current prices)
Birth Rate[3]	28.48	21.24	17.8
Death Rate[4]	6.35	5.86	4.2
Density of population[5]	6352	9340	11297
Literacy Rate[6]	75.29%	81.67%	86.34%
Sex Ratio[7]	827	821	866
Infant Mortality Rate (IMR)[8]	32.37	24.49	30
Work participation rate (%)[9]	31.64	32.82	33.87 (2005-06)
Households' access to safe drinking water	95.8%	97.2%	N.A.
Urban population[10]	52.76%	93.18%	95.14% (2007-08)
No. of villages	209	165	N.A.

1. Per capita income = National income / mid-year population
2. The second highest in the country, after Goa whose per capita income in 2012 is estimated at Rs 1,92,652 (current prices). Delhi's contribution to GDP of India in 2012 is 3.8 per cent whereas its share in the country's total population is only 1.4 per cent
3. Birth rate = Number of live births per thousand population
4. Death rate = Number of deaths per thousand population
5. Density of population = Number of people per square kilometre of area
6. Literacy rate = (Number of literates/Size of the population) x 100
7. Sex ratio = Number of females per thousand males
8. IMR = Number of children dying before their first birthday per thousand live births
9. Work participation rate measures the number of people working as a percentage of total population
10. Percentage of urban population in India is the highest in Delhi (Census, 2001)

Source: Economic Survey of Delhi, 2008-09, Economic Survey, 2011-12, NSS 64TH Round Survey & Census data, 2011.

Delhi and its Population

The population of Delhi rose sharply from 94,20,644 in 1991 to 1,38,50,507 in 2001 to 1,67,53,235 in 2011 (Census data). According to the Economic Survey of Delhi 2005-06, Delhi has the highest population density among the states of India. It has become 11,297 per sq.km in 2011 compared to 9340 per sq. km. in the 2001 census or 6352 in 1991 (Economic Survey of Delhi, 2005-06: Table 3.6(1) & Census data, 2011). The exponential decadal growth rate for Delhi between 1991 and 2001 was 3.85 per cent whereas the All India figure for the same was 1.93 per cent (Economic Survey of Delhi, 2005-06: Table 3.4).

Table 3.2
Exponential Annual Growth Rate of Delhi's Population

Period	Delhi	India
1901-1911	0.2	0.56
1911-1921	1.66	(-)0.03
1921-1931	2.64	1.04
1931-1941	3.67	1.33
1941-1951	6.42	1.25
1951-1961	4.22	1.96
1961-1971	4.25	2.22
1971-1981	4.25	2.20
1981-1991	4.15	2.14
1991-2001	3.85	1.93
2001-2011	1.92	1.76

Source: Registrar General of India (Census data, 2011)

Out of a total population of 1,38,50,507 in Delhi in 2001, according to official statistics, 82,04,230 were born within the geographical boundary of Delhi suggesting that a significantly large number of migrants (53,18,362), born elsewhere, settled down in Delhi (Census, 2001).

There has been a constant inflow of people from the other states to Delhi since 1911 when the British made it their capital. Immediately after Independence a large number of refugees from West Punjab settled down in Delhi outnumbering Delhi's original residents concentrated around Chandni Chowk in Old Delhi. The post-reform period saw an influx of people from all over the country to come and settle down in the Capital stretching its boundary and creating the National Capital Region (NCR). NCR is the urban agglomeration of Delhi encompassing the bordering cities of Noida, Ghaziabad,

Faridabad and Gurgaon. The National Capital Region has attracted a large number of migrants because land is more easily available and rules less stringent in the outlying areas of the city than within. The demographic picture of Delhi had metamorphosed beyond recognition with waves of influxes in the wake of Partition and subsequent industrialisation outnumbering its original population in the Walled City of the Mughals. The migrants over the time, therefore, have created and influenced a mixed cosmopolitan culture and way of life in the Capital.

The decadal growth rate of population in Delhi has marked a decline in 2011. The census report, 2011 explains the development in the following terms:

- Removal of slums from Yamuna Pushta (spread along the riverbanks across New Delhi, Central, North and East Districts), Kalka Mandir, Gautam Nagar in the South district and several clusters in the NDMC area resulted in a significant fall in the city's population. The slum population in Delhi, in fact, has come down since 2011. Although exact data are not available, the census report claims that a 25 per cent depletion in the New Delhi district's population occurred in 2011 primarily due to the wiping out of slum clusters in the NDMC areas as part of a so-called beautification drive before the previous year's Commonwealth Games.
- Commercialisation of older residential areas like Chandni Chowk, Paharganj, and Sadar Bazar in Old Delhi and Karol Bagh in Central Delhi compelled their residents to relocate to newer areas, often the NCRs. This, combined with the cleanup drive in Yamuna Pushta, has reduced the population of the Central district by 10.5 per cent.
- But there is a 31 per cent population growth in the South West District due to the emergence of Dwarka sub-city as a new hub of the migrant population, particularly in the urbanised villages of Najafgarh, Kapashera and Bijwasan.

According to the 2001 census, 15.7 per cent of Delhi's population lived in slums. In 2011 it grew to almost 24 per cent. Experts estimate that the 2011 figure would have been much higher but for the demolition of slums as part of the preparation for the 2010 Commonwealth Games.

Delhi had an estimated 44,92,939 children in the 0-14 age group, and 14,27,979 in the 15-19 age group in 2001 (Census of India, 2001: p. 253). According to the 2011 Census, 19,70,510 children (11.76 per cent of the total population) in Delhi are in the 0-6 age group. Although it marks a marginal fall from the 2001 figure of 20,16,849 children (14.56 per cent of the total population) in the same age group (2011 Census, Data for Delhi: Chapter 2, Tables B & C), the challenge of providing education to all of them remains both tough and daunting.

Linguistic Division of Delhi

Although the main official languages of Delhi are Hindi and English, the people here love speaking a language which is a fair mix of Hindi and English referred to as *Hinglish* by college students. Hindi is found to be the most commonly spoken language in the markets and other public places. Punjabi refugees, who made Delhi their home after Partition, form a major segment of the city's population and thereby Punjabi is a dominant language spoken in the city. A large number of people have migrated to the Capital from UP and Bihar whose mother tongue is Hindi. Historically, the exposure to foreigners through trade, social and diplomatic interactions as well as tourism has influenced a culture of speaking English among the upper-middle and high-income groups. The sizable presence of people from the southern states has strengthened the trend because of their unfamiliarity with Hindi. The public-school culture, spawned by demands of the rapidly growing professional classes and the spread of computer literacy has contributed to the growing acceptance of English as a medium of communication. The South Indians and Bengalis in Delhi stick to their own mother tongues at home because of their strong affinity to their own culture and out of a concern that unless spoken to in the mother tongue, their children would lose their link to their rich cultural heritage and cultural roots. The educated among them prefer to speak English outside whereas the less educated ones pick up Hindi for communication. A large number of students from the Northeast, in Delhi for college and University education and job opportunities, prefer to speak their language among themselves. Kashmiri Pandits fondly retain their own sweet language as their link to the troubled valley they were forced to leave. The Muslims prefer Urdu and tend to see the language as an identity rubric, an attestation of their culture. The four officially recognised languages in Delhi are: English, Hindi, Urdu and Punjabi.

Table 3.3
Main Languages Spoken in Delhi

Language	Percentage of population using the language	
	1991	2001
Hindi	81.64	80.94
Punjabi	7.94	7.14
Urdu	5.45	6.31
Bengali	1.29	1.51
Tamil	0.90	0.67
Malayalam	0.69	0.66
Maithili	0.00	0.62

Source: Economic Survey of Delhi, 2008-09

The author has discerned an interesting dichotomy with regard to the language issue. In institutions where Hindi is used for official purposes the language question does not pose a problem. Everybody quickly picks up Hindi and adjusts to the new situation. Language is no constraint for the students in the government schools where Hindi is the medium of instruction. The migrants from Bihar, Uttar Pradesh, Uttarakhand and Rajasthan speak the same language and those from the non-Hindi areas adapt to it fast. It proves a hindrance and causes some kind of bipolarity in private schools where the medium of instruction is English. Language creates a barrier for the migrant children studying in such schools and adversely affects their academic performances.

Economics of Delhi

A comparison of average minimum wages in scheduled industries in Delhi and the states of UP, Bihar and West Bengal in 2009-10 testifies to the wide divergence in the minimum wages for the unskilled workers across the country.

Fig 3.1 Wage differentials : Delhi and other states in 2009-10

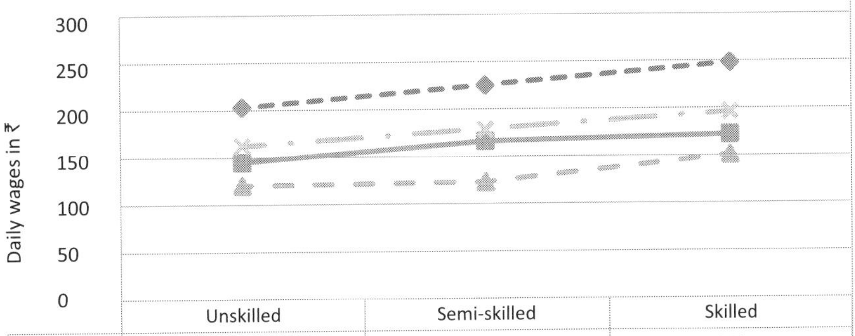

	Unskilled	Semi-skilled	Skilled
Delhi	2032	25	248
UP	144.76	166.11	172.23
Bihar	120.08	122.78	150.8
WB	162.23	178.46	196.3

Source: www.labourbureau.nic.in

[Note: Data for 2010. From April 2012 Delhi's minimum wages got further revised upwards. Unskilled—₹270, Semi-skilled—₹298, Skilled workers—₹328 www.zeenews.india.com, 28 June 2012)]

Minimum wages for an unskilled worker in Delhi are higher than that of a highly skilled worker in Bihar and skilled workers in UP and

West Bengal. By the rule of economics the wage differentials naturally attract people in large numbers from those states to Delhi.

Not only higher wages but the wide diversity of jobs has also pulled workers and artisans from different fields to Delhi and its sprawling industrial belt. Besides, the rapid growth of the unorganised sector in the post-reform period made Delhi an obvious destination. With growth and diversification of industries, the income and purchasing power of the households increased significantly. This in turn boosted the consumer goods industries and services sector. Many auxiliary services required for maintaining consumer durables are available at a cheaper price in the unorganised sector and preferred by the consumers. For example, automobile workshops, units for repairing washing machines, air conditioners and similar white goods offer employment opportunities to skilled workers migrating from other places. This in turn led to the mushrooming of the roadside car mechanics' kiosks offering services at a rate much lower than that of the service centres run by the big auto manufacturers or their franchisees.

Without any support or intervention by the government, thousands of skilled workers from different parts of the country earn their living as mechanics and repairers of mobile phones and scores of other appliances and offering services such as plumbing, private security and elevator maintenance. Electricians and car washers combine another such sector absorbing a large workforce from the rural hinterland of the adjoining states. However, a major section of the workers in Delhi is underemployed, underpaid, exploited and subjected to harassment by their employers. But most migrants find employment—even though often at lower wages. In fact, this prospect of employment brings such a big workforce from the poorer states to the capital almost on a daily basis.

The author confined the study to poor migrants living in the slums of Delhi and its adjoining areas. Most of them have come from Bihar, UP and West Bengal and earn their wages as construction workers, domestic helps, rickshaw pullers and vegetable vendors. They work as domestic helps, cooks, malis, tea-stall assistants, car cleaners or parking-lot assistants, security guards, lift operators, canteen boys, shop assistants, sweepers and garage assistants. The skilled ones find employment as drivers, tailors, masons, plumbers, painters and carpenters enjoying a marginally higher standard of living.

Indices of Development

The indices of development in Delhi are much higher than the national average in almost every respect. In an important profession like teaching women outnumber the men impressively—221:100. The following table compares the values of important indices of development in Delhi vis-à-vis the national average.

Table 3.4
Development Indices: Delhi vis-à-vis India

Index	1990-91		2000-2001		2010-2011	
	Delhi	India	Delhi	India	Delhi	India
Net State Domestic Product/ GDP per capita (Nominal)	₹ 5972	₹2213	₹6478	₹2840	₹11,318	₹4570
Per Capita Consumption Expenditure	₹777.01 (1993-94 prices)	₹328.18 (1993-94 prices)	₹1316.30	₹590.98	N.A.	N.A.
Urbanisation rate	89.93	25.71	93.01	27.78	95.14 (2008)	29 (2008)
Literacy rate (Total)	75.29	52.21	81.82	65.20	86.34	74.04
Male Literacy	82.01	64.13	87.37	75.64	91.03	82.14
Female Literacy	66.99	39.29	75.00	54.03	80.93	65.46

Index	1990-91		2000-2001		2010-2011	
	Delhi	India	Delhi	India	Delhi	India
Sex Ratio	827	927	821	933	866	940
IMR	49	72	40	63	30	47
Total Fertility Rate (TFR)	1.8	3.7	1.6	3.4	1.9	2.62
Persons in labour force (employed or unemployed population above 15 years of age as a percentage to total population)	50.8% (1993-94)	64.5% (1993-94)	47.6% (1999-2000)	61.8% (1999-2000)	49.9% in (2007-08)	41.3
Growth in annual employment rate	3.9% (1983 to 1994)	2.1% (1983 to 1994)	2.9% (1994 to 2000)	1.6% (1994 to 2000)	N.A.	N.A.

Sources: NHDR, 2001, Census reports, 1991, 2001 & 2011, NSS 64TH Round Survey, Economic Survey, 2011-12. Data compiled by the author.

It is said that a picture is worth a thousand words. A look at the following figures will show that the level of development in Delhi is much higher than the national average in almost all the areas. The data to illustrate the point have been sourced from the Economic Surveys, HDRs, NSSs and Census Documents.

Fig 3.2 Census highlights for Delhi, 2011

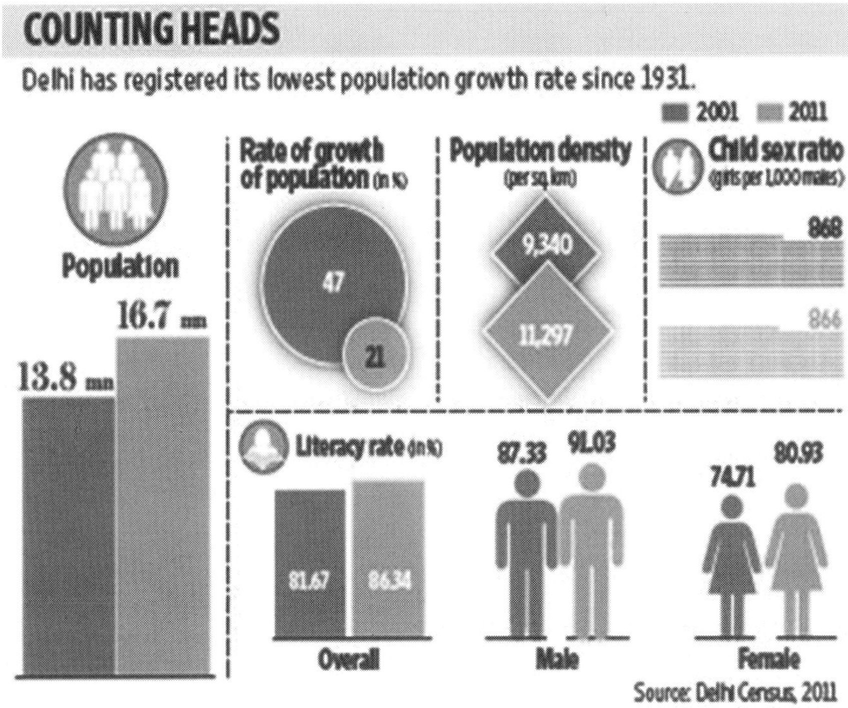

Courtesy : www.livemint.com December 25, 2011

Fig 3.3 Annual average growth rate of population

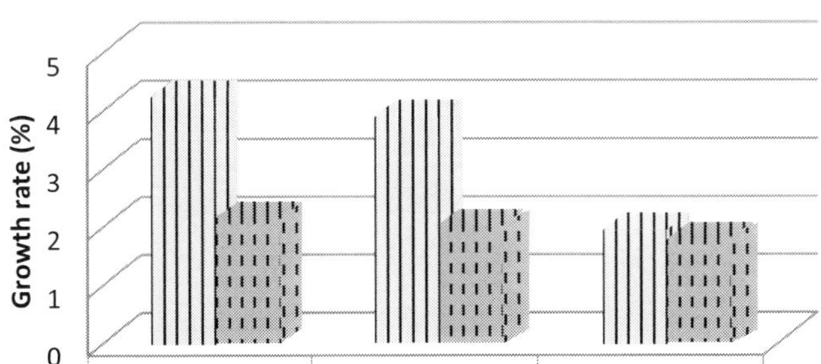

	1981-1991	1991-2001	2001-2011
Delhi	4.24	3.88	1.92
All India	2.13	1.95	1.76

Fig 3.4 Rate of Urbanisation

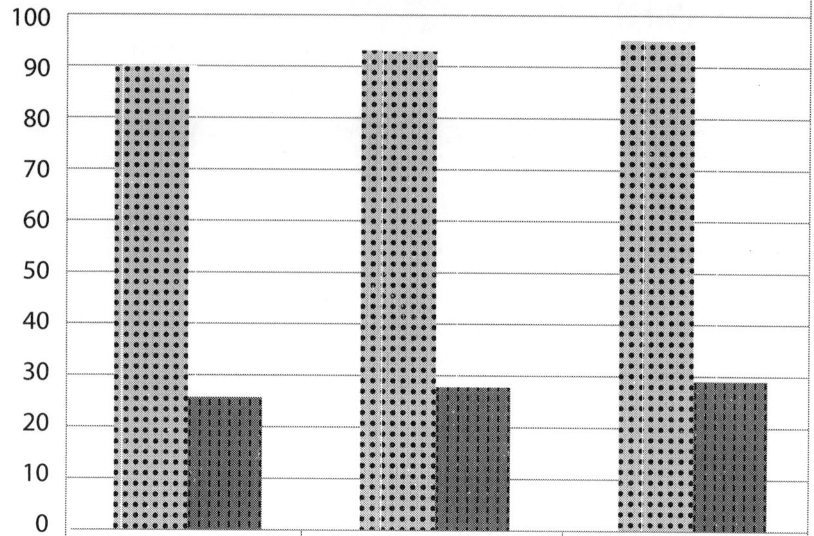

	1991	2001	2008
Delhi	89.939	3.01	95.14
India	25.712	7.78	29

Delhi has a much higher literacy rate than the national average. This is particularly noteworthy with respect to female literacy rates.

Fig 3.5 Literacy Rate

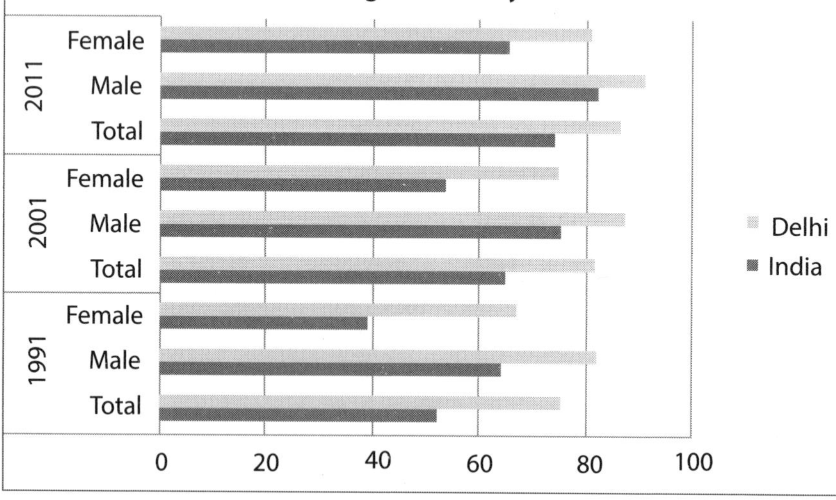

Fig 3.6 GER : Delhi vis-à-vis India

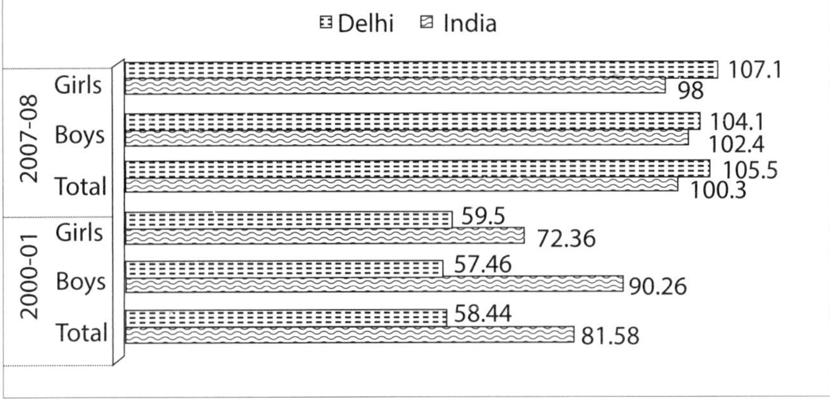

Fig 3.7 Total Fertility Rate

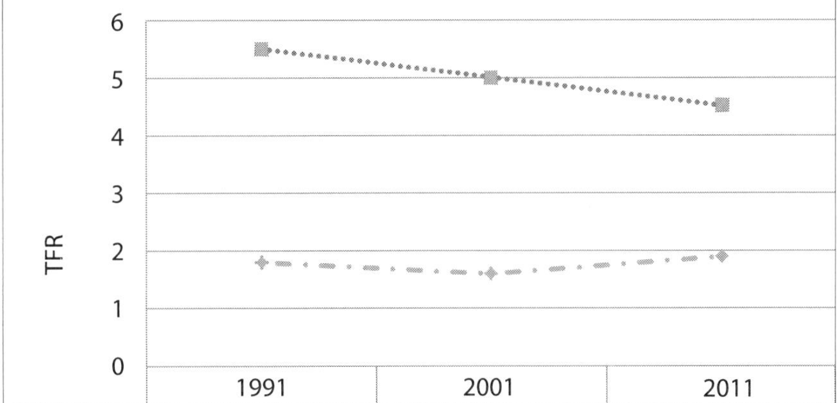

	1991	2001	2011
All India	3.73	3.4	2.62
Delhi	1.81	1.6	1.9

Fig 3.8 Per capita consumption

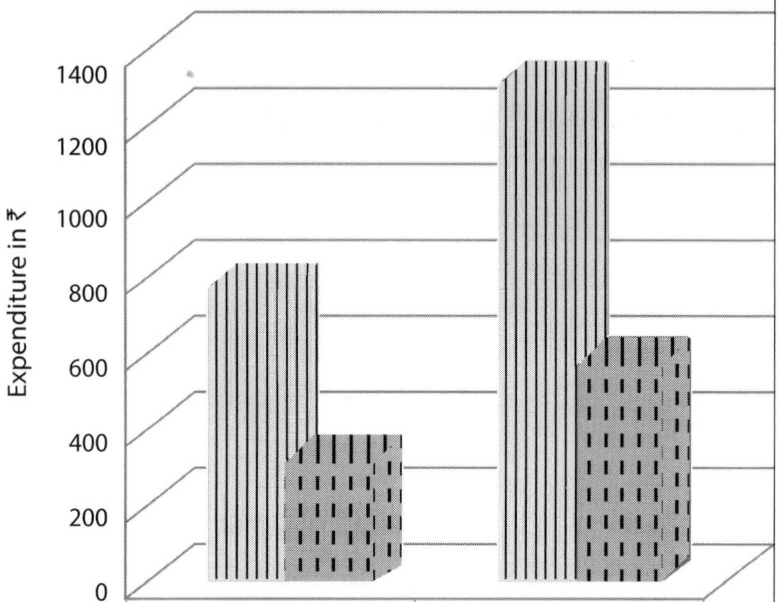

	1991	2001
Delhi	777.01	1316.3
All India	328.18	590.98

Fig 3.9 Labour force

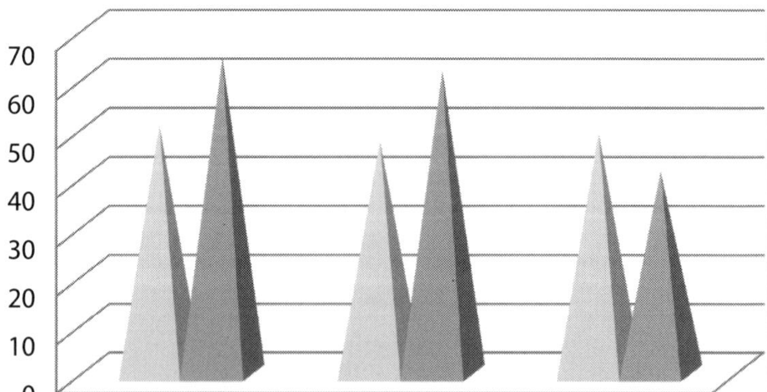

	1993-94	1999-2000	2007-08
Delhi	50.8	47.6	49.19
All India	64.5	61.8	41.3

Fig 3.10 Growth in annual employment

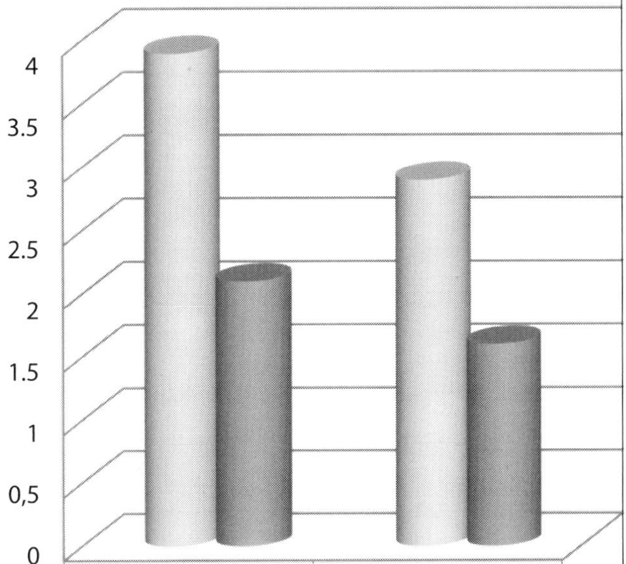

	1983-1993	1993-2000
Delhi	3.9	2.9
All India	2.1	1.6

The annual employment growth rate in Delhi when compared with the national average, confirms the fact that the opportunities created in this city attract every year not just the migrant workers from the other states but from the other big cities as well.

Where Delhi lags behind the other developed states is at the critical social-sensitivity level. Going by a high degree of gender bias working against women in the city, it, not surprisingly, has a disconcertingly low sex ratio, more appalling than the national average. In 1991, Delhi had a sex ratio of 827 against the national average of 927 which came down further to 821 in 2001 when it was 933 for the entire country. In 2011, the sex ratio somehow rose to 866 but is still much lower than the national average of 940. This causes concern and appears strange given the fact that female GER and female literacy rates—two major determinants of women's status in a society—in Delhi are much higher than the national averages. In fact, Delhi ranked sixth in India with respect to literacy in 2001. The low sex ratio is a major cause for violence against women in the city and makes the capital quite unsafe for working women and college or schoolgirls travelling alone. Domestic violence against women is also high in Delhi. The low status of women in turn makes the birth of a girl child unwelcome to its parents. Sex determined abortion, though legally banned, continues in the capital although illegally, contributing to this vicious cycle.

Fig 3.11 Sex Ratio

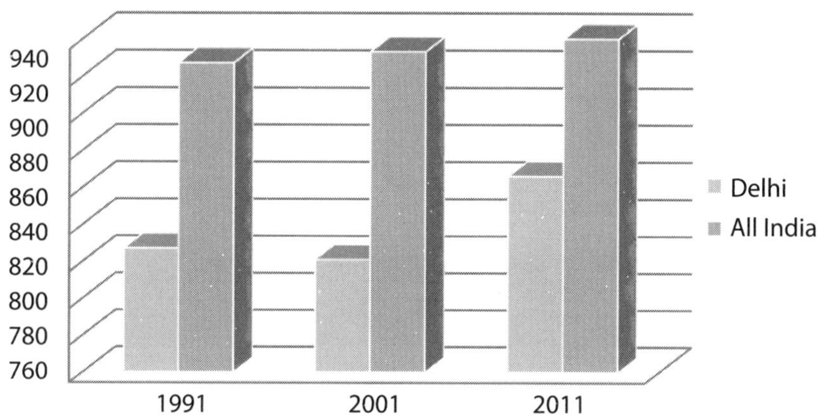

The National Curriculum Framework 1986 and 1992 stressed improvement in the literacy rate for girls as a way of raising their status in society—'a decisive intervention to bring about a basic change in the status of women' (Ministry of Human Resource Development [MHRD], GoI, Annual Report, 2010-11: p. 21). It seems the link is not that automatic as it is supposed to be. In the event of social conservativeness disapproving of women's empowerment, an equal status for them in the workplace and at home making economic and other decisions would be resented. Men would cling to their privileges pushing the women to a lower position.

Delhi's Human Development Index (HDI)

A comparison between the human development Indices of Delhi and the other states clearly points to the state's superior achievements and explains why people from elsewhere prefer Delhi over the other big cities closer home or state capitals while making a choice for migration. In fact, Delhi's level of human development, as indicated by the values of HDI, is much higher than the national value.

Table 3.5

HDI for Delhi and Migrants' States of Origin

States	HDI (Rank)		
	1981	1991	2001
Delhi	0.495 (3)	0.624 (2)	0.737
Uttar Pradesh	0.255 (29)	0.314 (31)	0.388
Bihar	0.237 (32)	0.308 (32)	0.367
West Bengal	0.305(22)	0.404 (20)	0.472
All India	0.302	0.381	0.571

Source: National Human Development Report, 2001, section 1 & Economic Survey of Delhi, 2001-02

Table 3.6

School Connect: DISE Data for Delhi

	2004-05	2005-06	2006-07	2010-11
Total No. of schools	4267	4542	4742	5021
Govt. schools	2779	3000	2985	2772
Private schools	1488	1542	1757	2249
Enrolment in govt. schools	13,90,051	15,14,267	15,64,288	16,78,331
Enrolment in private schools	6,56,814	7,04,685	7,80,626	10,32,152
Total enrolment	20,46,865	22,18,952	23,44,914	27,10,483
Percentage rise in enrolment	-	8.41	5.68	-

Source: DISE reports for the respective years. Data compiled by the author.

Political Patronage and Media Support to Slums

Another significant factor attracting the underprivileged migrants to Delhi is political support along with the media attention enjoyed by the slum dwellers in the city. Across party lines, political leaders count on these 'vote banks' and therefore, offer direct or indirect patronage in terms of security or facilities. Newspapers and television news channels on their part highlight government high-handedness or eviction drives to focus on human rights abuses and official insensitivity in dealing with the most vulnerable segment of society. Projecting human-rights violations is an important component of the strategy to win the support of civic society.

Role of Delhi Development Authority

The growth of slums in a sense is a measure of a city's growth. It is the industrial progress of an urban centre that induces labourers from other places to migrate looking for new jobs there. This leads to the creation of urban agglomerations with the city at its centre and also growth of slums within its periphery and in the outlying areas. The burgeoning professional classes, too, require a steady supply of cheap labour to meet their various requirements.

Delhi has an urban agglomeration surrounding it from all sides. The National Capital Region stretches from Gurgaon in the south to Noida and Ghaziabad in the east, and Faridabad in the south-east. Within the city and on its outskirts live the distressed migrants in steamy slums and JJ clusters.

Delhi Development Authority (DDA) has the responsibility for making the shanties a little more humane and habitable by providing basic infrastructure. It is mandated to look after the development and rehabilitation of the slums and JJ clusters. From 409 in 1981, the number of such clusters had gone up to 1080 in 1994 but came down marginally to 1000 in 1998. The slums cover 2390 acres of area inhabited by 4,78,175 households (www.dda.org.in). In

2011, it came down further to 685 clusters with 4,18, 282 *Jhuggis* (www.delhishelterboard.in) or shacks during a drive to *clean up* the Yamuna Puhsta—the city's largest slum spread— prior to the Commonwealth Games.

The Master Plan of Delhi 2010 (MPD 2010) proposed allocation of three per cent of DDA land for JJ clusters and slum rehabilitation and earmarked areas in Dwarka, Rohini, Narela and Bakarwala for this purpose. DDA issued a no objection certificate (NOC) to acquire and develop slums in Bawana (100 acres), Holambikalan (70 acres), Bhalaswa (200 acres), Savda-Ghevra (257 acres) and Kadipur (65 acres). Proposals for slum and JJ transit and rehabilitation in Madanpur Khadar Phase I and II and Hastsal have also been taken up by DDA (www.delhishelterboard.in).

Industrial Policy Reforms in Delhi since 1991

The number of industrial units in Delhi has gone up considerably since NEP 1991. In 2005 the capital city had close to one lakh manufacturing units generating employment for around six lakh people although the majority of them are in the unorganised sector.

Industrial Policy 2010 was initiated by the Government of the National Capital Territory in response to an urgent need for relocating industries to bring down the level of pollution. Keeping in view the growing concerns over the high carbon levels in the city air, the government moved to revise the 1982 policy in this respect. It was felt that to keep pace with the growth impulses triggered by the reforms, norms for globalisation and its emphasis on IT, ITES, and knowledge industries, Delhi needed to modify its old policy framework. In appreciation of the huge prospects of Business and Knowledge Process Outsourcing (BPO & KPO), the policy makers also wanted to create the right environment for Delhi to become a destination for the developed outsourcing countries. The new policy's effectiveness is evident from an analysis of the sector's contribution to the state's GDP confirming its fast growth trajectory. From 25 per cent in 1982, the share of the secondary sector in NSDP rose to 80 per cent in 1999-2000. Interestingly, the share of the secondary sector declined to 20 per cent again in the following years giving way to 80 per cent share of the tertiary sector (Industrial Policy of Delhi, 2011-2021).

The Industrial Policy Report of Delhi Government points out that the state has a large presence of garment manufacturing units followed by electrical machinery production and repairing services. As manufacturing is a small-scale industry and does not require high skills, these sectors attracted a large number of migrant workers from nearby areas (Industrial Policy of Delhi, 2011-2021: p.10). The industries in Delhi, particularly the small-scale and household ones, largely operate from non-conforming areas instead of the 28 designated industrial estates spread over the city. This, over a period of time, has given rise to the development of slums close to the industries to accommodate the flow of migrant labour. The policy statement also deplores the tardy growth of alternative, new-generation businesses like knowledge-based industries in Delhi and the NCRs leading to the outflow of professionals to the IT hubs in some other states. This, it was noted, led to contribution to the economy of states like Andhra Pradesh, Karnataka and Maharashtra. In this regard, the policy suggests, an integration of the industrial policy with the academic institutions, particularly those engaged in higher studies and research (Industrial Policy of Delhi, 2011-2021: P. 9).

Post-Reform Trends in Migration and Delhi's Slum Population

One important trend in the post-reform rural—urban migration is the shifting of the entire family from rural to urban areas contrary to the earlier practice of the head of the household going to a city to earn and send money back home. This has been witnessed in the post-reform China as well, raising hurdles for the schooling of the migrant children. In China education is funded by the local government. When rural households in China come to urban areas they are not entitled to social benefits provided by the local bodies in the cities as their domicile status remains unchanged as rural households. This is not the situation in India. Within the domestic boundary of the country the child's right to education has been acknowledged by the Indian government as a fundamental right. Every child is entitled to free education and facilities in any school in India (RTE Act, Section 5). RTE has brought into the limelight the obligations of the government as well as the private providers of education in making available schooling facilities for all (RTE Act, Chapter III).

Delhi has 1.9 million people living in the slums, second only to Greater Mumbai Municipality Area which has 6.9 million slum dwellers. Among the metro cities Kolkata has the third largest slum population (1.5 million) in the country.

These slums and JJ clusters are the cheap sources of labour for the capital city. Not only unskilled domestic helps or construction workers but a large number of skilled migrant workers live in these slums and eke out a living from mostly unorganised sectors.

Census 2001 recognises the fact that the 'slum dwellers contribute significantly to the economy of the city being a source of affordable labour for the production process in both the formal and informal sectors of the economy. Comprehensive information on the slums is thus essential for formulation of an effective and coordinated policy for their improvement and rehabilitation (Census of India, 2001).'

An interesting finding of the 2001 census was an impressively high literacy rate in the slums—73.1 per cent. While the percentage for men is a satisfactory 80.7, for women it is an encouraging 64.4. This compares well with the overall non-slum literacy rates of 81.0—87.2 for males and 74.2 for females (Census of India, 2001). It indicates that the literacy programmes among slum dwellers in the post-reform period have yielded results.

Out-of-School Children and Non-Formal Education

After the World Education Forum in Dakar in 2000 the member States took several determined initiatives and policy measures to achieve Education for All by 2015 which reduced the number of out-of-school children in the world substantially by 2010—from 105 million in 1990 to 61 million in 2010 (EFAGMR-UNESCO, 2012). But it is disconcerting, according to EFAGMR-UNESCO statistics, to see India placed in the group of 19 countries having more than 500,000 out-of-school children in 2010, most of the other countries belonging to sub-Saharan Africa.

Table 3.7

Countries With More than a Million Children Out of School in 2010

Country	Out-of-school children (in thousands)
Nigeria	10,542
Pakistan	5,125
Ethiopia	2,390
India	2,278
Philippines	1,460
Ivory Coast	1,161
Burkina Faso	1,128
Niger	1,086
Kenya	1,010

Source: EFAGMR-UNESCO Institute for Statistics (UIS)

A Household Child Census in 2009 was conducted under the supervision of the ministry of human resource development, Government of India, in all the JJ clusters, resettlement colonies, slums, unauthorised areas, subsidised housing for the depressed classes, and low-income-group pockets of Delhi which covered about 15 lakh households. The findings point to the fact that a large number of children in Delhi are still out of school—35,642 in the 6-10 age group (18,949 boys and 16,693 girls) and 18,578 children in the 11-13 age group (9,757 boys and 8,821 girls).

But the observations made by the Planning Commission in its Eleventh Five Year Plan shows a steady decline in the number of drop-outs, particularly in the past 10 years.

Table 3.8

Reduction in Drop-Out

Year	No. of Drop-outs (in crores)
2001-02	3.20
2002-03	2.49
2003-04	1.16
2004-05	1.35
2005-06	0.95
2006-07	0.70

Source: Eleventh Five Year Plan, Fig 1.1.2 (p.4), Planning Commission, GoI

This clearly implies that more and more children from the marginalised households are coming into the folds of formal schooling.

The National Policy on Education, 1986 had laid a major emphasis on universal access to and retention of children in the 6-14 age group in school and took it up through its flagship programme, Sarva Shiksha Abhiyan (SSA) in collaboration with the states and Union Territories. The 86TH amendment to the Indian Constitution in 2002 made education a Fundamental Right for the children and consequently binding on and obligatory for the State to provide eight years of free and compulsory elementary education to each and every child in the said age group (Juneja, Nalini, NIEPA Occasional Paper No. 33). Section 4 of the RTE Act, 2009 makes specific provision for special training for age-appropriate admission of out-of-school children (www.edudel.nic).

The SSA policy paper titled 'Alternative and Innovative Education for Out-of-school Children' in 2011 mentions that a majority of these children belong to the disadvantaged communities like 'SC,

ST, Muslims, migrants, children with special needs, urban deprived children, working children, children in other difficult circumstances. Girls comprise a bulk of out-of-school children'.

The urban out-of-school children can be broadly classified into: (i) street children, (ii) children of migrant workers living in slums, (iii) children of sex workers and (iv) juvenile delinquents. Most of the research on the disadvantaged children focused on migrant children too but there was not much of an inquiry into the educational aspirations of the migrant children as a group so far (Govinda, R., 2002).

How Much Ownership has been Taken by the Government in Delhi?

Delhi is divided into three segments with respect to administrative control. The heart of the Capital, the VIP district known as the New Delhi Municipal Council (NDMC) area, comes under the direct control of the Union government. The city areas outside the core Lutyens Bungalow Zone, under the purview of the Municipal Corporation of Delhi (MCD), are the responsibility of the Delhi Government. The National Capital Region (NCR), comprising Delhi and its adjoining areas falling within the geographical border of Haryana and Uttar Pradesh, is looked after jointly by all the three state governments with the Centre playing a catalytic role. This has often created confusion of accountability. NDMC, MCD and the Delhi government together run a total of 3,100 schools. Providing secondary and higher secondary education is primarily the responsibility of the Delhi government with the Delhi Directorate of Education being the controlling authority.

The issue that concerns observers and experts is the level of seriousness and commitment of the multiple agencies in implementing literacy programme. Delhi Government has taken up the RTE Act and ordered all the schools, including the private non-aided ones, in the city to conform to the Act. A recent verdict of the Supreme

Court also directed the private unaided schools to provide free books and uniforms to EWS students and strictly prohibited them from segregating these children by putting them in separate sections (*Indian Express*, 30 March 2011). A vigilance cell in the Delhi Directorate of Education is also active monitoring implementation of the directive.

Delhi Government proposed to cover 23,536 out-of-school children during the year 2011-12 partly through Dakhila Abhiyan (direct admission of 5,896 such children to various schools) and through Special Training Programmes for the rest. A district-wise distribution of these children was made by the Delhi Directorate of Education to keep the target more focused.

Table 3.9

Out-of-School Children to be Covered in 2011-12

Revenue District	Out-of-school children to be covered
East	2380
North East	3760
North	0960
North West	3200
West	3665
South West	2520
South	5751
New Delhi	0160
Central	1140
Total	23,536

Source: www.edudel.nic.in

The Delhi Directorate of Education has announced a number of schemes to lure the slum children to school. Clearly the attempt is to incentivise schooling to enrol them and fight dropout tendencies. The schemes are:

- Free supply of text books
- Book banks and improved school library facilities
- Subsidies to economically weak students for uniforms
- Free transport to girls from rural areas
- Improvement in quality of school buildings
- Pratibha Vikas Vidyalayas for bright children from underprivileged families
- Strengthening of correspondence courses and opening of State Open Schools modelled on the National Institute of Open Schooling
- School extension programmes like science teaching, SUPW activities, educational and vocational guidance and population education etc.
- Computer education
- Awards to best schools, students and teachers
- Scholarships to educationally backward minorities, girl students from rural areas and JJ colonies
- Coaching facilities for academically weaker students
- Public-private partnership
- UEE
- Mid-day meal programme
- Promotion of sports and games facilities, etc.

[Source: http://www.edudel.nic.in]

Although there are no specific programmes (except serial No. 11) under the DDE schemes to directly cater to the slum children, the initiatives mentioned above, if implemented properly, will in a significant way touch the lives of the poor slum children. As the cost of education in government schools is almost nil or very low children from most of the slums can attend those schools only. Hence the government efforts to improve the quality of education in its schools as well as setting up of neighbourhood schools will surely benefit the slum children.

A successful initiative by MCD was the Tigri project in Janata Jeevan Camp, a slum in South Delhi. The project, Vikas, is basically a self-help programme for the welfare of the 7000 odd families of this slum. Guided by Prof. N. K. Singh of Delhi School of Business this MCD project has involved the residents directly in the uplift of their own situation. Vikas has created employment opportunities, particularly for women and built a non-formal school for children up to Class V. About 400 children from the slum have been attending this school regularly. Each family contributes one rupee a month towards the welfare of their slum and the funds thus collected has helped create a cleaner environment and support the education for their children. The integrated welfare plan has taken into its fold sanitation and family planning as well. Inspired by the success of the Tigri project, MCD is now expanding the programme to other slums as well (*The Hindu*, 21 April 2002). SSA, a flagship programme for UEE, aims to use it as an opportunity to ensure social justice through basic education. It also talks about involving slum-level committees, among others, in the management of education. Innovative activities under SSA covers deprived urban children among others for which ₹15 lakh per district has been allocated. Special programmes under SSA to cover out-of-school children: Khul Ja Sim Sim, Chalta Firta School, Residential Bridge Course for out-of-school children, special drives for minority education, hostel facilities for girl children under the KGVB scheme, setting up of Early Childhood Care and Education Centres (ECCEC), Alternative Innovative Education (AIE) centres, BaLA—an initiative to make schools learner friendly, Computer Aided Learning (CAL), grants and material supports.

In order to improve management of schools the SSA has introduced the following programmes: (a) Community Leaders' Training, (b) In-service Teacher Training, (c) appointment of resource persons to take care of children with special needs, (d) Urban Resource Centres and Cluster Resource Centres and monitoring tools, (e) creating an effective and updated website for the Directorate of Education to encourage e-governance.

The state of Delhi claims to be the first in the country in the following educational initiatives under SSA (SSA Report, 2009):

- Chalta Firta (mobile) Schools
- Khul Ja Sim Sim Project: Computer-based learning stations for Alternative Innovative Education Centres for out-of-school children and adult learners
- Implementation of Building as Learning Aid (BaLA) in all government schools
- Setting up of multimedia classroom or lab in all government schools
- Development and implementation of YUVA-a school life skills programme
- In-house development of multimedia animated classroom content
- In-house development and implementation of online modules for online school management
- Constituting and empowering Vidyalaya Kalyan Samithis with the participation of community and students
- Online collection of DISE data: The DISE and the other relevant data pertaining to all levels of schooling in Delhi is being collected online. The attempt has been successful and the data so collected is used for educational planning
- School Audit Report containing all school related data in respect of all government schools

Educational Responsibilities Shared by the Non-Governmental Organisations

A large number of non-government organisations (NGOs) in Delhi have been working in the field of education. In fact, the NGOs have made a deeper dent in the area of non-formal education than the government. Their success in taking care of the out-of-school children is more remarkable than the government initiative.

The educational NGOs took upon this responsibility on themselves. Not only did they set up Nonformal Education (NFE) centres for the disadvantaged children of Delhi, but also took care of their lives in a comprehensive way. They created income opportunities for the slum dwellers so that they could afford to send the children to go to school or attend an NFE centre. They trained the young children at the pre-school centres and made them suitable for formal schooling. The NGOs played a commendable role in the children's skill development so that after school they could find profitable employment. With newly acquired skills they were in a position to bargain the terms of employment. In order to make the programme useful and attractive the groups trained their team of teachers, introduced innovative, child-centered methodologies, age-appropriate techniques of learning and interesting teaching tools to attract and retain the children in the fold of education. Instead of incentives they introduced rewards to make the school a place of sustained interest for the child. Free transport, mobile learning centres and community involvement yielded the targeted results. Being in the private sector, the NGOs did not have any constraints in raising funds and levels of efficiency. Hence the NGO-run NFE centres or schools work more efficiently than the government-run NFEs.

In fact, in certain programmes for the out-of-school children Delhi Directorate of Education has involved reputed NGOs to assist, organise and implement a number of its non-formal education programmes like Khul Ja Sim Sim (NGOs involved being Whole-in-the-Wall Education Ltd. and IL & FS), Chalta Firta School (NGOs involved being Salam Balak Trust and Butterflies), Residential Bridge Courses (NGO involved: Samya Centre for Equity Studies), Alternative Innovative Education (AIE) centres run by a number of NGOs, BaLA guided by the NGO VINYAS.

The author would like to take note of the commendable work done by some prominent educational NGOs working successfully for the welfare of the slum children in Delhi.

✣ Katha Khazana

The NGO was set up in 1990 by the publishing house Katha. It caters to slum children in Govindpuri, one of the largest shantytowns in Delhi, and also runs a programme in Arunachal Pradesh. Katha Khazana, at the time of its inception, realised that parents would start sending their children to school only when their economic contribution was supplemented somehow by other sources. Therefore, they started with training and empowerment of the mothers of the targeted children. Within a few years the initiative bore fruit. Today Katha Khazana has 7000 beneficiaries. The elegantly simple school building with murals and tribal motifs on its outer walls stands out as an emblem of hope in the midst of squalid clusters of the Govindpuri slum.

The NGO is working towards spreading its base to 50 slums and bringing more and more women under its fold. It has earned international recognitions by winning the Social Enterprise Laboratory Award and NASDAQ Stock Market Education Award 2002. Their initiatives have been appreciated by the media as well. *The Week* magazine writes: 'The name (Katha Khazana) could not have been more apt as the endeavour has contributed to stories of women's empowerment, stories of would-have-been school dropouts becoming school toppers, and now the story of how despite being housed in a dirty slum, a wonderfully clean bakery churns out delightfully tasty biscuits ... It is also a story of struggle waged by women such as Manjula and Urmila to cast away the veil that shrouded their existence and step out of their homes to establish their worth, not just to the outside world, but also to themselves... Katha is an epicentre of activities that have transformed the Govindpuri Basti.'

✣ Sankalp

Initiated by Commandar K. K. Choudhary, a retired navy officer, the NGO was set up in 1996. They cater to the children of construction workers and migrant workers in Gurgaon. From a rudimentary structure providing education to a handful of children, Sankalp now operates from more than one place and provides education to 900-odd children of the target group. An impressive 40 per cent of these children are girls. The students are mainly the children of construction workers who migrated from West Bengal, Bangladesh, Uttar Pradesh and Madhya Pradesh and stayed in slums in Sectors 56 and 53 of Gurgaon. Sankalp has identified the problem of transportation as a hindrance for underprivileged children from the slums to come to school. Keeping that in mind they have made pick-and-drop arrangements for the children. In addition to providing education from its premises Sankalp introduced the Mobile Schooling system in 2005. The school on wheels is a specially designed bus functioning as a classroom. It also works in partnership with the Department of Education, Haryana and helped improving the school infrastructure with government assistance. The NGO is efficiently run by a group of management professionals who work as volunteers for the organisation.

Smile Foundation

Smile Foundation was set up in 2002 to cater to the needs of slum children in Vasant Kunj in South Delhi with a special emphasis on girls of school-going age. Nai Disha is working in collaboration with Smile Foundation for the education of slum children in South-West Delhi. The organisation believes that the mothers' health plays a crucial role in ensuring girls' education. Nai Disha, along with Smile Foundation takes care of the educational needs of the children of the maids and drivers working in 12,000 households of Vasant Kunj and coming from the slums of Kisangarh, Bhawani Kunj, Shanti Kunj, Andheri More and Rangpuri Pahadi. Apart from taking care of their educational needs, the organisation also trains the children in various skills to enhance their future employability. Currently it has 244 beneficiaries with 84 more awaiting admission. The organisation also has a tie-up with NOW (New Opportunity for Women)—a non-profit organisation working towards the welfare of poor and marginalised women in Delhi—to bring adolescent girls under the fold of education.

✣ Deepalaya

It is one of the oldest educational NGOs in Delhi working in the slums of Kalkaji and Okhla since 1979. Deepalaya has tie-ups with public schools and engages their children in a conversation with the slum children in constructive ways. They evolved a unique way of fundraising from the public schools by collecting old newspapers from the students and creating funds for their schools either by selling them or making paper bags. Along with formal education, it also provides basic health facilities to children. Recently their Kalkaji school has got government recognition and now works as an aided school.

Deepalaya also provides financial assistance to women of the Kalkaji slums. They make jute bags and other such handicrafts which are marketed through Deepalaya. This eco-friendly initiative is a step towards economic self-reliance for the poor women living in the slums.

✣ Childreach International

The NGO is an international charity which runs many programmes in India. It is working towards sustainable education for the slum children in Delhi, Ahmedabad, Dharamshala, Hissar and Darjeeling. In Delhi, Childreach International has built its own team of trained young teachers to coach the slum children going to the MCD schools. The first-generation learners who are not able to cope with regular studies in class are identified and grouped for special classes. CRI volunteers take their classes using innovative techniques of teaching. The methodology adopted caters to individual needs and use of ICT enables them to understand in a sustainable way. Child Reach International is also involved in creating awareness among slum children on different issues affecting their lives. For this purpose, they have tie-ups with schools in Delhi. Children from the well-known public schools interact with slum children and inform them through discussions, paintings, street theatre (*nukkad natak*) and so on. The NGO does not encourage any kind of donations either in cash or kind to the underprivileged children as they are concerned about the impact of handed-down money or commodities on their self-esteem and value system. They raise funds through sponsorships and other innovative programmes like 'Ek Din Swadeshi' where students from public schools go on a village trip organised by CRI to acquaint themselves with the rural India and its problems and part of the earning from the trip goes to the welfare of slum children. The NGO is also working extensively on the problem of female foeticide in Delhi, Haryana and Himachal Pradesh.

Pratham

This NGO, started in 2000, adopted an interventionist approach. They train the pre-school children in East Delhi to prepare them from early childhood for formal schooling. The training helps the children adjust comfortably to the school environment. They also provided bridge classes to out-of-school children in the 6-14 age group in the same area. By 2009-10 Pratham's efforts spread across 260 slums in Shahdara and Karol Bagh bringing under its fold dropouts from 650 MCD schools across the city.

Pratham also has library programmes to encourage reading habits in slum children and improve their communication skills. It runs Balwaris in slums and in some Anganwaris to provide pre-school care to three- to five-year-olds from the community. It also runs learning centres for slum children who cannot afford paid tuitions to cope with their studies in school. This helps them overcome the possibility of dropping out. Its interventions, the NGO claims, has touched the lives of 80,000 slum children in the past decade.

Salaam Balak Trust

This organisation works for homeless and street children. It has created six shelters in Delhi for street children with specific target groups (for example, one for girls only). Salaam Balak Trust provides need-based education to its children through both formal and non-formal methods. They have tie-ups with National Institute for Open Schooling (NIOS), formal schools and also provide bridge courses. Not only education, SBT also trains them to be skilled workers so that they could earn more making a difference to their situation. The shelters are an attempt to give back to the street children what they have lost in the grime and squalor of the city slums, and inculcate in them self-esteem and a sense of social responsibility.

Aarohan

Set up in 2005, it has been working for remedial and bridge classes for slum children in South Delhi. Their Malviya Nagar camp offers coaching to the children attending the municipal schools. They also run a pre-school to prepare children below five years from the nearby slums for formal schooling. They assist them to get school admission.

SARD & Oxfam

Two other NGOs—Oxfam and SARD—have collaborated with MCD to provide education and medical care to slum children (www.indiaedunews.net).

In 2010, 20 MCD schools tied up with Oxfam, an international NGO and SARD (Society for All Round Development), a Delhi NGO, to improve the quality of teaching in their schools located near or in the slum areas of the city's west and southwest. The innovative teaching method of SARD has caught up with the enthusiasm of slum children in these schools.

The author was told by a SARD official informally that they first identify the weak students and put them in a separate class called 'Anandadaayi Kaksha' (Class of Joy). These children are provided assistance in Mathematics, English and Computers through innovative and experimental teachings. Once they are at par with the rest of the class they are sent back to regular classes. SARD uses imaginative teaching aids and methodology to make the classrooms interesting and child-friendly. For example, instead of moving from letters to words to sentences in language teaching they move in the opposite direction. They say that the children can relate better to a simple sentence than individual words and letters. From the sentence to words is a step from the familiar to the unfamiliar. That way they grasp it more easily. So far about 600 slum children from 20 MCD schools have benefitted from the initiative.

Arpan

Set up by the House of Pearls, a non-profit, in 2006, this NGO provides schooling to poor children from the Vasant Kunj slums. They provide food and clothing to students to incentivise schooling. Picnics, monthly gifts and outings are intended to make school going an enjoyable experience. They also provide tutorials for Mathematics and English to the older children. They organise free medical check-ups for them regularly. The organisation is funded by donations from various sources.

Raasta

Set up in 1994, the NGO caters to slum children of East Delhi and Ghaziabad (Khora village). Raasta primarily provides remedial classes. Its programme, the NGO claims, has benefited 7000 children in the past decade. Of late it has widened its activities to areas such as health and social awareness.

These NGOs, most of them established in the 1990s and 2000s, have not only helped the migrants to educate their children but also created subsidiary employment opportunities for them to make education sustainable for the indigent households. Some of them help the children in finding work after schooling. Their encouragement and organisational efficiency have increased the level of the migrants' aspiration for their children's education.

Conclusion

Faster pace of growth and better economic opportunities have made the NCT a favoured destination for the migrants. The uprooted community living in slums, may have a deep sense of deprivation but their situation is definitely better than what it was in their villages. Higher wages and exposure to the ambience of middle-class living raise their aspirations for a better future for their children. This has created a demand-pull factor for the migrant children to attend school. There are about 5000 schools in Delhi. The Right to Education Act, 2009 has created enough space for the slum children to pursue their dreams. Now, with a little more planning and sincere implementation on the part of all the stake-holders the migrant children's dreams may come true.

References

- 'A news report on EWS admission.' *The Indian Express*, 30 March 2011.
- 'MCD keen to replicate Tigri slum development project,' *The Hindu*, 21 April 2002. Retrieved from https://www.thehindu.com/todays-paper/tp-national/tp-newdelhi/mcd-keen-to-replicate-tigri-slum-development-project/article27843183.ece
- Census of India, 2001. 'Metadata and Brief Highlights on Slum Population,' p. 2.
- Census reports, 1991, 2001 & 2011.
- Department of Industries, Govt. of National Capital Territory of Delhi. 'Industrial Policy for Delhi, 2011-2021,' pp. 9-10. New Delhi: Government of NCT of Delhi.
- DISE reports for the years 2004-05, 2005-06, 2006-07 and 2010-11.
- Economic Survey of Delhi, 2001-02.
- Economic survey of Delhi, 2005-06, Table 3.4, 3.6(1).
- Economic Survey of Delhi, 2008-09.

- EFAGMR-UIS. 'Reaching out-of-school children is crucial for development.' Policy Paper 4 June 2012. Retrieved from http://unesdoc.unesco.org/images/0021/002165/216519e.pdf.
- GoI. 'National Human Development Report, 2001-2002.' New Delhi: Planning Commission.
- Govinda, R. Ed. 'India Education Report,' pp. 60-66. New Delhi: NUEPA, 2002.
- Institute of Applied Manpower Research. 'India Human Development Report, 2011.' New Delhi: Planning Commission, GoI.
- Juneja, Nalini: 'Constitutional Amendment to Make Education a Fundamental Right.' NIEPA Occasional Paper No. 33, as cited in Reading Material for the Workshop on Management of Child Rights to and in Education, held at National University of Educational Planning and Administration (NUEPA), New Delhi, September 2009.
- Ministry of Human Resource Development, GoI. 'Annual Report, 2010-11,' pp. 21. New Delhi: MHRD, GoI.
- Planning Commission, GoI. 'Eleventh Five Year Plan,' Vol. II, PP. 3-4, Fig. 1.1.2. New Delhi: OUP.
- UEE Mission, SSA Report (2009), retrieved from www.edudel.nic.in
- www.dda.org.in
- www.delhishelterboard.in
- www.edudel.nic.in
- www.labourbureau.nic.in
- www.livemint.com
- www.mapsofindia.com
- www.zeenews.india.com

4

FROM ANCESTRAL VILLAGE TO SHANTYTOWN

Life of a Migrant Child in a Slum

How does it feel to be at the bottom of the pyramid?

The author met Sakina (name changed), growing up in a cramped shanty with seven more siblings. An open drain skirting the row of ratholes in the sprawling Govindpuri slum in South Delhi washes away Sakina's dreams and ambitions. The second of eight children, this nine-year-old wants to be a dancer. The dreamy-eyed girl does not yet get bothered by the harsh world around her, but Rani, her 15-year-old sister, a Class X student, understands that it is beyond the capacity of their vegetable-vendor father to support their education above the school level. All of them go to free government schools.

The picture is not that grim for Rubina and Shama (names changed), both studying in Class X. Their father, a tailor, is eager to support their education as long as they want to study and shares their ambition. Rubina wants to be a teacher. And Shama, her father feels, is intelligent enough to prepare for the Civil Services Examination. He even thought of his third daughter Sheeba (name changed) to be trained as a dancer but there is no such opportunity in that slum. Migrated from Shivpur village in Uttar Pradesh 15 years ago with the hope of a better education, Md. Rais (name changed) did not have luck on his side. As he could not study beyond the primary level, Rais is very particular about sending his children to school. He wants to work harder to earn more to support his children's education. He and his wife believe that sending their children to school will ensure a higher level of income for them in the future.

In the middle of the dilapidated shanties of the sprawling Govindpuri slum, there stands tall the Katha Khazana School. Started by the NGO Katha in 1990 this school looks like an oasis in a desert, complete with murals and mud-plastered walls with Madhubani motifs and the bulletin boards displaying the story of crossing hurdles and reaching milestones. Katha Khazana caters to the children of empowered slum women. The NGO appreciated the need for supplementing the incomes of indigent households in order to ensure sustainable education to the migrant children and started the programme for the economic empowerment of slum women. The school got government recognition a few years ago and at present works as a government-aided school.

The contrast between Govindpuri and SIM Slums was too sharp. SIM Basti at Mori Gate near Delhi University is a JJ colony of about 200 migrant families from South India, some of them living there for two generations now. The Aayappa temple guarded the entry to a neat and tidy square of tenements where the migrant 'Madrasis' lived. To a common man in Delhi any South Indian is a 'Madrasi', and hence the name. Each household kept its few pieces of furniture and other meagerly possessions clean and dusted. One had to take off the shoes to enter the rooms—not because it was their custom but the cleanliness was so compelling. The distinct culture of the south was reflected in the well-organised slum life. This shantytown was remarkable for its cleanliness and sense of hygiene. Despite poverty there was no sign of gender discrimination. It was evident that the families with one or more daughters did not go for sons, rather, had been taking good care of the girls. In fact, there were more girls playing around than boys. All of them went to school. The parents, whether a Hindu working in a canteen, a Muslim daily wage-earner or a Dalit sweeper, were eager to support their children's education as far as they wanted to pursue. The children did not have a clear idea about their career prospects but insisted that their parents would back them in realising their goals. A common thread running through the households in this slum was the assurance to the children that they would not miss out on the opportunities their parents had never got. Going to school, the men said that Sunday afternoon in early winter, was the only way to a better life for their kids. What the author saw as a sign of rising aspirations in the new generation of migrants was their preference for white-collar jobs. One girl who had already passed the Board examinations, had collected the application form for a constable's job in Delhi traffic police. Her friend wanted to do a nursing course for a job in a government hospital.

Nehru Camp in Patparganj, East Delhi, offered a very different picture. It was not as cohesive and progressive a social group as the slum community at Mori Gate, but perhaps more intense and closer to the larger social reality. The slum received a lot of political patronage. Situated between National Highway 24 and the high-rise apartment blocks of Patparganj, the politically sensitive slum had maintained the electoral roll of all its eligible voters. Everybody here was acutely aware of the crucial importance of their vote. While talking to the people, the author noticed a young man carefully counting the voter identity cards issued by the Election Commission. He was counting them reverentially, the way a priest would the coins collected in the temple, or a warrior his weapons. He was reading out the name of every voter in the community and then looking at their picture on the ID.

It's here that I met Deepak Kumar, the lightly-built young man with a quiet demeanour. I told him about my project and sought his help to collect data from the slum.

Most of the children from a total of 260 families in the slum went to school, mainly the nearby government-aided ones. Some of the older boys were pursuing higher studies. One of them went to the prestigious Hindu College of Delhi University for a degree in History. Another teenager the author met was doing BBA from Sikkim Manipal University through correspondence. The shanties were numbered, piped water and electricity available and at least one member of every family had a mobile phone. Most of these migrants were from Bihar, Uttar Pradesh and West Bengal. Caste or religious lines were not rigidly drawn. In fact, the norms of segregation along the caste or religious lines were rather relaxed in the slum. The divisions were more pronounced along political affiliations. Additionally, poverty and migration had brought them closer; uprooted from their villages, alienated in an indifferent city, the migrants knew they needed to stand together in the battle for survival in an unfamiliar place which did not see their coming kindly. The children spoke the Hindi of the city variety rather than the dialects of their ancestral places. All the people whether Hindu or Muslim, were keen to send their children to school. A community feeling prevailed in the slum. Those who had not sent their older children to school were determined to make sure that the younger ones did not miss the freedom of education. The few college students, it was apparent, were influential and had a big say in the affairs of the slum. Even the community elders gave much importance to their opinion on an issue. The girls attending school were quite ambitious and could articulate their roadmap well. Their main obstacles were inadequate parental support and the high cost of private coaching which they could barely afford. As a consequence, despite their considerable talent, big dreams and a high level of enthusiasm, these children's achievements were poor to average.

Their financial incapacity notwithstanding, the migrant workers were enthusiastic about their children moving into the big world to change the narrative.

While collecting data in February 2010, the living conditions of the slums appeared to the author as far above the level of gnawing poverty. But a revisit in the summer of 2011 told a different story. The health and hygiene levels were far from satisfactory. The entrance to the camp was littered with garbage piled up for days and human excreta. Children were running around oblivious of the stink and squalor.

The slum cluster of Shiva Kunj on the outskirts of Delhi presents a different picture. Situated between the swank apartment blocks and an open sewer, it combines the hope and despair of its surroundings. Tucked away behind a glitzy shopping mall and multiplexes, Shiva Kunj in Vaishali is a blotch on the affluent landscape of this upwardly-mobile neighbourhood in the NCR. But the aspirations of the enterprising professionals living in the high-rise apartment buildings—in a sense also migrants but from higher income group—have influenced the thought processes of the adolescent children in this *jhuggi* cluster. Rukshar (name changed), a Class XII student, wanted to be a 'successful software engineer' and showed the kind of determination required to achieve this goal. Lata (name changed) had just passed her Class XII Board Examination and doing BBA from a private college in West Delhi with the dream of becoming a senior executive in a multinational company one day.

The shantytown milieu significantly changed with the locale. A slum that had quietly grown over the past few decades behind the National Sports Club of India in the NDMC area adjacent to Purana Qila Road, not even a kilometre from India Gate, had a confident mien about it. Among its residents were servants, maids, chauffeurs and *mali*s of senior officials and Members of Parliament living in the sprawling bungalows across the road. Known as NSCI JJ Colony, the cluster also accommodated the lower-level employees of the club and Class IV staff of the nearby schools. They were mostly skilled workers in the organised sector and not migrant workers doing physical work. Walking down the dirt track to the slum, the author saw quite a few Maruti 800 and other small cars parked here and there, young men riding motorcycles. They had a confident look about them. Patronised by powerful people, enjoying social benefits of being close to the power centre, going to good schools, these teenagers could follow English.

Perhaps because they lived behind the National Sports Club of India, some of the youths in the slum aspired to pursue a career in sports. Most of the children here attended school and cherished a life better than their parents. One of them, son of a plumber working at a well-known school, even visited China as part of a youth exchange programme. An Economics (Honours) student at a reputed Delhi University college, his social circle has far surpassed his immediate surroundings.

The residents of this *jhuggi* cluster in the heart of the Capital's VIP district were better off than their counterparts in the outlying areas. The government agencies within the New Delhi Municipal Corporation (NDMC) were more active than their counterparts elsewhere. There is also the added factor of vote-bank politics compelling those in power to appreciate the crucial support of such people in any election. The signs of well-being were everywhere around the place. The shiny bikes and little Marutis are more than anything else pointers to a new possibility.

The Why and How of this Narrative

This project had been embarked upon out of a quest, to find out about the migrant community's aspirations for their children's education in Delhi in the post-reform period. Many experts believe that the economic liberalisation of 1991 was the single-most impactful event in the life of the nation since Independence. The New Economic Policy of Liberalisation, Privatisation and Globalisation was adopted by the Indian government shaking off the deadwood socialism to bring about a structural change. The forces triggered by the reforms consequently pushed the economy into a higher trajectory of growth.

The Terms — Their Meanings and Subtexts

✣ Educational aspirations

Oxford Advanced Learner's Dictionary of Current English (OUP) defines 'aspiration' as a strong desire to have or do something. 'Educational aspiration' can, therefore, be defined as the strong desire or willingness of a set of people to educate themselves or their children, mainly through formal schooling.

✣ Occupational aspiration

The term similarly refers to the strong desire or willingness of people to get themselves gainfully employed at the end of their education and training. Occupational aspirations are fulfilled by the achievement of educational aspirations whereas educational aspirations are guided by the occupational aspirations of a social group. It is a proven fact that chances of getting better employment and earnings increase proportionately with one's educational achievements.

In the present context, the educational and occupational aspirations of the migrants and their children in Delhi have been the subject of investigation.

✣ Migrant population

Migration: It is the movement of people from one place to another in search of a better standard of living. Migration can take place across national boundaries or from one place to another within a country. Accordingly, we can define international migration and internal migration.

International migration: The movement of people from the country of their birth to some other part of the world.

Internal migration: 'It includes any movement within the political boundaries of a nation which results in a change of usual place of residence. It may consist of the crossing of a village or town boundary' (Census, 2001).

The present study solely focuses on internal migration. In the context of this research internal migration refers to the movement of people from the other states of India to the national capital territory of Delhi. A large number of people not only from the adjoining states of U.P., Uttarakhand or Haryana, but also from far-off states like West Bengal, Bihar or Tamil Nadu migrate to Delhi to eke out a better living. The study delimits itself to this internal migration and movement of people permanently from their own places of origin to the national capital.

Migrants: A migrant is usually defined as a person who has moved from one politically defined area to another similar area. In the Indian context, these areas are either villages in a rural area or a town in an urban agglomeration. Thus, a person who moves out from one village or town to another village or town is termed a migrant provided his or her movement is not of purely temporary nature on account of casual leave, visits, tours and so on (Census 2001).

This study concentrates on the migrants from the lower income groups only. They are the underprivileged people from different states, either skilled or unskilled who along with their families come to the city of Delhi in search of a better life.

Non-migrants (Immobile): People, who live their entire lifetime and die in the same village or town in which they were born, are defined as Immobile or non-migrants (Census report, 2001).

In the true sense of the term there will be hardly any non-migrants in Delhi. The city, barring its small group of residents in the Walled City and the minuscule Jat community in the rural segment, grew with the continuous inflow of people from the outside. For the purpose of this research the second-generation non-slum migrants, who were born and brought up in Delhi, have been taken as non-migrants. As the purpose of including the non-migrants in the study is to compare the aspirations of the marginalised migrants with that of the non-migrants, the latter group has been chosen from the non-slum population of Delhi and without attaching any income condition to them. For the purpose of the study, therefore, non-migrants are the non-slum population of Delhi residing in the city for at least two generations.

Slums: A compact area for a population of at least 300 or about 60-70 households of bare, congested tenements, in an unhygienic environment usually with inadequate infrastructure and lacking in proper sanitary and drinking water facilities.

This includes:

(a) All specified areas in a town or city notified as 'Slum' by a state or local government or UT Administration under any Act including the 'Slum Act'.

(b) All areas recognised as 'Slum' by a state or local government or UT Administration, Housing and Slum Boards, which may have not been formally notified as slum under any Act.

To decongest the city and put a check on unlimited flow of migrants into the city, the Delhi Master Plan 2021 talks about Counter Magnet Areas with a 120 km radius around Delhi. This is viewed as the future National Capital Region which will be developed to attract and absorb migrants instead of allowing Delhi to get overcrowded by them (Retrieved from www.ncrpb.nic.in).

Table 4.1

Migrants in Delhi: Population Classified by Place of Birth

Birth place	Census 1991	Census 2001	Census 2011
Delhi	57,09,750	82,04,230	N.A.
Uttar Pradesh	17, 04,197	23,16,731	22,96,367
Bihar	2,67,567	7,37,867	7,25,565
Haryana	4,40,275	5,45,811	5,55,173
Uttaranchal	-	3,06,503	N.A.
Punjab	2,35,142	2,51,091	N.A.
West Bengal	78,811	1,69,165	N.A.
Other States	3,75,313	6,03,127	N.A.
Total Population in Delhi	94,20,644	1,38,50,507	-

Source: Economic Survey of India, 2005-2006, pp. 262-63, Table 3.14, Migration Data; Census 2011, migration data (www.censusindia.gov.in)

The study is delimited to marginalised migrants living in the slums of Delhi. The sample took into consideration nine slums chosen at random from five administrative zones of Delhi. From each slum on an average 10 households were picked up. Children studying in Classes IX-XII from such households comprised the sample base of migrant children. From each slum five parents were chosen as part of the sample for migrants.

The Methodology

The methodology used in this study is the descriptive survey method. Descriptive research describes the present events and establishes causal-relationships between observed variables. It is not possible to control any variable in this type of research. Although it describes the present it may often use events from the past as factors that might have influenced the present variables under study. In case of this particular research project the economic reforms of 1991 has been used as one such past event which has affected the educational and occupational aspirations of the migrants and their children in the period under study.

Statement of the Problem

This is a study of educational aspirations of the migrant population in Delhi in post reform India. Therefore, the Title of the study has been formulated as 'Educational Aspirations of the Migrant Population in Delhi'.

As educational aspirations and occupational aspirations are closely linked the study also observes and analyses the occupational aspirations of the migrant children living in the slums of Delhi.

Objectives

The Objectives of this research work are framed as:

1. To assess the educational and occupational aspirations of the students and their parents.
2. To assess the enrolment and success rate of the children of migrant labourers for the past decade.
3. To analyse the academic and vocational programmes available for the children of migrant labourers in terms of their level of aspiration and specific requirements.
4. To examine how the process of economic reforms has impacted the educational aspirations of the migrants and their children.

Hypotheses

The following hypotheses have been constructed to empirically observe and analyse the objectives of the study:

(i) Null Hypotheses for objective 1:

Ho1.1 There is no significant difference in educational aspirations of the migrant children and their parents

Ho1.2 There is no significant difference in occupational aspirations of the migrant children and their parents

Ho1.3 There is no significant difference in educational aspirations of the boys and girls of the migrant children

Ho1.4 There is no significant difference in occupational aspirations of the boys and girls of the migrant children

Ho1.5 There is no significant difference in educational aspirations of the migrant and non-migrant children

Ho1.6 There is no significant difference in educational aspirations of the migrant and non-migrant parents.

Ho1.7 There is no significant difference in occupational aspirations of the migrant and non-migrant children

Ho1.8 There is no significant difference in occupational aspirations of the migrant and non-migrant parents

(ii) Hypothesis for objective 2:

H2. The enrolment and academic success rate of migrant children have gone up in the past decade

(iii) Hypothesis for objective 3:

H3a. The migrant children prefer vocational education to general education

H3b. Education system has not yet fulfilled the aspirations of the migrants fully

(iv) Hypothesis for objective 4:

H4. Economic reforms have thrown open larger opportunities for the migrants who are skilled or educated and boosted their aspirations

Population & Sample

The poor migrants living in the slums of Delhi have been considered the target population of this research. To understand their educational and occupational aspirations in post reform India, a stratified random sample has been drawn out of this population. The sample consists of 100 migrant children and 50 migrant parents. In order to compare the migrants' aspirations with the non-migrants, a random sample of same size has been drawn from the non-migrant, non-slum population of Delhi. To analyse the role the school plays in fulfilling the aspirations of the migrants a random sample of 100 teachers including Head teachers has been drawn from the schools situated across the city.

Hence, the total size of the sample is 400 consisting of 200 children and 200 adults.

Table 4.2

Composition of the Sample

Categories of respondents	Migrant	Non- Migrant	Total
Parents	50	50	100
Students	50 (Class X) 50 (Class XII)	50 (Class X) 50 (Class XII)	200
Teachers (Including Head of the Institution)	100		100

Sampling method

Stratified random sampling has been followed to choose the migrants. Delhi is divided into five zones for administrative purposes—North, East, South, Central and West. They are further subdivided into nine revenue districts—North-West, North, North-East, East, Central, New Delhi, South, South-West and West. From each zone two slums were chosen at random. East and South revenue districts have larger concentration of slums, hence two slums from each of these districts were picked up. New Delhi district's slum population is insignificant, so it has been merged with the Central. From each slum approximately 10 households were randomly selected.

Table 4.3

List of Slums from Where Data Related to Migrants Have Been Collected

Administrative Zones	Revenue Districts	Slums	No. of interviewees	
			Children	Parents
North	North-West	Shankar Camp, Rangpuri Pahari	10	05
	North	South Indian Madrasi Slum, Mori Gate	10	05
East	East	Nehru Camp, Patparganj	12	06
		Shiva Kunj, Vaishali	10	06
Central	Central	JJ Colony NSCI, near Purana Quilla	20	08
South	South	Bhuvin Camp, Govindpuri	10	04
		Batla House, Ashram	10	05
West	South-West	Mahavir Enclave JJ Colony, Dwarka	10	06
	West	Rattanpuri Chowk, Pusa Gate , Patel Nagar	08	05
Total			100	50

Fig 4.1 Zone wise sample for migrant children and parents

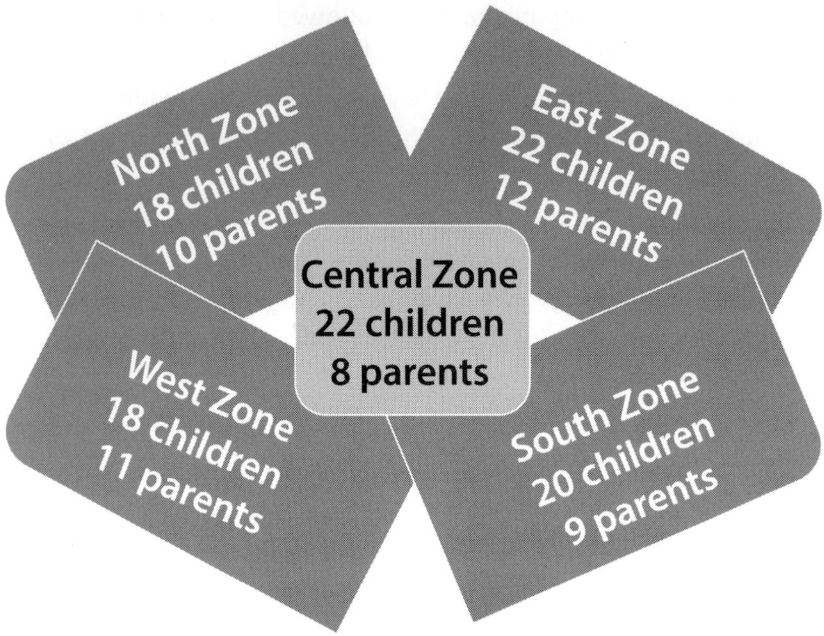

The sample of 100 non-migrant children was collected by random sampling method from across the city. The teachers' sample was drawn at random from across the schools of Delhi.

In all three samples direct personal interview method was followed to collect data with the help of the questionnaires. For majority of the migrant children and all of their parents the author had to explain the questions in Hindi and fill in the answers for them. Some of the respondents among migrant children, particularly in NSCI JJ Colony, could understand English and fill the questionnaires themselves. Non-migrants and teachers filled in the questionnaires themselves. Data from a few teachers were collected via e-mail.

Tools

Tools are used to satisfy the objectives of the study. Following are the tools that have been formulated and used for the purpose of this study.

- A questionnaire to interview the migrant labourers (Annexure A)
- A questionnaire to interview the school-going children of the migrants (Annexure A)
- A questionnaire to collect information from school teachers including the head teacher (Annexure A)
- Educational aspiration scale (Annexure B)
- Occupational check list and rating scale (Annexure B)
- Same questionnaires & scales were used to collect data from non-migrant children and their parents for comparing the data
- Secondary data from various authentic sources have been used to follow trends and interpret tendencies

Validity and Reliability of tools:

- The questionnaires were assessed by five eminent educationists and economists and changes were made according to their advice. The tool thus has content, criterion and consensus validity.
- The educational aspiration scale was derived from the scale used by Prof. Kevin Marjoribanks of Department of Education, University of Adelaide, Australia, in 2000, to find out the link between educational aspirations and achievements of Australian young adults (Published in International Education Journal, 2005). Educational aspirations were measured by him on a 5-point scale with the adolescents indicating when they planned to leave school and how much education they hoped to attain afterward. The derived scale, as modified with respect to Indian situation, measures very low educational aspiration as 1 and very high as 5. Very low or 1 indicates 'eager to drop out before class X or already a drop out' whereas very high or 5 indicates

the aspiration when the respondent 'wants to complete post graduation'.

- The occupational check list and rating scale were developed by Banerjee and Roy in 2010. Here 1 indicates very low occupational aspirations when the respondents aims to get lowly ranked jobs requiring no special skills whereas 5 indicates that the respondents target the occupation which requires higher level of skills or professional training.
- For secondary data the authenticity of the sources was kept in mind. Main sources were:
  - Economic Surveys, 1989-90 to 2010-11
  - Human Development Reports, 1996 to 2012
  - National Human Development Reports, 1991 and 2011
  - Budget Documents of India, 1991 to 2012
  - Census Data of India, 1991, 2001 and 2011
  - Planning Commission reports
  - National Sample Survey data
  - DISE data
  - Gazette of India
  - Official websites of:
    - Delhi Directorate of Education (www.edudel.nic.in)
    - Ministry of Human Resource Development (www.mhrd.gov.in)
    - Ministry of Labour (www.labourbureau.nic.in)
    - Planning Commission (www.planningcommission.nic.in)
    - Sarva Shiksha Abhiyan (www.ssa.nic.in)
    - Central Board of Secondary Education (www.cbse.nic.in)
    - National family and Health Survey (www.nfhsindia.org)

    - India Education Review (www.indiaeducationreview.com)
    - Delhi Urban Shelter Board (www.delhishelterboard.in)
    - www.ncrpb.nic.in
- Major Newspapers and Magazines
    - *Time magazine*
    - *The Economist*
    - *The Times of India*
    - *The Indian Express*
    - *The Hindustan Times*
    - *The Pioneer*
    - *The Hindu*

Reliability indicates whether the questionnaire performs consistently. The reliability of the questionnaires for this study was tested through pilot survey. Test-retest method was followed in an interval of two weeks for the pilot survey group. The correlation between responses found between two points of time was very high (0.881) indicating high degree of reliability of the questionnaires.

Delimitations

This study is delimited to:

- The area National Capital Region i.e. Delhi and its neighbourhoods
- The post-reform period from 1991-92 to 2011-12
- Internal migration
- Poor migrants living in the slums of Delhi

5

ANALYSES OF DATA

From Ancestral Village to Shantytown: Why did they Migrate?

The majority of migrants under study came to Delhi driven out of their rural life by grinding poverty and for the prospect of earning more. Some of them, mainly women, came after marriage. A small percentage was forced to leave their ancestral places by natural calamities or loss of land or property. But it was very obvious from the long sessions the author had with these people that all of them had left their villages hoping to see a better life for themselves and their children in the national capital.

Table 5.1

Causes of Migration

Cause of migration	Percentage of respondents
Prospect of better income	61
Marriage	18
Loss of land or property	05
Natural calamities	07
Any other	09
Total	100

Source: Primary Data

Fig 5.1 Causes of migration

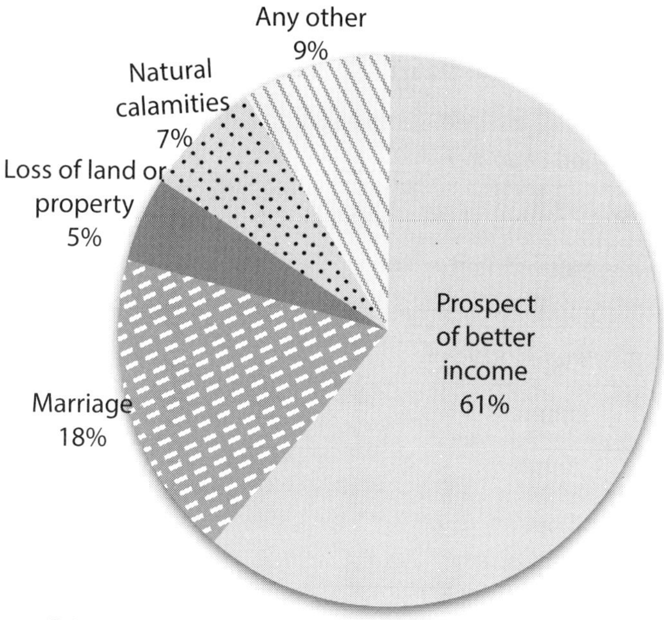

Source: Primary Data

After they settled down in the capital city, they looked for employment mostly in the unorganised sector as skilled or unskilled workers. Many among the women remained unemployed looking after the households.

But the migrant children and their parents revealed that they saw education as a tool for realising their ambitions. The study found out that for them education was a vehicle to ride to a better life where they could find the jobs they preferred. An analysis of the current occupational status of the migrant parents and the favoured occupation of their children presented in the Tables below would bring out the sharp contrast between the realities and their hopes.

The analyses of data subsequently established that schooling could act as the bridge between the two.

Table 5.2

Occupational Status of the Parents of Migrant Children

Parents' occupational status	Father (per cent)	Mother (per cent)
Unskilled Labourer	25	18
Skilled Labourer	43	03
Self-employed/Petty business	18	05
Unemployed/Housewife	10	73
Others	04	01
Total	100	100

Source: Primary Data

Fig 5.2 Migrant parents' occupations

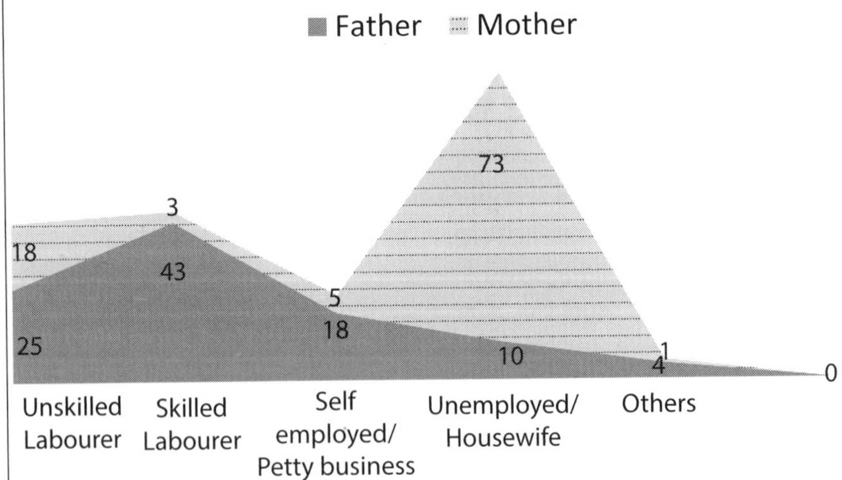

Source: Primary Data

Table 5.3

Desired Occupations of Migrant Children Surveyed

	WHAT DO YOU WANT TO BE?							
Occupation → / Slums ↓	Doctor	Engineer	CA/Lawyer/ Manager/ Pilot	Govt. Officer	Teacher	Non-Conventional	Others (Business/ Self empt/ Petty jobs etc.)	Total
Rangpuri Pahari	1				7	1	1	10
SIM Basti			1	2	4	1	2	10
Nehru Camp	3	1	1	2	3	1	1	12
Shiva Kunj		1	3	2	1		3	10
NSCI JJ Colony	2	5	2	2	5	3	1	20
Govindpuri	1	1	1	2	3	1	1	10
Ashram		1			5	3	1	10
Mahavir Enclave	1	4	1	1	2		1	10
Pusa Gate	1	1		4		2		08
Total	09	14	09	15	30	12	11	100

Source: Primary Data

Objective 1

To assess the educational and occupational aspirations of the students and their parents.

Testing of Null Hypotheses

Table 5.4

Educational Aspirations of the Interviewees

Educational aspirations	Migrant children			Migrant parents	Non-migrant children			Parents of non-migrant children
	Boys	Girls	Total		Boys	Girls	Total	
1	2	2	4	5	0	0	0	2
2	1	2	3	4	0	0	0	2
3	6	9	15	10	5	3	8	3
4	17	19	36	16	13	13	26	19
5	22	20	42	15	30	36	66	24
Total	48	52	100	50	48	52	100	50

Note: Scale used: 5 point scale with 1 as the lowest aspiration (wants to leave school anytime) and 5 the highest (willing to study up to university level). (Detailed scale has been shown in Annexure B).

Table 5.5

Occupational Aspirations of the Interviewees

Occupational aspirations	Migrant children			Migrant parents	Non-migrant children			Parents of non-migrant children
	Boys	Girls	Total		Boys	Girls	Total	
1	2	2	4	4	0	0	0	2
2	4	2	6	5	0	0	0	2
3	3	7	10	6	0	0	0	10
4	12	21	33	25	12	7	19	15
5	27	20	47	10	36	45	81	21
Total	48	52	100	50	48	52	100	50

Note: Occupational aspirations were measured on a 5-point rating scale with 1 indicating very low aspiration and 5 very high with respect to the job checklist. (Annexure B).

Data derived from the Tables 5.4 and 5.5 have been used for testing the null hypotheses. Chi-square (χ^2) has been used for the non-parametric statistical analyses. The formula for Chi-square is:

$$\chi^2 = \Sigma [(f_0 - f_e)^2/f_e]$$

where f_0 is the observed frequency and f_e is the expected frequency. The estimated chi-square values have been shown in Table 5.6 below.

Table 5.6
Estimated Chi-Square Values

Hypotheses	Chi-square value (with degrees of freedom)
$H_0 1.1$	6.245* (df4)
$H_0 1.2$	11.371* (df4)
$H_0 1.3$	3.368* (df4)
$H_0 1.4$	5.622* (df4)
$H_0 1.5$	16.076**(df4)
$H_0 1.6$	8.056* (df4)
$H_0 1.7$	32.802**(df4)
$H_0 1.8$	9.356* (df4)

* Accepted at .01 level of significance
** Rejected at .01 as well as .05 levels of significance

On the basis of Chi-square values estimated null hypotheses H01.1 to H01.4 have been accepted indicating the lack of gender influence on educational and occupational aspirations of the migrant children. They also show the parental support behind the migrant children in achieving their goals. But the rejection of H01.5 and H01.7 indicates that contrary to the hypotheses of the author there is significant difference in the educational and occupational aspirations between migrant and non-migrant children. On the other hand, acceptance of H01.6 and H01.8 signify that the parental ambitions for children for their education and occupation are similar for the migrant and non-migrant parents.

Qualitative Analysis: Descriptive Statistical Analyses of Survey Questions

The author used three sets of questionnaires to analyse the rising educational aspirations of the migrants in the post-reform period from the points of view of the migrants themselves, their children and the teaching community. They are presented in Tables and Diagrams in the section below.

The migrants who now send their children to school, would not have done so a quarter century ago. Most of the respondents felt that sending their children to school was a sure way of changing their lives. They were eager to support their children's education as long as possible. Even their children believed that this would improve their families' standards of living.

Analyses of their responses confirm this.

Table 5.7

Desire of Parents for Same Type of Occupation for their Children

Response	Number of respondents (migrant parents)			
	Illiterate	Literate	Total	Percentage
Yes	2	1	3	6
No	13	33	46	92
Can't say	1	0	1	2
Total	16	34	50	100

Source: Primary Data

Fig 5.3 Do the migrants want their children to follow the same occupation as theirs?

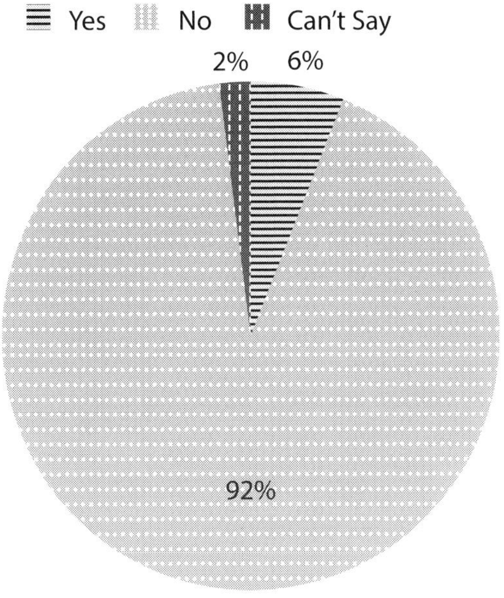

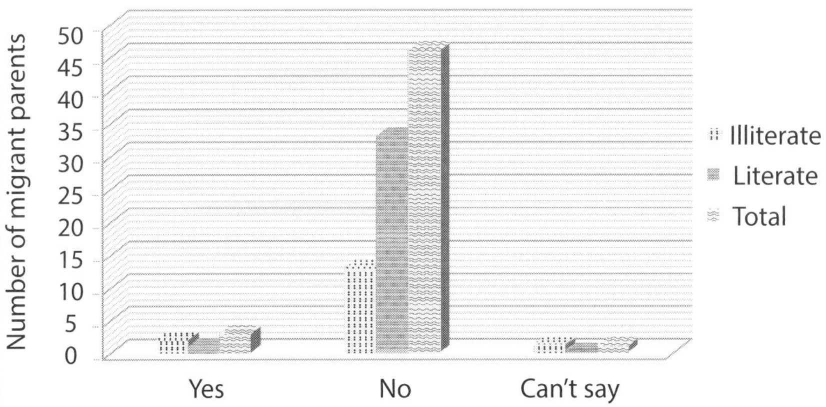

Source: Primary Data

Note: Information on parents' educational qualifications as obtained through the questionnaire helped the author segregate them into two categories—literate and unlettered. Literate parents at least had attended school up to some level whereas the illiterate ones had never gone to school.

Most of the parents interviewed were unskilled or semi-skilled workers, as shown in Table 5.2, employed as maids, drivers, lift operators, canteen assistants, vegetable vendors, masons, carpenters, guards and so on. Almost all of them (92 per cent) whether literate or unlettered, did not want their children to do the same kind of hard physical work, and wanted them to start at a higher level.

The parental aspirations influenced the children whose response to new opportunities came as a kind of morale booster for the elders. When the migrant children were asked whether their parents shared their ambitions, 87 per cent said yes.

Table 5.8

Sharing of Ambition among Migrant Parents and their Children

Responses	Percentage of migrant children
Yes	87
No	05
Can't say	08
Total	100

Fig 5.4 Do your parents share your ambition?

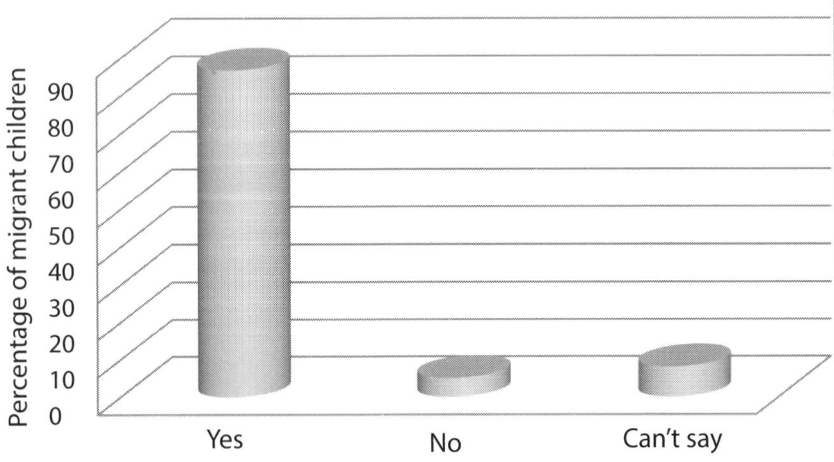

Source: Primary Data

Most of the migrants (84 per cent of the respondents) put their children in government schools. A small number of parents (16 per cent) sent their children to private schools as well. Whether they sent their children to private or government schools the predominant considerations for the choice were either cost or quality. A small percentage of parents considered the distance from home as a factor deciding their selection of the school.

Table 5.9

Considerations for Choosing the Child's School

Criteria	Percentage of migrant parents
Money/ Financial costs	30
Quality of education provided	48
Distance	22
Any other	0
Total	100

Fig 5.5 Considerations for choosing the child's school

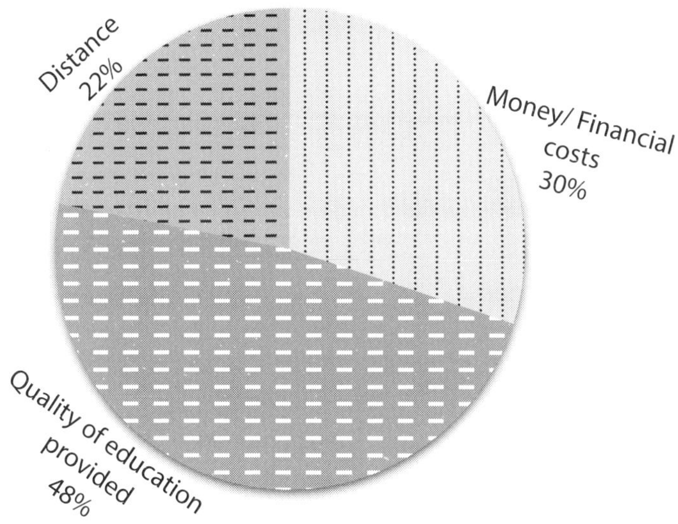

Source: Primary Data

Not only the migrants shared their children's dreams, they were willing to financially support their children's education as well. Asked how they supported their children's education, 41 per cent of them said that they paid the tuition fees from their own incomes while 59 per cent of the parents admitted their children had access to free education. No one seemed to take financial help from relatives or sponsors for their children's education.

Whether they themselves had the knowledge of the Three R's or not, the migrant workers were keen to see their children move upwards availing the new opportunities through education.

Table 5.10

Level of Education as Desired by Migrant Parents for their Children

Responses	Number of respondents			Percentage of respondents
	Illiterate	Literate	Total	
School leaving	5	0	5	10
Graduate	6	5	11	22
Postgraduate	1	2	3	06
Technical education	1	7	8	16
As far as the child wants	3	20	23	46
Total	16	34	50	100

Fig 5.6 How far do you want your child to study?

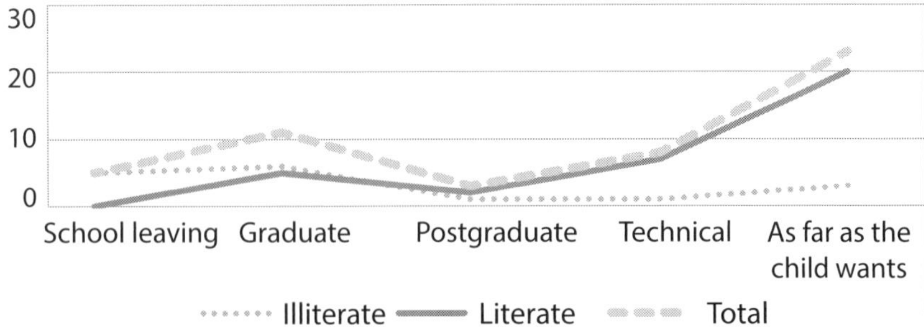

Source: Primary Data

The parents were ready to work even harder to support their children's education although a small section of them would not mind if the children could share their financial burden a little by doing odd jobs to assist themselves.

Table 5. 11

Parents' Opinion on Part-Time Odd Jobs for their Children

Responses	Percentage of migrant parents
Yes	27
No	30
Only when he/she goes to high school	07
Only when he/she passes out of school	36
Total	100

Source: Primary Data

The children, on the other hand, believed that going to school could get them everything and pull them out of their sub-human existence in the slums. They dreamt of earning good money, settling down to a life of dignity—having access to everything that they had missed so far. They felt that going to school would pave the way to freedom from their gloomy existence in the slums. They also feel the urgency of going to school to improve their families' standard of living and moreover social status. This sentiment was reflected in their response to the author's question about why they wanted to be what they wanted to be.

Table 5.12

Reasons Behind the Desired Occupation and Educational Aspirations

Response	Percentage of migrant children
To earn money	28
To become famous	29
To have dignity of life	17
To improve the standard of living of my family	26
Total	100

Source: Primary Data

Fig 5.7 Reasons behind the desired occupation for the migrant children

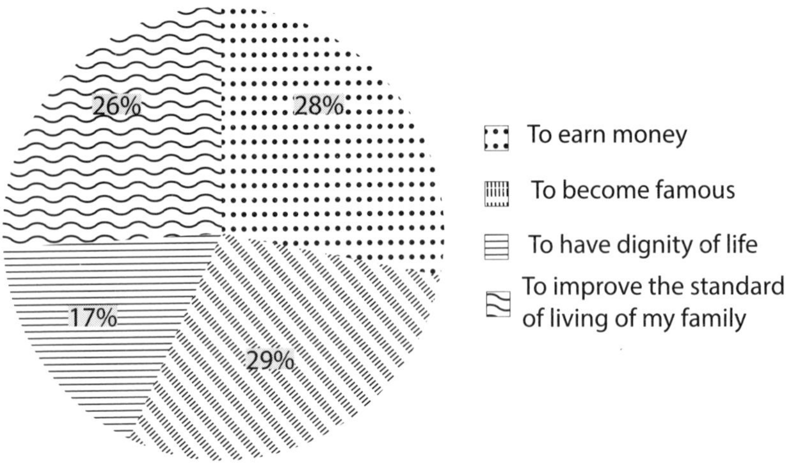

Source: Primary Data

While interviewing the school teachers, including the Head Teachers, it was apparent that the number of admission requests from the migrant children had gone up significantly after the year 2000. They testified to a growing eagerness among the migrants to send their children to school in the recent years (2000-2010).

Table 5.13

Confirmation by Teachers of Migrants' Rising Aspirations

Response (Migrants' educational aspirations rising in recent years)	Percentage of respondents (Teachers/ Principals)
Yes	95
No	0
Can't say	5
Total	100

Source: Primary Data

Fig 5.8 Teachers' observations on migrants' rising aspirations

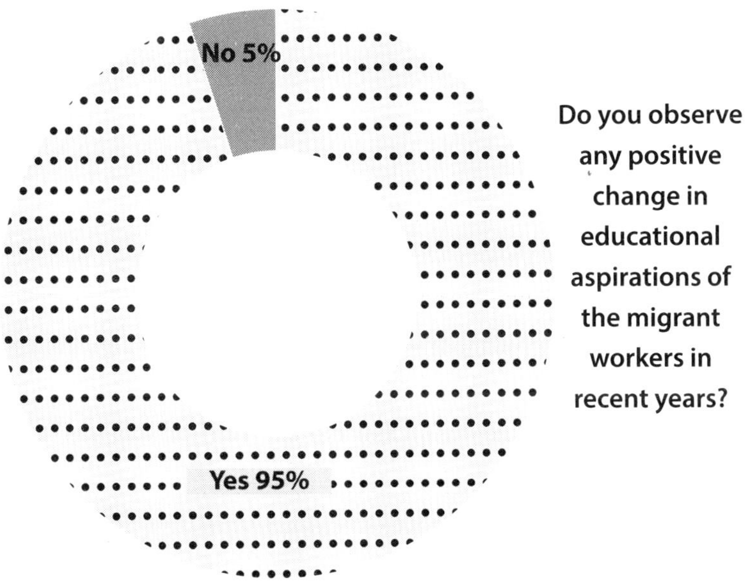

Source: Primary Data

Table 5.14
Bigger Flow of Migrant Children to School in Post-Reform Years

Response	Percentage of teachers/ Principals
Yes	90
No	0
Can't say	10
Total	100

Fig 5.9 More requests for admissions in post-reform period?

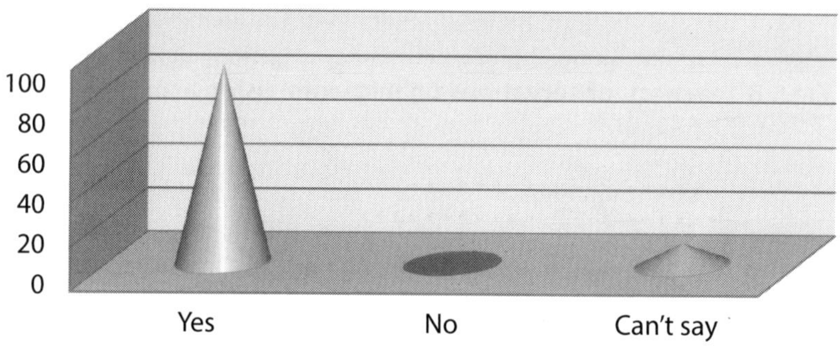

Source: Primary Data

An analysis of data from teachers' responses also confirmed the rising occupational aspirations of migrants for their children in the recent years.

Table 5.15
Increased Occupational Aspirations of the Migrants for Their Children (Teachers' Observations)

Response	Percentage of teachers/ Principals
Yes	87
No	5
Can't say	8
Total	100

Source: Primary Data

Fig 5.10 Teachers' view: Rise in migrant children's occupational aspirations

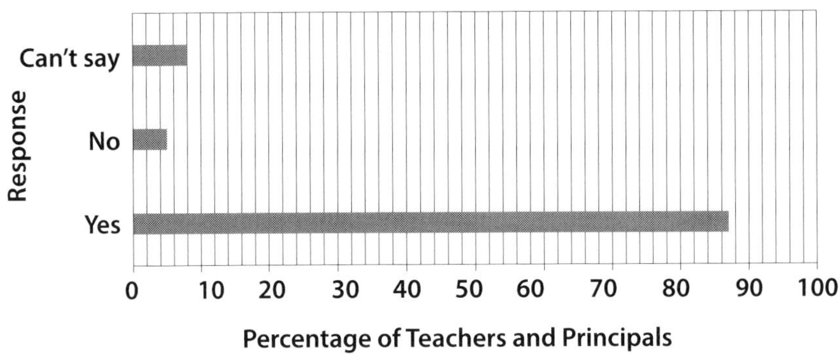

Source: Primary Data

However, a smaller number of teachers felt that the migrants were aware of new job opportunities opened up by call centres, retail, travel industry, telecom and a few others raising their occupational aspirations in the post-reform period. While 87 per cent of teachers confirmed a rise in the migrant students' occupational aspirations only 55 per cent of the respondents felt that the uprooted community was aware of the new sectors opening up in the economy creating jobs in the years following the reforms.

Table 5.16

Migrants' Awareness of New Job Opportunities in Post-Reform Era (Teachers' View)

Response	Percentage of Teachers/ Principals
Yes	55
No	20
Can't say	25
Total	100

Fig 5.11 Migrants' awareness of new types of jobs (Teachers' observations)

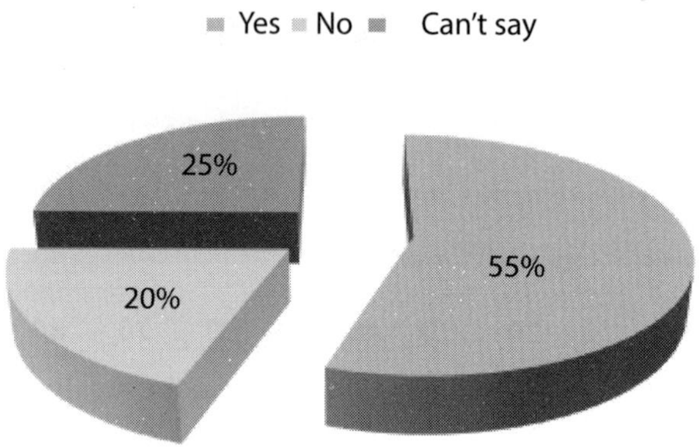

Source: Primary Data

Contribution of the NGOs

This research project would be incomplete without acknowledging the contributions of the non-governmental organisations (NGOs) in playing the crucial role of taking education to the underprivileged slum children of Delhi.

As the government provides free education, it was only natural that the children of migrant workers living in slums would take admission in the government schools only. But the poor quality of teaching, absenteeism among teachers and lack of basic infrastructure like proper classrooms, blackboards, stationery, toilets, etc. make these schools less attractive.

Non-formal education (NFE) for out-of-school children introduced by the government was a major step to universalisation of elementary education (UEE). It covers the children who dropped out or never enrolled for various personal or socio-economic reasons including migration (www.edudel.nic). But the government-run NFE centres are very few in urban areas. Delhi Directorate of Education has a plan for setting up 75 ICT-based non-formal education points along the boundary walls of government schools to bring out-of-school children and unlettered adults in the fold of education (SSA Document, p.5). The planning for the year 2011-12 included Dakhila Abhiyan for 5,896 out-of-school children and creation of Special Training Centres (STCs) on the government school premises led by the HOSs for the remaining 19,640[1]. But there is always a huge gap between planning and implementation as far as the government projects are concerned.

Here comes the role of the non-governmental organisations (NGOs) many of whom have taken the initiative to provide NFE to underprivileged children in Delhi and NCR. Although an NGO can get funds from the government to run an NFE centre, some of them professionally managed by the private organisations have fund-raising skills and collect sufficient funds for their programmes through various subsidiary activities and sponsorships. Many of them do proper research before starting NFE centres for the target groups and it helps achieve their objectives better. The drop-out rates in the NGO-run schools and at the NFE centres are low or almost nil (Govinda, R., India Education Report, OUP, Delhi). They achieve this by making school life interesting for the child. They also reduce the opportunity cost of sending the child to school for the parents by providing them alternative sources of income, particularly the mothers, who were previously unemployed. For example, Katha first created work opportunities for women in the Govindpuri slums before bringing their children into the fold of their Katha Khazana school set up there.

---

1 According to government estimates through Household Child Census there were 25,536 out-of-school children in Delhi in 2010-11. (Alternative and Innovative Education for out-of-school children, SSA Document, p. 3 retrieved from www.edudel.nic.in)

These NGOs have not just helped the migrants educate their children but created subsidiary employment opportunities for them to make education sustainable for these underprivileged households. Some NGOs provide free transport from slums to the education centres so distance or transport cost does not act as a deterrent. Some of them help the children get college admission and find work after completion of their courses. Their encouragement and organisational efficiency have increased the level of educational aspirations of the migrants and their children. In fact, the sharp rise in the literacy rate between 1991 and 2001 to a great extent could be attributed to the efforts of the education NGOs working for the out-of-school children. Work done by some prominent education NGOs in Delhi has been highlighted in Chapter 3.

The government recognises the role and contribution of the NGOs in improving the level of literacy among the marginalised. The SSA in its documents on 'Programme for out-of-school children' mentions:

> 'In the education sector, non-governmental organisations have been making very meaningful contributions. Work related to pedagogy, mainstreaming out of school children, developing effective teacher training programmes, organising community for capacity development for planning and implementation, expressing gender concerns, work in the sphere of disability among children, are some such examples' (Alternative and Innovative Education for Out-of-School Children, SSA document, retrieved from http://www.edudel.nic.in/ssa/7.pdf).

A large number of prominent educational NGOs are operating very effectively in the slums of Delhi to bring the disadvantaged children into the fold of education. (Details in Annexure C). In fact, for the Special Training Programme under SSA in 2011 the government itself has involved some reputed education NGOs to complement its efforts (ibid. at p. 6).

Table 5.17

List of NGOs Assisting Delhi Government in Running Special Training Centres for Out-of-School Children

Sr. No.	NGO	No. of centres run by this NGO	Revenue District
1	Sakar Outreach	6	South
2	STOP	2	North West
3	Multi Vision Foundation	3	North West
4	Tamoha	10	West
5	Nature	8	West
6	Nai Disha	8	South West
7	Prayas	21	20 in South, 1 in South West
8	R. S. Rohini Education and Charitable Society	4	North West
9	Urvi Vikram Charitable Trust	5	South West
10	International Centre for Women and Child	3	South West
11	Invigorator Development Research and Action	3	South West
12	Waruda	8	West
13	Natural's care	15	South West
Total		96	

Source: http://www.edudel.nic.in/ssa/7.pdf., Data compiled by the author.

The statistical as well as qualitative analyses of data corroborated by case studies of NGO projects prove that the educational and occupational aspirations of the migrants are high today. Whether the parents are literate or not and irrespective of the child's gender, the migrants as a community feels that sending the children to school is the only way to improve their lot.

Rising Enrolment and Academic Success Rate of Delhi's Migrant Children

Objective 2

To assess the enrolment and success rate of the migrant children for the past decade.

Hypothesis (H2)

The enrolment and academic success rate of migrant children have gone up significantly over the past decade.

Empirical observations and data analyses

Human Development Report 2009 observes that the migrant children tend to perform less impressively than the privileged city children. However, 'the next generation—children of migrants who are born in the destination place—generally do better.' (HDR 2009, pp. 59)

Data related to enrolment or success rates of migrant children are not available in schools in Delhi as the criteria for classification of school students by the Directorate of Education do not consider them as a separate group. Children's records have been maintained according to gender, and categories such as SC, ST, OBC, disabled, religion and economically weaker sections (EWS), but schools are not encouraged to differentiate between the children with respect to parental occupations or place of birth. The schools, therefore, do not maintain records of a family's migration. So it was not possible to assess the enrolment and success rates of the migrant children directly from school data.

Dr Sunita Chugh, a professor at NUEPA in a recent paper[2] laments that 'one of the significant reasons for the inability to plan for the urban disadvantaged is non-availability of data'. She points out that as the underprivileged migrants live in unauthorised slums, the official surveys do not cover them and therefore schools are not intended to cater to them.

Regretting the unavailability of migration data, and the governmental indifference towards maintaining them properly, Human Development Report 2009 said, 'Unfortunately, migration data remain weak. It is much easier for policy-makers to count the international movements of shoes and cell-phones than of nurses and construction workers.' (HDR, 2009, ch 32, p. 328)

The author wanted to take EWS data as a substitute for that of poor migrant children. Although a migrant child living in a slum will definitely figure in the EWS category, it is not the other way round. As the income limit for the EWS category is Rs 1 lakh per annum, the underprivileged people living in the neighbourhood of a school are normally covered in this category. As compulsory admission of EWS students in schools is a recent decision, a proper record of their numbers is not yet maintained in most of the schools. Even the DISE form did not enquire about the data related to EWS students till the 2009-10 session whereas it had columns for religious and social groups (SC/ST/OBC) to identify the number of students belonging to minority social or religious groups in a school. While collecting data for the year 2011-12, however, DISE created a column for the EWS. Even the Delhi Directorate of Education so far has not maintained any data with respect to enrolment and success of EWS students. When contacted, the office of one of the Directorates of Education in November 2011, to enquire about the publication or website for accessing data about the enrolment and success of the EWS students, the author was told that this kind of record had not yet been generated

2 'Data Needs for Achieving UEE in Urban Areas: Focus on Disadvantaged Groups'.

though the process would start soon. In fact, after the RTE Act was introduced in Delhi schools in 2010, the newspapers focused on the admission records of the EWS students. One post on the Delhi Directorate of Education website revealed the availability of seats for the EWS students in the private unaided schools in Delhi for the session 2009-10. Out of 54,316 seats reserved in various schools, only 7,797 were filled. In other words, only 14.35 per cent of the EWS children actually got admission against the quota allocated for them. A news report in *The Pioneer* on 29 April 2012 mentioned that 9,706 seats were still vacant in various schools in Delhi for the EWS category for the session 2012-13 (*The Pioneer*, 29 April 2012). However, a post on the DDE website www.edudel.nic.in in May 2012 claimed that at that point only 704 seats remained to be filled in for the session 2012-13.

Whether we can entirely depend on the contradictory statistics or not, it is clear that in the past few years the media and social pressure forced the government to play an active role in enrolling the EWS and other backward and disadvantaged students into the folds of formal schooling. In the beginning of the session 2012-13 the Deputy Directors called meetings of the heads of schools of their zones and collected data about vacant EWS seats in each school and planned to bridge the gap. The zone-wise statistics for EWS seats on the DoE website authenticated by the DDEs in May 2012 seemed to be part of that effort. This, however, clearly indicates the increase in enrolment of EWS students in schools.

The new government policy of Rashtriya Madhyamik Shiksha Abhiyan (RMSA) which is a step forward from SSA aims at putting all children in the 14-16 age group in school by 2017. Accordingly, the Delhi government has been taking measures to ensure greater school accessibility for the EWS students. Some of those measures are:

- Scientific micro-planning
- School mapping

- Involvement of the community in planning and NGOs in conducting Special Training Centres and for special admission drives
- Mobile schools to reach out to the unreached
- Offering education to out-of-school children through ICTs
- E-governance

If they are implemented properly the enrolment drive will get boosted very soon.

From the year 2010 the marking system has been replaced by the grading system up to Class X by the CBSE. Hence the assessment records of children in school are no longer maintained in terms of marks. Although marks only get converted to grades in CCE, but that is only for internal assessment, not to be revealed publicly. Also, the Delhi Directorate of Education has a policy of not retaining any child up to Class VIII. Moreover, as identification of migrant children in school is not possible from the available records, accessing their performance records from school data is ruled out. The author, therefore, had to depend mostly on primary data collected by herself to analyse the academic performance of the migrant children under study.

Table 5.18

Academic Performance of the Migrant Children Surveyed

Performance		Percentage of migrant children
Good	Scoring above 60%	47
Average	Scoring between 40% and 60%	49
Poor	Scoring below 40%	4
Total		100

Fig 5.12 Academic performance of the migrant children surveyed

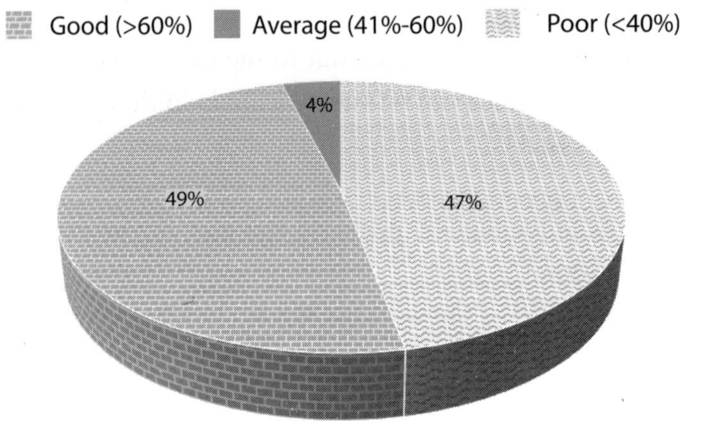

Source: Primary Data

The above table shows the performance of the children interviewed on the basis of their school reports. Being the first-generation literate with almost no assistance available at home and cost of private tuition unaffordable for most of them, their performance can be seen as entirely the outcome of their own efforts.

As most of the impoverished migrant children living in slums attend government schools a time series analysis of enrolment and success rates of students in such schools at this point will be relevant and indicative of the trend.

Table 5.19

Time Series Analysis of Enrolment and Success Rates in Class X in Government Schools in Delhi

Year	Enrolment/ appeared	Pass percentage
1997-98	88,846	32.1
1998-99	89,746	34.57
1999-2000	91,422	38.95

Year	Enrolment/ appeared	Pass percentage
2000-2001	72,278	40.2
2001-02	83,086	46.14
2002-03	79,069	48.87
2003-04	79,330	50.77
2004-05	85,479	48
2005-06	96,551	59.73
2006-07	95,309	77.12
2007-08	1,05,332	83.69
2008-09	1,16,054	89.44
2009-10	1,32,020	90.99
2010-11	1,75,023	99.09

Source: www.edudel.nic.in

Fig 5.13 Enrolment in government schools in Delhi (Class X)

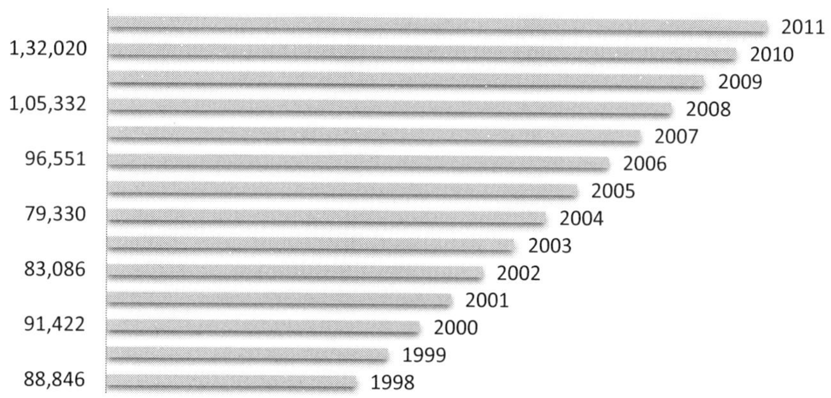

Source: www.edudel.nic.in

Fig 5.14 Pass percentage in government schools in Delhi (Class X)

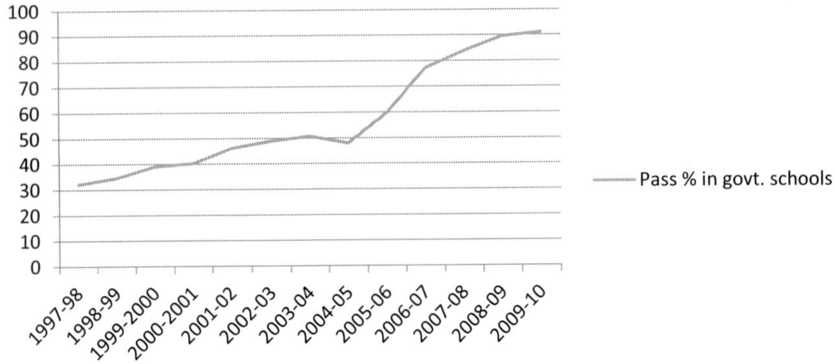

Source: www.edudel.nic.in

Fig 5.15 Government vs. Public schools – A comparative result analysis for Class XII

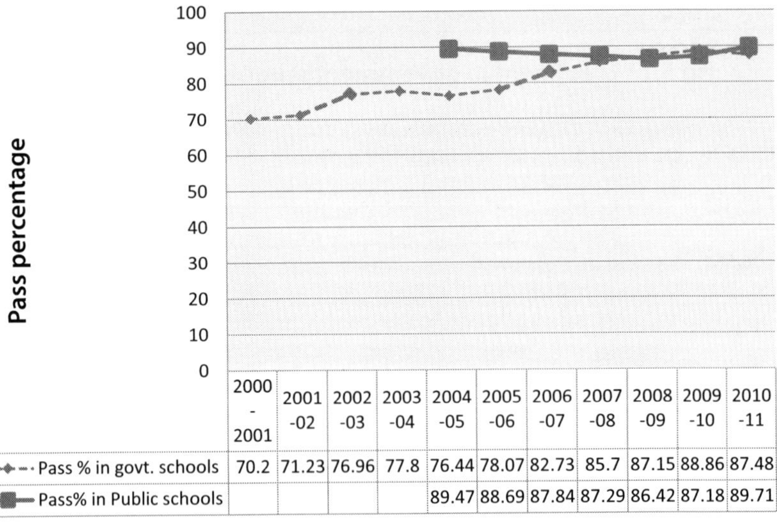

	2000-2001	2001-02	2002-03	2003-04	2004-05	2005-06	2006-07	2007-08	2008-09	2009-10	2010-11
Pass % in govt. schools	70.2	71.23	76.96	77.8	76.44	78.07	82.73	85.7	87.15	88.86	87.48
Pass% in Public schools					89.47	88.69	87.84	87.29	86.42	87.18	89.71

Fig 5.16 Govt. vs. public schools – A comparative result analysis for Class X

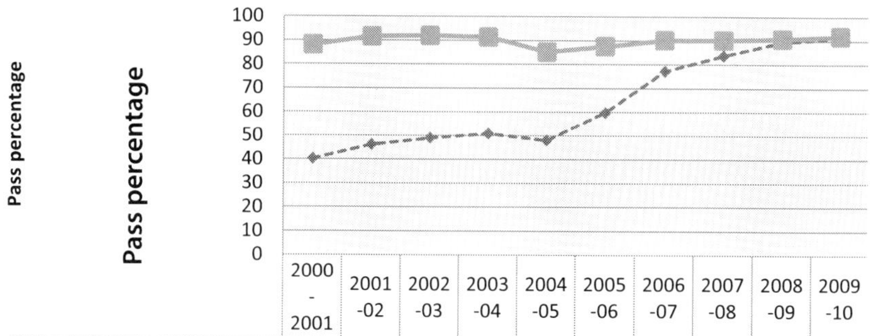

	2000-2001	2001-02	2002-03	2003-04	2004-05	2005-06	2006-07	2007-08	2008-09	2009-10
Pass % in govt. schools	40.2	46.14	48.87	50.77	48	59.73	77.12	83.69	89.44	90.99
Pass% in Public schools	88	91.54	91.87	91.37	85.1	87.47	90.11	90.14	90.71	91.83

Source: www.edudel.nic.in , data compiled by the author

A rise in enrolment and increased pass percentage for the period 1998-2010 indicates positive change in the education scenario of the capital which definitely has brought the migrant children into its fold.

Data collected from secondary sources confirm the rise in the slum literacy rates over time. It is a testimony to the fact that migrants have been sending their children to school and their educational aspirations have gone up since 1991.

Table 5.20

Slum Literacy in Delhi

Year	Slum literacy rate
1991	57.18
2001	64.4
2006	65.2

Fig 5.17 Slum literacy

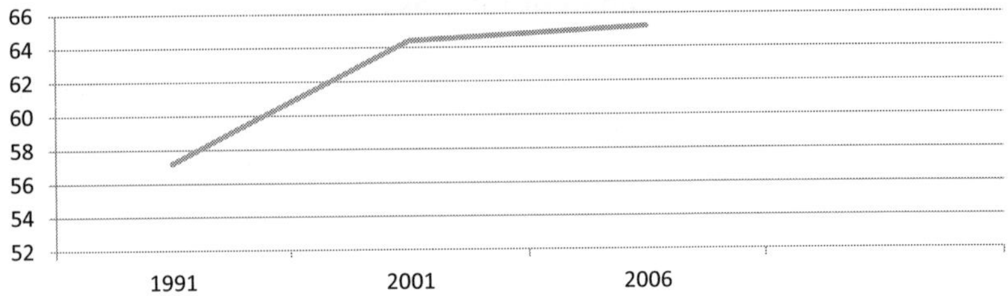

Source: National Family Health Survey 3, 2005-06

The findings of National Family Health Survey 3 (NFHS3) in 2005-06 reveal that in Delhi (urban as well as the rural segments of the capital) 'eighty per cent of children in the 6-17 age group attend school.' In the regular city areas inhabited by the middle class it is 84 per cent, for the slums the rate is only 65 per cent. But the attendance figures of the children offer interesting insights into the newly emerging gender patterns. This is true for the slum children as well. In both situations—slum as well as other children—in the 15-17 age group girls are more likely than boys to attend school.

Table 5.21

Slum Vs. Non-Slum Literacy in Delhi—A Comparative Analysis

Age group (Years)	Boys		Girls		Total	
	Slum	Non-slum	Slum	Non-slum	Slum	Non-slum
6-10	81.0	91.5	79.0	92.8	80.0	92.1
11-14	70.1	88.4	67.4	89.3	68.8	88.8
15-17	32.6	64.1	44.1	70.9	36.8	66.8
6-14	76.1	90.0	73.7	91.2	75.0	90.5
6-17	63.3	82.4	67.5	86.2	65.2	84.0

Fig 5.18 Slum vs. non-slum literacy in Delhi

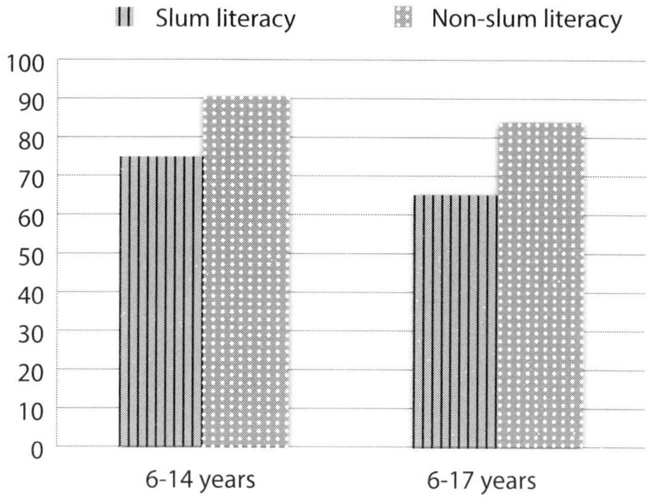

Source: NFHS3, Delhi, p. 33, Table 6, data for the year 2005-06

An analysis of some of the responses obtained from the migrant workers by the author also reveals their eagerness not only to send their children to school but also to support their education in the long run.

Table 5.22

Migrants' Support for their Children's Education

How long can you finance your child's education	Percentage of migrant parents
Up to School	24
College	46
University	06
As far as the child wants	24
Total	100

Fig 5.19 Parental support to migrant children's education

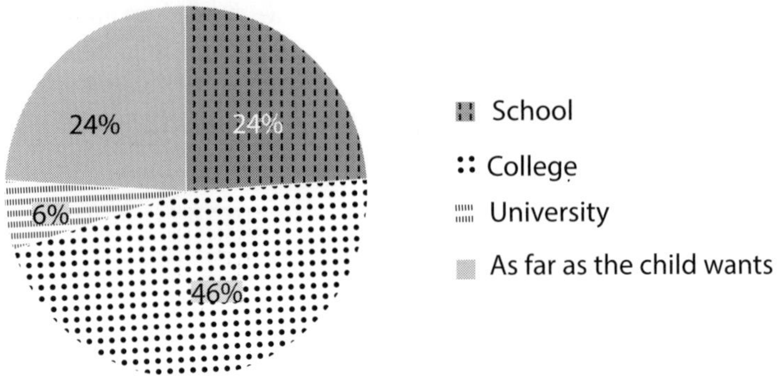

Source: Primary Data

An analysis of the above data clearly indicates that the parents are not just eager to send their children to school but a significant percentage (46 per cent) of them are willing to support them financially at least up to college level.

That the parents are willing to spend on their children's education also gets confirmed by the amount children spend on an average per month on stationery which counts as private cost of education.

Table 5.23

Monthly Average Expenditure on Stationery by Migrant Children

Average monthly expenses on stationery	Percentage of migrant children
Less than ₹100	25
₹100 to ₹200	36
More than ₹200	39
Total	100

Fig 5.20 Monthly expenses on stationery by migrant children

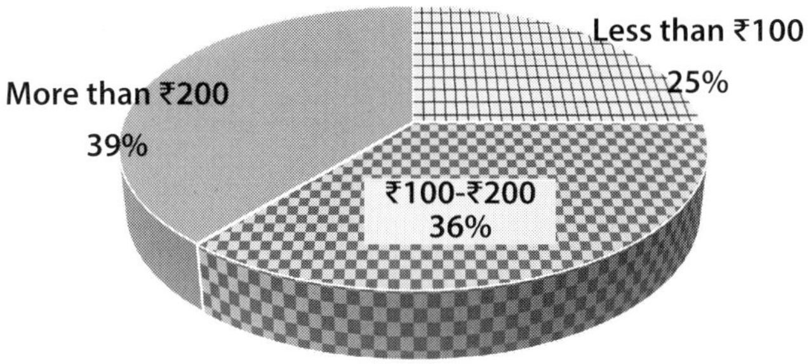

Source: Primary Data

Most of the migrant children interviewed study in the Hindi-medium schools (60 per cent of the respondents). As the mother tongue for most of them is also Hindi, language did not come in their way of following instructions by the teachers in class. A reassuringly 60 per cent of the children claimed that they could always follow the class procedures without difficulty. Another 24 per cent followed most often. Among those who found it difficult to follow the class activities, only 27 per cent had a language problem. These were mostly the children going to the English-medium schools. Another 43 per cent of the children who could not follow the class instructions well had other reasons, like attention deficiency, teacher's inability to explain a point or sharing a more interesting talk with the classmate sitting next than the topic being discussed by the teacher. This guided the study to observe that unlike migrants in other places, the language problem was not a major hindrance in the path of success for the migrants in Delhi.

Table 5.24
Medium of Instruction in School

Language of instruction	Percentage of migrant children
English	37
Hindi	60
Vernacular	03
Total	100

Fig 5.21 Medium of instruction for migrant children

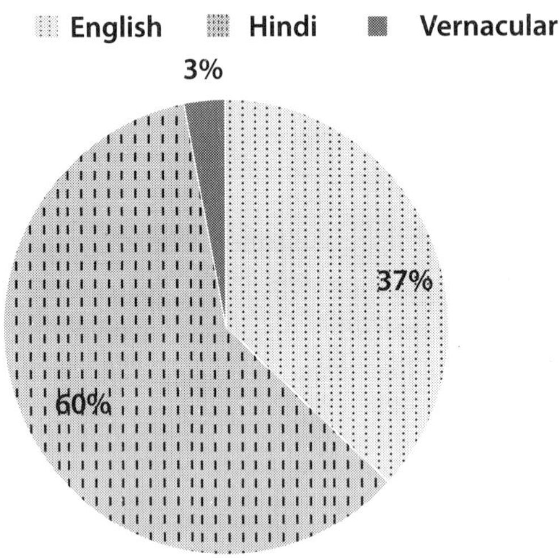

Source: Primary Data

Table 5.25

Instructions Followed in Class

Response	Percentage of migrant children
Yes, always	60
Most often	24
Sometimes	16
Never	00
Total	100

Fig 5.22 Hello, are you with the class?

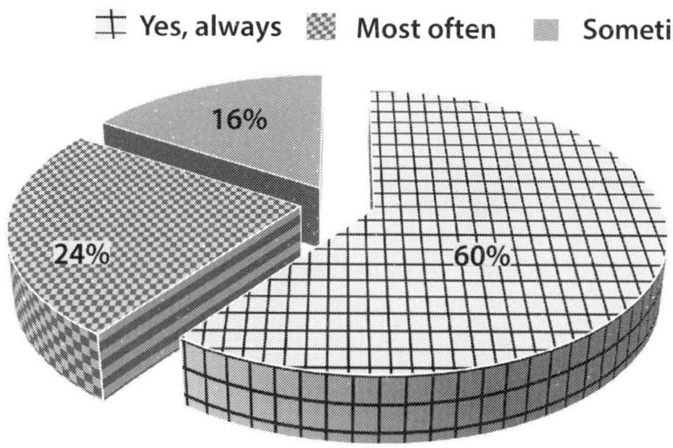

Source: Primary Data

A conversation with a group of migrant children brought out interesting facts: about 16 per cent of the respondents could not follow class instructions; the most cited reasons being the teacher's indifference and uncaring attitude, way of teaching being dull and boring, and also distractions caused by peers, language or cultural gaps for some and so on. However, the majority of the migrant children could follow the class always or most often.

This to the author is a picture of hope—enrolment rates climbing as a result of migrants sending their children to school in the post-reform period. As most of them attend Hindi-medium government schools, instructions were easy to follow, and therefore, in no way affected their performance. Despite other constraints in their lives majority of the migrant children were able to cope with their studies. Their success rates, although much lower than that of other children, are showing a rising trend over time.

Academic and Vocational Courses vis-à-vis Migrants' Aspirations

Objective 3

To analyse the academic and vocational programmes available for the children of migrant workers in keeping with their level of aspiration and specific requirements.

Hypotheses

H3a. The migrants prefer vocational education to general education.
H3b. The education system has not yet fulfilled the aspirations of the migrants fully.

Data analysis

With respect to hypothesis H3a it was found that most of the schools in Delhi do not provide any vocational course at Class X or XII level. Out of 100 teachers interviewed only 29 said that they offer some such courses in their schools at +2 levels.

Table 5.26
Vocational Courses in School

Vocational course available in their school	Teachers' response (percentage)		Total
	Yes	No	
At Secondary level	2	98	100
At Higher Secondary level	29	71	100

Source: Primary Data

Samples were collected randomly by the author from the DDE website for daily attendance of government school students to find out the availability of vocational courses at the +2 level. Out of 60 schools only seven had offered some kind of vocational courses and out of 6319 students enrolled in Class XII in these schools only 230 had taken up vocational courses. None of these schools had any such option for Class X students.

Although the Central Board of Secondary Education listed 34 subjects under vocational courses to be offered at the +2 level and 15 pre-vocational courses for Class X (Annexure D), there is lack of awareness as well as apprehension among students and their parents about the future employability of these courses. Parents still prefer the traditional career areas for the safe and secure future of their children. For example, two courses, Geospatial Technology and Mass Media, recently introduced by the CBSE as vocational courses at the +2 level have huge employability but not yet gained popularity among students.

The teachers surveyed also said there was no demand for vocational subjects not just from the migrant children but others as well. Even when offered, these subjects are taken as an additional and not a main subject.

Table 5.27

Teachers' Observations Regarding Course Preference by Children

Stream		Pursued by percentage of migrant students	Pursued by percentage of non-migrant students
General	Science	21	39
	Commerce	25	31
	Humanities	16	18
	Sub Total	62	78
Vocational		38	12
Total		100	100

Source: Primary Data

Fig 5.23 Course preference of students

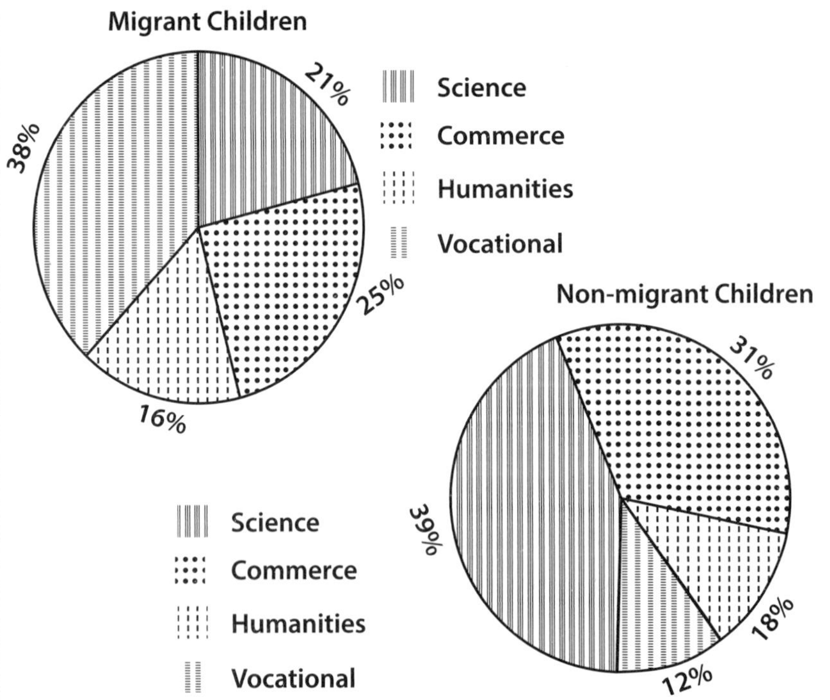

Source: Primary Data

When asked if they would prefer a non-conventional career for their children, 74 per cent of the migrant parents said 'no'. They would prefer their children to become a teacher or a doctor or an engineer rather than a dancer or musician or a sportsman.

Table 5.28
Non-Conventional Career Choice by the Migrants for their Children

Response	Number of respondents	Percentage of respondents
Yes	13	26
No	37	74
Total	50	100

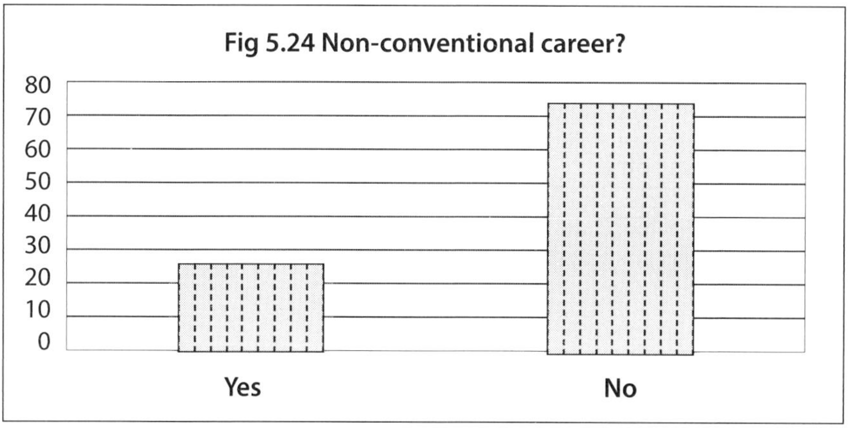

Source: Primary Data

The data tabled above show that only 13 migrant parents out of 50 were open to the idea of some non-conventional career choices for their children. When asked what the reason for choosing this non-conventional career for the child could be, eight out of 13 replied that it would make the child famous. They had no idea about the expenses to support this kind of education.

Table 5.29

Non-Conventional Areas Parents Would Like their Children to Pursue

Areas	Number of migrant parents (Out of total 13)
Sports	5
Film	0
Music	5
Any other	3
Total	13

Source: Primary Data

Table 5.30

Reason for Choosing Non-Conventional Careers

Responses	Number of parents (out of total 13)
Huge money earned in short time	4
Fame	8
Any other	1
Total	13

Source: Primary Data

Table 5.31

Idea About the Cost of Pursuing a Non-Conventional Career

Responses	No. of parents (out of total 13)
Yes	2
No	11
Total	13

Source: Primary Data

The lack of enthusiasm for vocational courses seemed to be the main reason for schools not introducing them. The Head Teachers also mentioned non-availability of qualified faculty in many cases.

India Education Review carried an article by Abhay Anand in its March 2012 issue that only 15 per cent of students in India reach the senior secondary level of schooling, and out of them only seven per cent make it to college. Anand wondered about the fate of the remaining 85 per cent who cease to pursue their education and training after Class X. It also quoted Confederation of Indian Industry data to claim that 95 per cent of workers in organised and unorganised sectors are unskilled. He commented that despite 2500 Industrial Training Institutes (ITIs) run by the government and 5000 Industrial Training Centres (ITCs) in the private sector, the students graduated from these institutions did not get appreciative remunerations in the industry.

Although CBSE has introduced vocational courses at the school level, the universities do not consider the marks scored in the subjects for admission to conventional courses (Anand, Abhay, India Education Review, 6 March 2012).

While discussing the matter with a senior CBSE official in June 2012, the author came to know that CBSE was in the process of starting a Vocational Board which would make an integrated approach to the vocational subjects and pursue the universities to integrate the vocational subjects with the other ones. 'Only when the vocational subjects have vertical growth opportunities they will be taken up by the students,' the official said (personal interaction, 18 June 2012). For example, Fashion Designing (FD), a vocational course at +2 level, could be integrated with the Commerce stream at the graduation level giving the children who had studied FD at school some weightage for admission into the B.Com. course. In that case children willing to study Commerce may take up FD at the +2 level. The official also pointed out that the vocational courses would never be that popular in public schools where children from the middle- and upper-income groups study. For them the career path does not lie in vocational streams. These courses should be offered more to students from the lower-income strata studying in government schools; for them any of these courses can open up a source of income immediately after school.

All this works in forward and backward linkages and dissuades students and their parents to opt for vocational courses. Consequently, the underprivileged migrant children after 12 years of schooling may not be able to get the right career openings or maybe found unsuitable for the industry.

The next hypothesis H3b wanted to find out whether the school has fulfilled the aspirations of the migrants fully or not.

Surprisingly, the children's responses pointed to their deep faith in their teachers. An overwhelming 72 per cent of the migrant children said that they always got enough support from their teachers. Another 21 per cent got it 'sometimes'. The children acknowledged that the teachers helped them either by counselling (36 per cent), or by taking extra care in class (53 per cent) or by providing free coaching beyond school hours (11 per cent). Only seven per cent of children felt that they did not get enough support from their teachers.

Table 5.32

Support Received from Teachers

Options	Percentage of migrant children
Yes, always	72
Sometimes	21
No	7
Total	100

Fig 5.25 Support from teachers?

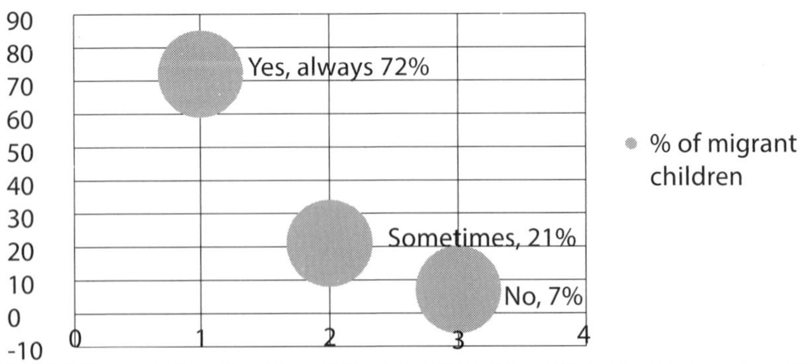

Source: Primary Data

Table 5.33

Teachers' Help to Students

Help from teachers	Received by migrant children (percentage)
Counselling	36
Extra care in class	53
Coaching beyond school hours	11
TOTAL	100

Source: Primary Data

Fig 5.26 Help from teachers

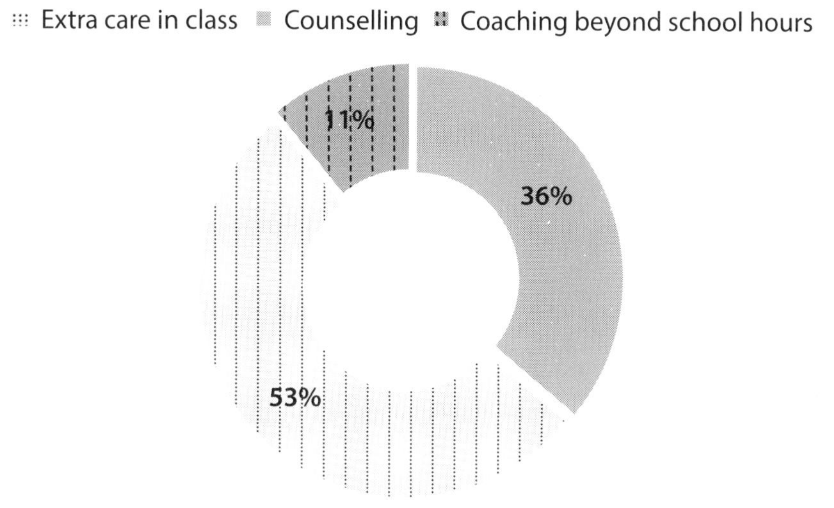

Source: Primary Data

For most of the migrant parents the teachers' feedback on their children's progress was very important. On the basis of primary data, the author observed that 81 per cent of the parents made it a point to meet the teachers regularly on PTM days. And 69 per cent of the children said that their teachers always gave the necessary feedback to their parents on their progress. However, the role of the Principals in the lives of the children did not seem very significant. Altogether 63 per cent of the respondents were of the view that their Principals met their parents if or whenever it was required, not on a regular basis.

Table 5.34

PTMs: Meetings of Migrant Parents with Teachers

Response	Percentage of migrant children
Yes	81
No	19
Total	100

Fig 5.27 PTMs

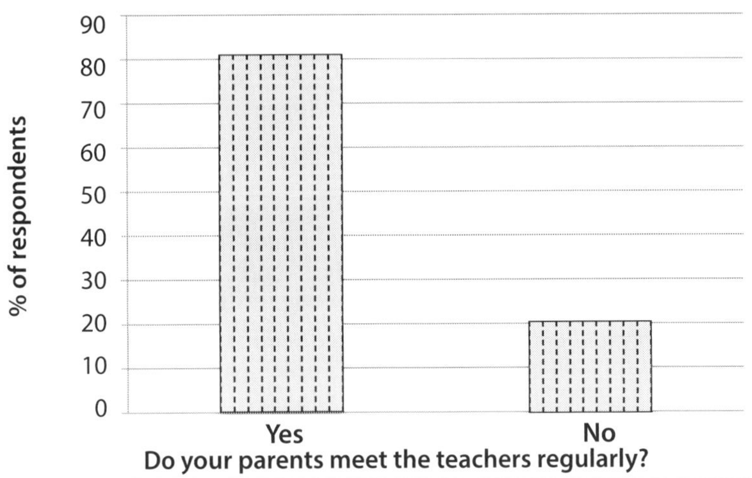

Source: Primary Data

Table 5.35

Meeting of Migrant Parents with Principal (as informed by migrant children)

Response	Percentage of migrant children
Once in a month	9
Whenever required	63
Does not meet	28
Total	100

Fig 5.28 Meeting with the Principal

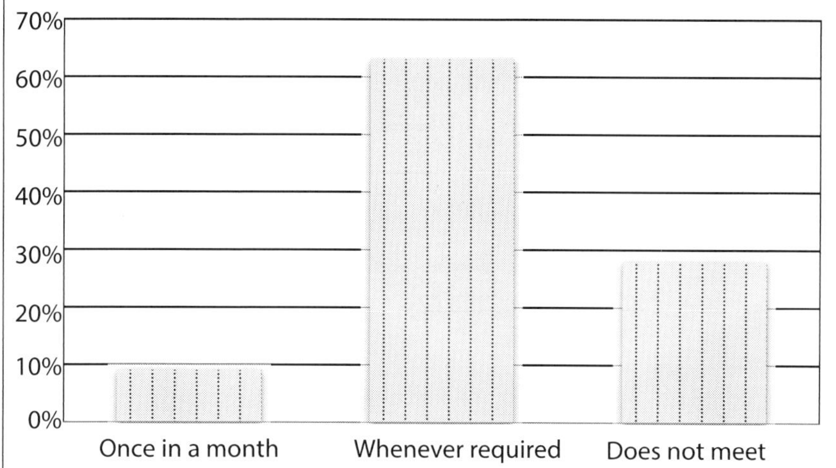

Source: Primary Data

The parents of such children also thought that schooling was essential for the fulfilment of their dreams. Altogether 52 per cent of the migrants interviewed understood that education and training could change the quality of their life. Another 23 per cent believed schooling would ensure better income for their children. Significantly, 19 per cent of the parents considered schooling a tool for moving upwards in society.

Table 5.36

Migrants' Reasons for Sending their Children to School

Reasons	Percentage of migrant parents
Education and training can change the quality of life	52
Schooling will ensure better income	23
It will open up new vistas in my child's life	06
It is the tool to move upwards in society	19
Total	100

Fig 5.29 Why schooling is essential?

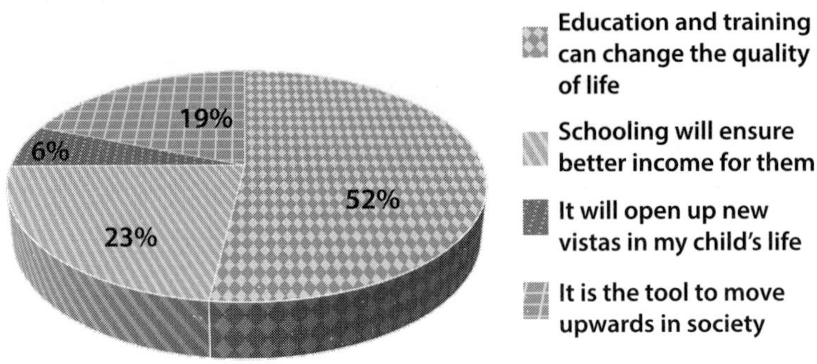

Source: Primary Data

A large number of migrant parents (67 per cent) admitted that they got cooperation from the school authorities in various ways. And 31 per cent of them got the right advice from the school about how to improve their children's performance. Exactly 28 per cent got fee concessions. Although 25 per cent of these parents said the school cooperated with them, they did not specify in which way and how.

Fig 5.30 Get cooperation from school?

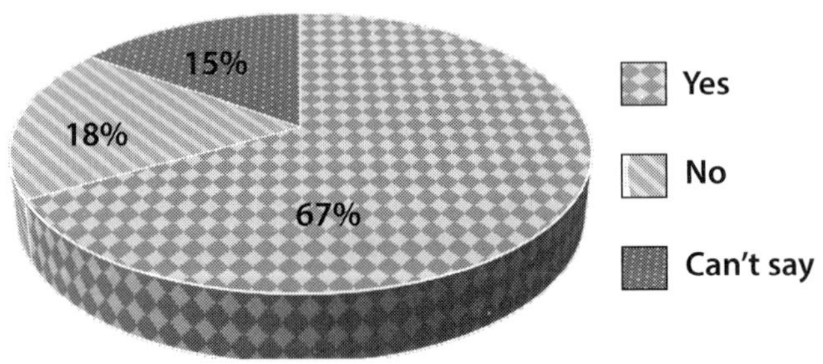

Fig 5. 31 If yes, how does the school help you?

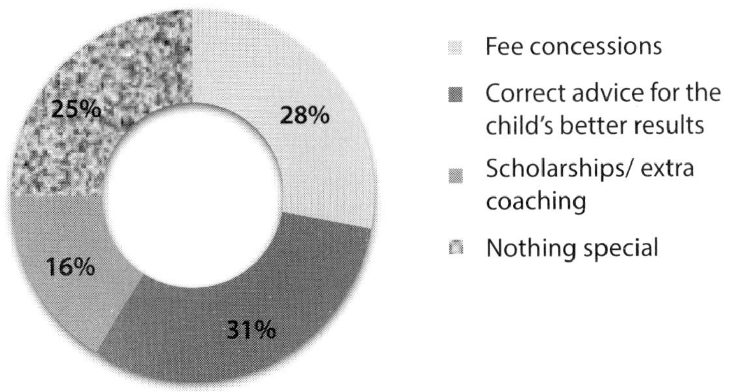

Source: Primary Data

Although the migrant children and their parents acknowledge the help from schools, an overwhelming 82 per cent of the teachers and school principals surveyed pointed out that the social gap between the migrant and non-migrant children posed a set of problems to them.

Table 5.37

Social Gaps Between Migrant and Non-Migrant Students

Response	Percentage of teachers and principals
Yes	82
No	18
Total	100

Fig 5.32 Any problem arising from the social gap between migrant and non-migrant children? (Teachers' responses)

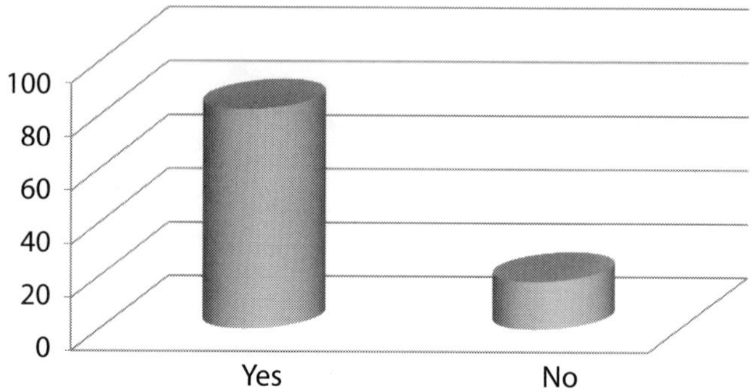

Source: Primary Data

However, they also confirmed that they took extra steps in their schools to resolve the problems and cater to the needs of the migrant children. It was comforting that 33 per cent of the respondents said they provided their students with extra coaching in school. Another 43 per cent of teachers and principals informed that their schools gave fee concessions and cash scholarships to the brighter ones among the migrant students. Another 21 per cent talked about appointing counsellors in school to help them adjust to the school environment. Only 3 per cent of the respondents mentioned that there was no such specific programme in their schools.

Table 5.38

Special Steps Taken by Schools for Migrant Students

Steps	Percentage of respondents
Provide extra coaching	33
Give fee concessions and cash scholarships to brighter ones	43
Appointment of a counsellor to help them settle down in school	21
Nothing very specific	3
Total	100

Fig 5.33 Steps taken by schools to cater to migrant students

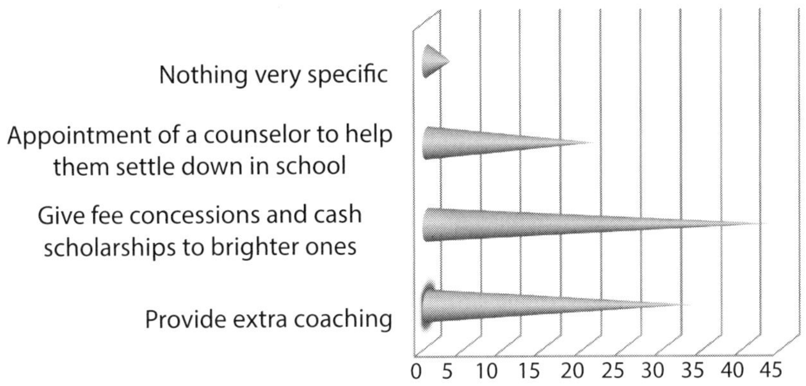

Source: Primary Data

We can, therefore, come to the conclusion that although the schools could not fulfil the disadvantaged migrants' aspirations fully the bond between them was growing stronger. For the migrants the school is the beacon of a future they cherish. The school authorities need to understand this and play a more assertive role in guiding this new social trend in the right direction.

Economic Reforms Opened More Opportunities for the Skilled and Educated Migrants

Objective 4

To examine how the process of economic reforms has impacted the educational aspirations of the migrants and their children.

Hypothesis

Economic reforms have thrown open more opportunities for the migrants who are skilled or educated and triggered their aspirations.

Data analyses

Economic reforms raised income levels of people, more so in Delhi

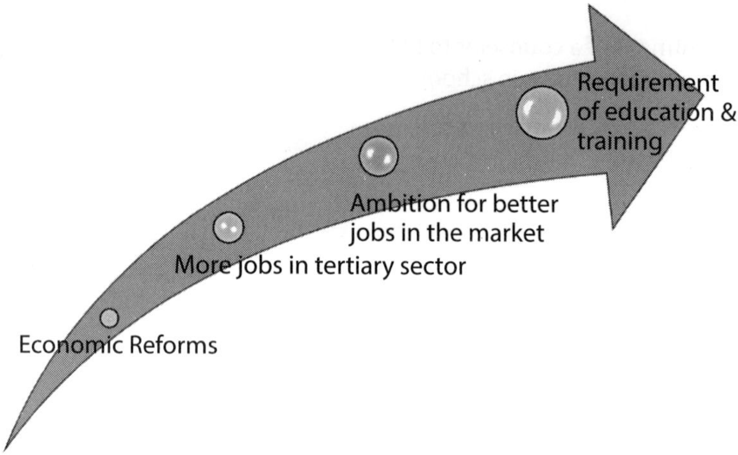

As observed by the earlier researchers (Tilak, 2009, Drèze and Kingdon, 2001) poverty acts as a disincentive for the disadvantaged people to send their children to school. On the other hand, HDR 2009 had found that 'in 13 out of 16 countries internal migrants had higher incomes than non-migrants. In Brazil and Panama, a series of studies found income gains for indigenous groups who had moved. Studies across a range of countries suggest that internal migration has enabled many households to lift themselves out of poverty' (HDR, 2009, p.50-51).

Economic reforms in India initiated in 1991 have changed the general living standards of people, particularly in the capital city of Delhi. It is interesting to note that Delhi became a state only in 1992. Being predominantly urban (76.2 per cent urban population), this state does not have the retarding factors of a rural sector influencing its growth. Its Net State Domestic Product (NSDP) growth (8.9 per cent) was more impressive than the national average (7.1 per cent) in the past decade. Its per capita NSDP grew at 5.7 per cent vis-à-vis the all-India average of 5.4 per cent in the same period.

A close examination of the statistics in Table 1.1 in Chapter 1 points to a sharp rise over the past two decades in Delhi's per capita income which is much higher than the national average. Keeping in mind the target group, the household income of the Delhi slums can be observed at this point.

Table 5.39

Income of the Migrant Households Interviewed

Income level (₹ per month)	No. of migrant households	Percentage of households
Less than 2000	1	2
2001-5000	22	44
5001-10000	17	34
More than 10000	10	20
Total	50	100

Source: Primary Data

Fig 5.34 Income of the migrant households

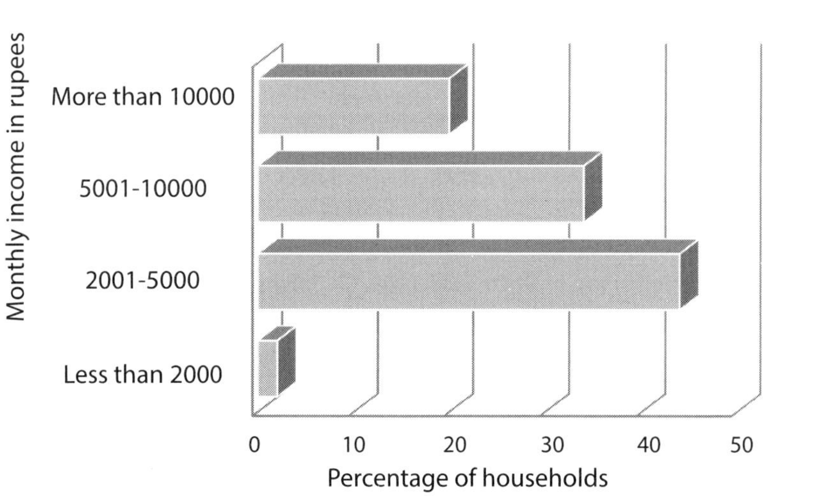

Source: Primary Data

It was heartening to see that very few households earned less than ₹2000 per month. In a recent article in *Time* magazine, Kurt Anderson observed that 'the two decades beginning in 1991 witnessed the greatest rise in the living standards that the world has ever known' (Anderson, Kurt, *Time* magazine, annual issue, 2011). This global trend has also been observed by the author in the Delhi slums.

Reforms Created More and Diverse Job Opportunities Particularly in the Tertiary Sector and Attracted Migrants to Delhi

The economic reforms have created a range of diverse work opportunities. The number of jobs created in the organised as well as unorganised sectors in the past two decades increased the number of workers significantly in the capital city.

Table 5.40

Increased Work Participation in Post-Reform Delhi

Year	No. of workers (all categories, in lakh)		Work participation rate (employment as a percentage of total population)	
	Delhi	India	Delhi	India
1991-92	29.80	3141.40	31.64	37.11
2001-02	45.45	4023.60	32.82	39.11
2007-08	57.07	4961.79	33.65	36.15

Source: Economic Survey of Delhi 2008-2009, Ch 5: Employment-unemployment, pp. 69, 72; NSS 64TH Round Data (State Sample, Government of NCT of Delhi), Statements 4.2.1, 4.3.1 and 4.3.7 & http://mospi.nic.in/mospi_new/upload/nsso/531_533_Highlights.pdf

The increase in the number of workers in Delhi between 1991-92 and 2007-08 was primarily due to a large-scale inflow of migrants from the neighbouring states. A study by the Planning Commission in

1998 showed that 43 per cent of the people registered with the Delhi Employment Exchange were from the neighbouring states (Economic Survey of Delhi, 2008-09, chapter 5, p. 69). The following table shows the migration data for Delhi. The states from where a large number of people have migrated to Delhi have only been shown in the table.

Table 5.41
Migration Data for Delhi

States of origin	Migrant population in Delhi		Percentage growth in one decade	Migration in 2011
	1991	2001		
Uttar Pradesh	17,04,197	23,16,731	35.94	22,96,367
Bihar	2,67,567	7,37,867	175.77	7,25,565
Haryana	4,40,275	5,45,811	23.97	5,55,173
Uttaranchal (Uttarakhand)	-	3,06,503	-	N.A.
Rajasthan	2,31,856	2,74,392	18.35	N.A.
Punjab	2,35,142	2,51,091	6.78	N.A.
West Bengal	78,811	1,69,165	114.65	N.A.
Jharkhand	-	1,13,675	-	N.A.
Total number of migrants in Delhi	33,33,161	53,18,362	59.56	76,63,955
Total population of Delhi	94,20,644	1,38,50,507	47.02	1,67,53,235

Source: Census data for Delhi. Data compiled and analysed by the author

Although the largest number of migrants in Delhi have come from Uttar Pradesh, the rate of influx was very high from Bihar and West Bengal. The reason can be traced to a lack of economic growth and low level of wages in these states for a long period.

On the contrary, Delhi has seen a phenomenal employment growth in the post-reform period. The growth has been more spectacular in the private sector than in the public sector. In fact, the new thrust to privatisation and liberalisation in the reforms of 1991 led to a shrinkage of the public sector and its capacity to generate employment. While the public sector employment generation rate fell to an annual 0.52 per cent, for the private sector it rose to 0.59 per cent (Economic Survey, 2008-09, p.75). A large number of people are also engaged in the unorganised sector or self-employed. In fact, it is the unorganised sector that absorbs most of the uprooted migrants.

Table 5.42
Job Creation in Delhi after Reforms

Year	Employment (lakh)		
	Public sector	Private sector	Total
1999	6.26	2.22	8.48
2001	6.24	2.17	8.41
2006	6.05	2.21	8.26
2008	6.00	2.36	8.36

Source: Economic Survey 2008-09, Chart 5.3. Data compiled by the author

Change in Employment Patterns

An overview of NSS 50TH round (conducted in 1993-94) and 61ST round (conducted in 2004-05) data with respect to employment patterns in Delhi clearly shows a rise in regular employment over self-employment or casual work. This in turn indicates a significant growth in the organised sector employment opportunities in the city.

Table 5.43
Distribution of Employed People (numbers in thousands)

Workers	NSS 61st round (2004-05)			NSS 50th round (1993-94)		
	Self employed	Regular wage/ salaried	Casual labour	Self employed	Regular wage/ salaried	Casual labour
Male	371	590	39	441	452	107
Female	159	796	44	242	576	182

Source: NSS Report no. 520: Employment and Unemployment situations in cities and towns of India, 2004-05

Minimum Wages – Delhi vis-à-vis Other States

The Committee on Fair Wages was set up in 1948 to provide guidelines regarding wage structures in the country. It came up with the landmark concepts of fair wages, minimum wages and living wages (Minimum Wages Act, 1948, Ministry of Labour and Employment, GoI). It proposed that the State ensure the right to work to its citizens and minimum wages to be decided with respect to a decent standard of living. Soon after the country's independence, the committee significantly called for removing discrimination between men and women doing the same work (equal pay for equal work) and providing the condition of work with full enjoyment of leisure, social and cultural opportunities.

Therefore, the minimum wages should cover the basic requirements of food, clothing and shelter for the workers in the scheduled industries (45 scheduled employments in the Central sphere and 1679 in the states) and additionally pay the workers the expenses for fuel, lighting and other miscellaneous expenses. It should also partly cover their children's educational expenses and take care of necessities like weddings, minimum recreation, medical expenses and old-age needs.

From 1948 to 2010 minimum wages got revised almost every year keeping in view the rising price level and adding increased percentage of dearness allowance to offset the rising cost of living for the workers.

As the standard of living gets influenced by local conditions, a minimum wage level for the entire nation is not feasible. It is, therefore, decided by the state governments and consequently varies from state to state. In order to reduce wage disparities among the states, a minimum national floor level was recommended by the National Commission of Rural Labour (NCRL). It can be observed from the secondary data used from the Ministry of Labour publications that wages have steadily increased over time, particularly after 1991.

Table 5.44

Minimum National Floor Level Wages

Year	₹ per day
1996	35
1998	40
1999	45
2002	50

Source: Ministry of Labour, GoI

Delhi, the capital city and the area of this research, has a much higher minimum wage level compared to many other states. Minimum wages in Delhi are many times higher than the floor level wages recommended by the NCRL. It ranged from ₹203 to ₹248 per day in scheduled industries in 2010. The Sixth Pay Commission recommendations implemented in this state have raised the wage level higher than those of the other states and therefore, made it lucrative for unskilled as well as skilled workers to migrate to this state.

An obvious reason for migrants flowing into the capital city from UP, Bihar and West Bengal is the wage differential. The Delhi Human Development Report, 2006 claimed that about 46 per cent of the migrants during 1991-2001 came from Uttar Pradesh and Uttarakhand and another 23 per cent from Bihar.

Table 5.45

Average Daily Wages in 2010 – An Inter-State Comparison (Values in ₹)

Average wages	Delhi	UP	Bihar	West Bengal
Unskilled workers	203	144.76	120.08	162.23
Semi-skilled workers	225	166.11	122.78	178.46
Skilled workers	248	172.23	150.80	196.30

Source: www.labourbureau.nic.in [Data compiled by the author]

Fig 5.35 Comparative wages: Delhi and other states

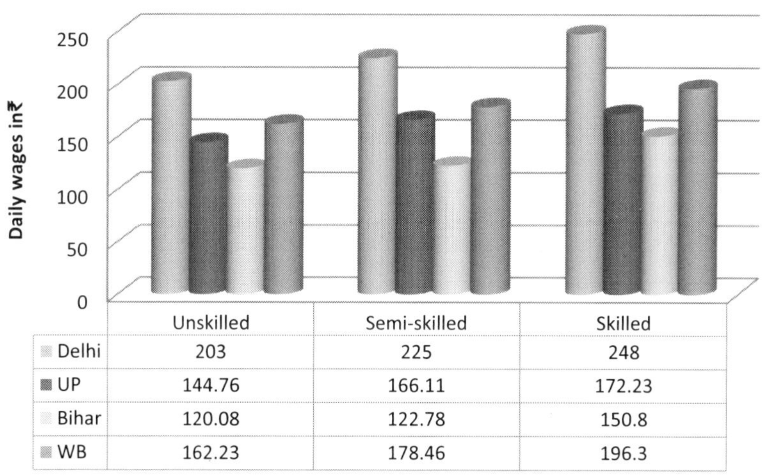

Source: www.labourbureau.nic.in

An analysis of per capita consumption expenditure in these states also confirms that the higher living standard in Delhi induces people from the other states to migrate here.

Table 5.46
Monthly Per Capita Consumption Expenditure for Delhi & Some Other States (values in ₹)

States	1983-84	1993-94	2004-05
Delhi	228.64	777.01	1047.54
UP	110.45	297.62	726.02
Bihar	99.53	236.78	446.38
West Bengal	122.03	333.36	712.19
Rajasthan	134.5	346.6	724.27
All India	125.13	328.18	700.33

Source: NHDR, 2011, Table 3A.9. Data compiled by the author.

Higher Incomes Coupled with Enhanced Job Opportunities Boost the Aspirations of Migrants

Improved living standards, higher per capita incomes combined with an increased share of the tertiary sector in Delhi's GDP to create employment opportunities pushed up the aspirations of migrants in Delhi.

India Human Development Report 2011 mentioned that the contribution of the tertiary sector to GDP was very high in Delhi as compared to its industrial sector. The tertiary sector contributes about 97 per cent to the Net State Domestic Product whereas the industrial sector's contribution is less than one per cent. According to economists, the high and rising relative contribution of the tertiary sector to GDP makes a qualitative change in the economic growth of a country or a place and implies an improved level of development. This is apparent from the value and ranks of the Human Development Index for Delhi.

Table 5.47
Human Development Index for Delhi

Year	India	Delhi	
		Value	All India Rank
1981	.302	.495	III
1991	.381	.624	II
1999	.387	.783	I
2008	.467	.750	II

Source: NHDR, 2001, pp. 140-141, Tables 1.1, 1.2 & NHDR, 2011, p. 24, Table 2.4

As the tertiary sector jobs require trained and skilled employees, the growth of this sector in the post-reform period has motivated the job seekers to get themselves trained and educated in order to seize the new opportunities.

The rising wage level has ensured a rising standard of living even for the uprooted migrants in Delhi. The homes in shantytowns often have televisions, cooking gas, refrigerators and desert coolers fitted onto windows to beat the summer heat. The author found such items of convenience and comfort in almost every slum. Besides, an increasing number of slum-dwellers in Delhi are in possession of motorbikes, adding speed and mobility to their lives. A reference can be made at this point to the findings of the National Family Health Survey (NFHS3) in 2005-06 with respect to the Delhi slums which shows a comfortable living standard for a significant number of slum-dwellers as compared to their counterparts elsewhere.

Table 5.48

Household Possessions in Delhi Slums

Household possessions	Percentage of slum-dwellers
Mattress	70.2
Pressure cooker	69.8
Chair	43.5
Cot or bed	77.6
Table	42.6
Electric fan	86.4
Radio or transistor	37.0
Television	68.0
Sewing machine	32.4
Cell phone	30.4
Refrigerator	30.9
Watch or clock	84.9
Motorcycle or scooter	12.5
Car	2.7
House	86.3
Bank account	43.8

Source: NFHS, 2005-06, compiled by the author

Fruits of Labour

Under the normal rules of economics fulfilment of the basic needs leads to the demand for items of comfort—education and healthcare among them. This was apparent from the study conducted by the author. Almost all the respondents send their children to school. The school-going children act as an influence on others. Some of the older boys and girls attend colleges, a few others are doing correspondence courses.

As already mentioned earlier, when asked by the author, the migrants at large responded by saying that they did not want their children to do the same menial work they had spent a lifetime doing. They wanted their children to go to school so they could access better job opportunities. And of course, they could now afford to send their children to school and were eager to support their education at least up to the college level. In return, they hoped the family as a whole would reap the benefit of this investment in their children's education. But how? Let us see their responses.

Table 5.49

Family's Benefits from the Child's Achievements

Benefits to the family	Percentage of migrant parents
Financial	19
In terms of elevated social status	36
His connections will pull up others in the family	08
All of the above	29
Family does not expect anything	08
Total	100

Fig 5.36 Benefits to the family

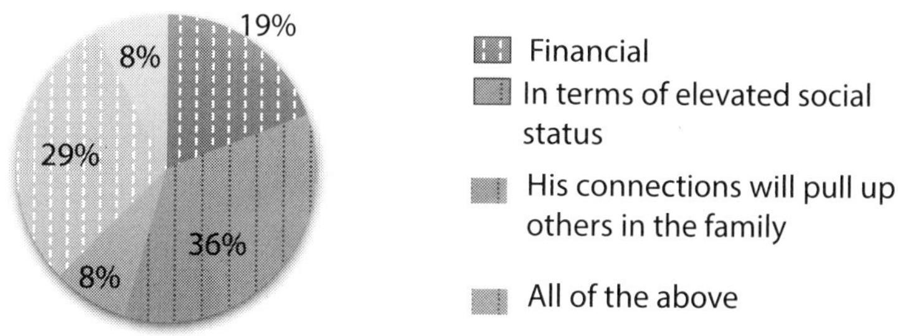

Source: Primary Data

'Suppose the child, when starts earning, does not take care of you? How would you feel?' Hearing this question from the author, the parents were seemingly caught off guard. But they did not express their frustrations. Rather, like the typical Indian parents, willing to do everything for their children without expecting anything in return, 52 per cent of them said, 'I will be happy if they can lead a life better than me, no matter whether they help the family or not.'

Table 5.50
Fruits of Labour if not Reaped

Responses	Percentage of migrant parents
That is absurd	14
I will blame my fate	16
I am not doing things for him/her for any future returns	18
I will be happy if he can lead a better life than me, no matter whether he helps the family or not	52
Total	100

Fig 5.37 If returns of labour is nil ?

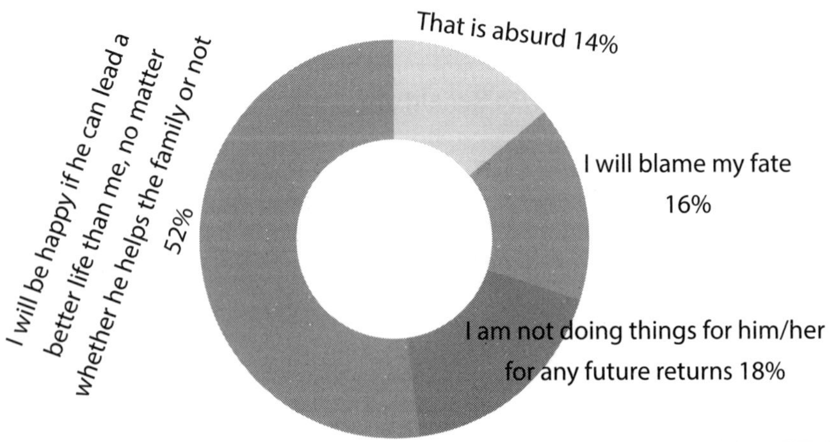

Source: Primary Data

March from Shantytown to School – A Silent Revolution

From the analyses of primary and secondary data the author draws the conclusion that the reforms of 1991 boosted the economic growth of the city of Delhi. This has led not only to enhanced job opportunities in the capital city but also an increase in private sector jobs. The scope of employment in the organised sector has also gone up creating a demand for the skilled, educated and trained work force. The underprivileged migrants who came to the capital city from other parts of the country to change their fate and worked mostly in the unorganised sector, have seen the prospect of better-paying jobs for their children and at the same time realised that it is possible only when they are trained and educated. As their earnings in the city are much higher than what they could have earned back in their villages, they do not require their children to work with them to make ends meet. Rather, after fulfilling the basic needs of life they can now afford to spend a little money on items of comforts like education for their children. The prospect of a better paying job at the end of school or college has greatly influenced these migrant workers living in the slums of Delhi and consequently, as observed by the author, their educational aspirations have gone up in the post-reform era.

References

- Anand, Abhay. 'Will Vocational Education provide a lucrative career option to the Indian youth?' *India Education Review*, 2012 Retrieved from http://www.indiaeducationreview.com
- Anderson, Kurt. 'The Protester'. *Time* magazine (Annual issue), 14 December 2011.
- Directorate of Economics & Statistics, Government of NCT of Delhi. 'NSS 64th Round Data, state sample.' Retrieved from http://des.delhi.gov.in.
- GoI. 'India Human Development Report 2011,' p. 24, Table 2.4. New Delhi: Planning Commission.
- GoI. 'National Family Health Survey 3,' 2005-06.

- GoI. 'National Human Development Report, 2001,' pp. 140-141, Table 1.1, 1.2. New Delhi: Planning Commission.
- GoI. 'NFHS3, Delhi,' p. 33, Table 6. Data for the year 2005-06.
- GoI. 'NSS 64th Round Data: Employment and Unemployment Situation in India (July 2007-June 2008): Highlights,' pp. H-i. Retrieved from
- Govinda, R. 'India Education Report,' p.6. Delhi: NUEPA, 2002.
- HDR, 2009, p. 59; Ch 2, pp. 28, 50-51.
- http://mospi.nic.in/mospi_new/upload/nsso/531_533_Highlights
- Ministry of Labour and Employment, GoI. 'Minimum Wages Act, 1948.' Retrieved from http://labour.nic.in/wagecell/mwact.pdf
- SSA Document. 'Alternative and Innovative Education for out-of-school children,' pp. 3, 7. Retrieved from http://www.edudel.nic.in.
- *The Pioneer*, 29 April, 2012
- www.edudel.nic.in. Visited on 4 and 16 June 2012.

6

INTERPRETING THE DATA

The wealth of data collected from the narrow lanes between rows of rabbit warrens with a foul odour floating around, however, revealed an absorbing story. Interpretation of the data yielded fascinating facts and offered insightful pointers.

The main cause for migration was the prospect of higher wages and more opportunities which the backward rural economy was unable to offer. For 61 per cent of the respondents that was the most compelling factor for moving out of their ancestral villages and leaving for the big cities. Although marriage, natural calamities and loss of property did influence 18, 5 and 7 per cent of the respondents respectively to migrate, the dream of earning better wages largely put them on the train.

The migrants, who live in the city slums, work mostly in the unorganised sector as unskilled, semi-skilled or skilled workers for relatively low wages. At the receiving end of social biases, economic exploitation, urban iniquities, they do not want their children to go through the same grind doing what they themselves have been compelled to do.

Empirical findings confirm the hypothesis that the migrants view school education as a means to a better life.

On the basis of testing the null hypotheses $H_0 1$ to $H_0 8$, the following observations were made:

- Educational aspirations of the migrant children are not gender specific.
- Occupational aspirations of the migrant children are also not influenced by their gender.
- Migrant parents share the educational aspirations of their children. There is no significant difference in this respect between the migrant children and their parents.
- There is no significant difference in occupational aspirations as well between the migrant children and their parents.
- Educational aspirations of migrant and non-migrant children differ significantly.
- There is a significant difference in occupational aspirations between migrant and non-migrant children.
- There is no significant difference in the aspirations of migrant parents and non-migrant parents for their children's education.
- There is no significant difference in the occupational aspirations of migrant parents and parents of non-migrant children.

An impressive 36 per cent of migrant children were found to have high and 42 per cent very high educational aspirations. And reassuringly, 87 per cent of the migrant children admitted that their parents share their ambitions.

While choosing the school for their children 30 per cent of migrant parents thought about the cost, 48 per cent attached importance to the quality of education whereas 22 per cent were concerned about the distance from home to school.

When asked whether the children should do some part-time job to assist their parents in financing their education, 30 per cent of the migrant parents answered in the negative. About 46 per cent of the parents were willing to support their children as far as they wanted to study. And 22 per cent of the parents said that they would support their children's education up to the college level. Significantly, an absolute majority—92 per cent—did not want their children to do the kind of work they were engaged in. The variation in this attitude was almost nil irrespective of the parents being literate or unlettered.

A reassuringly 33 per cent of the migrant children had high occupational aspirations and for 47 per cent this was very high.

Migrants also share their children's dreams for white-collar jobs and disapprove of any suggestion that they pursue any vocational courses.

An absolute majority of the educationists (teachers and principals)—90 per cent—confirmed that they got more admission requests from this group now than 10 years ago. As high as 95 per cent of them agreed that they have observed a positive change in the migrants' educational aspirations in the recent years. And 87 per cent of the teachers and principals surveyed also observed rising occupational aspirations in migrant children in the recent years. But only 55 per cent of them felt that the children or their parents were aware of the new openings in the job market in the post-reform period. Case studies of different slums corroborated the observations of the author that the educational and occupational aspirations of the migrants were high now.

The initiative to spread education among the disadvantaged migrant children living in the slums of Delhi gained a new momentum with the active participation of a large number of educational NGOs (Listed in Annexure C). These NGOs involved in NFE and remedial teaching also generated supplementary work opportunities for the migrant families, particularly for mothers, which in turn would reduce the opportunity cost of sending their children to school. Because of their better managerial skills, the drop-out rates at the NGO-run schools or NFE centres are almost nil. Some of them even create skill-based training and placement opportunities for the children graduating from these schools. Some of them assist the government in providing training to out-of-school children (Table 5.17). These NGOs have boosted the ambitions of the migrants in Delhi.

As we have already pointed out, data for enrolment and success rates of the migrant children are not maintained separately in any school in Delhi as the parents' status as migrants is not yet considered a criterion to classify the school children here. A majority of the underprivileged migrant children study in government schools where they get free education. But as the quality of education is very poor in these schools, the better off among the marginalized have started sending their children to low-cost, unrecognised private schools. Since most of these schools are unrecognised, they cannot offer education beyond Class VIII. Parents have no choice but to move the children to government schools for the higher classes before the Board exam. Almost all the migrant children in the sample, studying in Class X or XII were found to be studying in government schools. But the Delhi Directorate of Education announced a 25 per cent quota for the EWS categories in private schools after the RTE Act, 2009 was adopted by Parliament. Consequently, the admission requests from EWS children in private schools have increased in the recent years.

The observation of the Human Development Report 2009 that the children born to migrant parents at destination places tend to do better academically than the first-generation migrants was found to be relevant for the slum children in Delhi as well. The author collected and analysed primary data with respect to the academic performance of the migrant children under study. Reassuringly 47 per cent of them scored above 60 per cent in their previous term-end examinations whereas 49 per cent of the respondents scored between 40 per cent and 59 per cent. Only four per cent of the respondents had scored below 40 per cent. But according to the instructions given by the Delhi Directorate of Education, no child can be retained up to Class VIII. Therefore, even when enrolment and pass percentage show an upward trend, there is a big question mark over the quality of learning for these children. Most of them feel they require tuitions or the support of a coaching centre. But in most cases their parents cannot afford it. Altogether 49 per cent of children's expectations from school, therefore, are not adequately met compelling them to look for supplementary teaching assistance elsewhere after school hours.

An analysis of the time series data for enrolment and pass percentage in the Delhi schools for the past decade established the growing trends in both. From 88,846 in 1987-88 enrolment in Class X in government schools has gone up to 1,75,023 in 2010-11. Pass percentage in the same period rose from 32.1 per cent to 99.09 per cent. As most of the slum children go to government schools this trend is indicative of their rising educational aspirations. This was supported by the higher rates of slum literacy over time. From 57.18 per cent in 1991 it has gone up to 65.2 per cent in 2006.

Good news is that almost a quarter of the migrant parents interviewed, exactly 24 per cent, want their children to study as far as they could. A more focused group of 46 per cent is hopeful that their children will go to college for a degree. But another 24 per cent can afford it only up to the school level. A mere 6 per cent of parents think about supporting their children's education up to the university level. The parental determination is reflected in their monthly expenditure on stationery like notebooks, pens, pencils, etc. for their children. A more reassuring 39 per cent of the migrant children spend more than ₹200 per month on such stationery items. However, 36 per cent spend between ₹100 and ₹200 whereas 25 per cent spend below ₹100 per month.

The medium of instruction for 60 per cent of the migrant children interviewed was Hindi and therefore, did not put a hurdle in the way of their following class proceedings. An impressive 37 per cent of migrant children attended English-medium schools and only three per cent had a regional language as their medium of instruction.

As high as 60 per cent of the children surveyed claimed that they were comfortable following instructions in class. Only 24 per cent said they did so most often. A mere 16 per cent of the migrant children admitted they found it difficult to follow class lectures though not due to any language problem. Among the reasons they mentioned were distractions by peers, apathy on the part of the teacher, absence of teachers or their decision to bunk.

Most schools in Delhi do not offer vocational courses. Primary data obtained by interviewing teachers and principals and analysis of secondary data revealed this fact. Almost all the teachers – 98 per cent – surveyed admitted they did not have the provision for offering vocational courses to Class X students in their schools. A random sample of 60 schools collected through secondary data from the website of the Delhi Directorate of Education confirmed this. Out of a total 6319 students enrolled in Class XII in these schools only 230 had opted for vocational courses.

There was no perceptible enthusiasm on the part of migrant students for vocational education (16 per cent) which may be due to lack of awareness about these courses or non-availability of vocational courses at the school level. Interestingly, teachers' observations reveal that even non-migrant children are not much inclined towards vocational courses. But lack of interest in vocational education in the case of non-migrant children can be attributed to their more affluent socio-economic background resulting in a higher level of aspirations. The issue has gained some kind of criticality for lack of an opportunity for vertical growth in the field of vocational education.

Migrants are also not very keen on vocational education or a non-conventional career for their children. Although 26 per cent of the respondents considered a non-conventional career path for their children, they did not have a clear idea about the financial obligations for sending a child to pursue such a career. But they could only think of either sports or music as an alternative career; areas like hotel management, tourism, mass communication, geospatial technology or retail management fell outside the orbit of their imagination. The majority (74 per cent) wanted their children to stick to the general stream of studies and choose a conventional career like medicine, engineering, banking or teaching. Understandably they could not afford to go off the beaten track.

It seems that lack of awareness about the vocational courses and the schools' inability to introduce them are the main reasons for the migrants not opting for them. Although the Central Board of Secondary Education (CBSE) listed 34 subjects under vocational courses to be offered at the +2 level and 15 pre-vocational courses at Class X (Annexure D), indifference to vocational courses seemed to be the reason for their being not in demand. The headteachers also mentioned non-availability of qualified faculty in many cases. This works in forward and backward linkages. Consequently, the children after 12 years of schooling may not be able to get the right career openings for them.

Migrant children see schooling as a means of grabbing new jobs made available by the newly-opened sectors after economic liberalisation, and thus change their grimy existence in shanties for a better life. Interestingly, 26 per cent of the respondents believed that education would improve their families' standards of living. For 28 per cent earning higher wages was the motivating factor pushing them towards the classroom; and for another 29 per cent it was the gateway to a new social respectability. In fact, a better life and improved living conditions were among the ambitions motivating them to go to school. Schooling, they somehow knew, could get them everything that they did not have at present.

Contrary to the prevailing notion, an overwhelming 72 per cent of migrant children acknowledged the support and encouragement from their teachers. Only seven per cent of them had a feeling that the teachers were unsupportive and indifferent. However, the remaining 21 per cent said they received support from the teachers sometimes. Asked about the kind of help they got from their teachers, 53 per cent of migrant students said that their teachers took extra care of them in class, another 36 per cent talked about having received counselling. A small number of them – 11 per cent – got coaching beyond school hours. It was important for the migrant parents to get feedback from school about their children's progress. A big majority of 81 per cent said that their parents attended PTMs regularly.

Although meeting the teachers was a regular affair for the migrant parents, access was not so easy to the school principal. Significantly 63 per cent of the children said that their parents met the principal only if required, implying that they would have access to the principal only in the event of great urgency.

In an attempt to appreciate the migrant children's new trek from shanties to school, the author found out that 23 per cent of the respondents expected schooling to help them earn more. And 52 per cent of parents felt it would change the quality of their children's life. For another 19 per cent it was a ladder to upward social mobility.

Although the migrants were appreciative of the schools' efforts to accommodate and support them, the picture was different when seen from the prism of the teachers and principals. As high as 82 per cent of them felt that the wide socio-economic gap between the migrant and non-migrant children posed various problems in the school environment and was a major concern for them. Interviews with other principals, teachers and the author's own experience as a principal pointed to the gap creating disciplinary and psychological problems for both groups. The prevailing tension had every possibility of widening a rift between two types of students and giving the migrant children a complex. Their social and economic disadvantages distanced them from others. They often felt alienated, even othered.

However, all the school teachers and principals interviewed mentioned that they did make extra efforts to see that no cracks appeared in the student community over the issue of social privileges. Reassuringly, 33 per cent of the respondents said that their schools provided extra coaching to the migrant children beyond school hours. And 43 per cent talked of fee concessions or other financial assistance while 21 per cent mentioned counselling by specially appointed experts.

Problems generally faced by the disadvantaged migrant children to pursue school education both at the secondary and senior secondary levels are:

- Lack of help in academics at home due to their parents' low level of education or its complete absence.
- Tuition which they required but could not afford. First, the cost of tuition is high; second, unavailability of efficient tutors in the slums where the social environment is not conducive to an academic culture. Consequently, they somehow make do with whatever assistance is available to pass their class tests. It leads to a kind of vicious cycle:

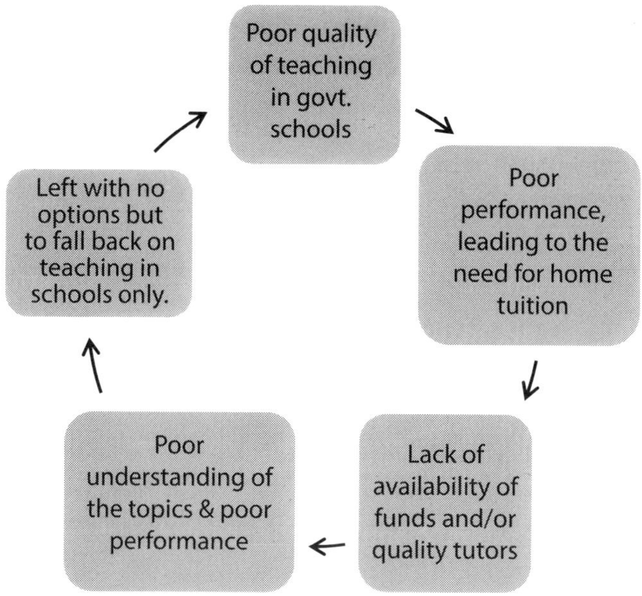

The Sakshar Bharat programme aimed at providing functional literacy to 70 million unlettered adults in the 15-35 age group, out of whom 60 million would be women, especially from the marginalized and disadvantaged sections, by 2012 (Annual Report, 2010-11, MHRD). If this programme became successful, these migrant children would have at least one literate parent at home. But the minimum literacy level does not technically empower the parents to help a child in their academic needs. While for a child from an educated middle-class home learning came as automatically as rowing for a boy growing up on the riverbank, for a migrant child it would be a steep uphill climb. Books, periodicals, dictionaries, atlases and newspapers are things the child from a middle-class home grows up with; for a migrant student such items would have to be acquired.

The 1991 economic reforms opened up the country to the rest of the world and boosted the growth of the export sector. This in turn generated a large number of jobs for skilled and trained workers in the export manufacturing sector. As Delhi's main industrial activity is textiles manufacturing, this has positively impacted the employment scenario creating more opportunities in the capital city.

Unlike the other states, Delhi does not have its rural burden as 76.2 per cent of its area is urban. The contribution of the tertiary sector to SGDP is almost 96 per cent, requiring huge manpower to feed this sector. Employment in the tertiary sector requires education, training and skill development. This has led to the realisation among the marginalized that education can give their children access to better jobs created in the tertiary sector and consequently will fetch better wages for them.

The reforms raised the wage levels of workers all over the country. The high wage rates in Delhi – higher than in the other states – spurred the inflow of migrants from UP, Bihar, Uttarakhand, Rajasthan, West Bengal and some other states. The minimum wage in Delhi for the unskilled workers is ₹203 which is much higher than the wages earned by even a skilled worker in UP (₹172.23), Bihar (₹150.80) or West Bengal (₹196.30). This trend is corroborated by the analysis of migration data contained in census reports. For example, between 1991 and 2001 there was 175.77 per cent rise in the number of migrants from Bihar to Delhi. From West Bengal it was 114.65 per cent during the same period. The massive growth of the workforce in Delhi in the post-reform period could be attributed to steady migration from the distressed parts of the country.

An analysis of the NSS data between 1993-94 and 2004-05 indicates that the economic boom following the 1991 reforms created a large number of regular jobs in the organised sector with the expansion of the services sector. This triggered a new rush to the sectors offering regular and assured wages. NSS data indicate that the number of self-employed people has been on the decline in the post-reform period. As jobs in the organised sector require trained and educated manpower, the new employment environment has induced the migrants to send their children to school.

The primary data collected for ascertaining the monthly earnings of the migrant households show that only two per cent of them have an average monthly income below ₹2000. For a substantial 44 per cent it is between ₹2001 and ₹5000 per month. Another 34 per cent earn between ₹5001 and ₹10,000 per month. Surprisingly, 20 per cent of these migrant households have a monthly income above ₹10,000. This earning was adequate enough for the migrants to meet the basic needs and gave them the cushion not to push their children into work to augment their income. With free education available in government schools they could afford their children spending the day in the classroom.

Delhi's Human Development Index is much higher than the national average and the state has always ranked among the top three. Higher wage rates have ensured better standards of living, even for the migrant workers. NFHS, 2005-06 data confirm that a significant number of slum-dwellers possess consumer durables like electric fans, televisions, refrigerators, motorcycles and so on. About 86.3 per cent of them live in their own houses.

The primers of economics tell us that a household would go for items of comforts once its basic needs are met. This includes education and healthcare for the family members. The slum community could not remain unaffected by the economic upturn in the years after the reforms. With the rise in their incomes and standards of living they could afford to spend a little on the children's education. The newly opened-up areas like call centres, retail or manufacturing export required a skilled and trained workforce. The migrants realised that with some education their children would be able to meet the new demands and earn higher wages and lead a life better than theirs. This has boosted their educational aspirations.

This study has sought to find an answer to the question raised in the sixth survey of the Educational Research: 'Can education in general and UEE in particular act as anti-poverty measure?' (Sixth Survey of Educational Research, p. 341)

The present study observed the strong possibility of raising the living standards of the impoverished slum-dwellers through the instrument of education. The migrant children were convinced that the road to school would lead them to realise their occupational aspirations. This conviction imbued them with a new optimism about scaling a new peak through the process of learning. The outcome of this journey changed mindsets and a lot about their life.

The trends are going to be strengthened in the coming years. Some of the older slum children doing undergraduate courses are hopeful of becoming part of the urban middle class with remunerative employment. The transition from the rural-migrant origins to the city-bred salaried classes has many implications. Their new status will have a direct bearing on the lives of their immediate families – parents and siblings. Importantly, 23 per cent of the disadvantaged migrants interviewed were of the view that schooling would ensure better income for their children in the future. There was a high degree of optimism that white-collar jobs would raise the families' standards of living. Even the readiness of the parents (24 per cent of the respondents) to support their children's education gave the new learners a positive push to work and earn well. Education has acted as a catalyst promising a better future and igniting the migrants' determination to earn more to support their children's studies. It has a motivational impact on the migrants' efforts to raise their present income levels.

The post-reform period has witnessed large-scale internal migration. People from the other states have been coming to Delhi due to wage differentials and job availability. A discernible change in the migration patterns has been noticed over the past two decades with the entire households moving out of the ancestral village to the city giving rise to the necessity of education for small children. The study finds that the migrants' higher levels of income and consumption compared to the situation back home have provided the basis for their determined move for a tryst with their destiny. Though limited, success has helped them see the big picture and provided the incentive for sending their children to school. In this context, the surge in the job market triggered by the processes of liberalisation, privatisation and globalisation of the 1990s has been an eye-opener for the uprooted migrant community of Delhi. They realised that better wages and living standards would only come along with education. They learnt the importance of schooling, that it was a precondition for enhancement of skills which could be the only avenue to higher wages in the tertiary sector.

The Union government's commitment to EFA by 2015 led to free and compulsory education for all children between 6 and 14 years. The initiatives taken by the Delhi government towards this goal have enabled the migrant children to pursue their education at no or almost negligible cost. Provisions of free books, uniforms and mid-day meals have acted as added incentives. The active participation of a large number of NGOs has streamlined the whole process giving the campaign an unprecedented pace and urgency. The enrolment level among the targeted groups has risen encouragingly. Unlike the past when slum-dwellers had to be persuaded to send their children to school, the push this time round has come from within. It is, therefore, more sustainable. The levels of educational aspirations for the majority of migrant children and their parents are high and so are their occupational aspirations. Despite difficulties and hardships, the migrants want to secure a better future for their children giving them both higher standards of living and a life of dignity.

7

THE FUTURE ROADMAP

On the basis of the observations during the course of the study the author would like to put forward her suggestions and recommendations which policymakers in the field of education may find useful. The author would also like to mention a few important areas which were beyond the scope of the present study but equally crucial from the viewpoint of the marginalized. Future researchers can take them up for detailed studies.

Challenges of Inclusion

The present study revealed that a majority of migrant children expected additional coaching from their teachers after regular school hours (49 per cent). This brought to the fore an acute absence of preparatory support at home and their eagerness to overcome the problem. Most of the respondents, aspirational – wanting to be doctors, engineers or teachers – did not, however, exactly know how to go about it. A significant number of them (37 per cent) expected the school to explain career prospects to them and provide adequate guidance.

Table 7.1

Children's Expectations from their School

Expects school to	% of migrant children interviewed
Provide remedial coaching beyond school hours	49
Explain career prospects and guide to reach it	37
Give financial assistance	14
Total	100

Fig 7.1 Children's expectatiions from school

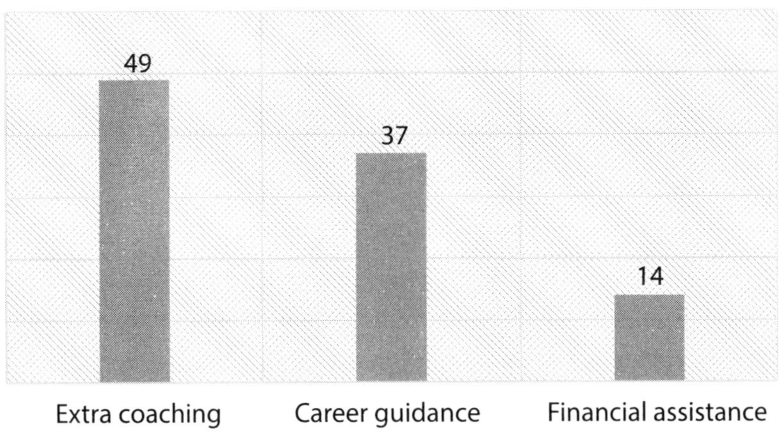

Source: Primary Data

With the government laying a big emphasis on more inclusive education today, there is a need to redraw the map to accommodate the concerns over the migrant children's education. It requires detailed data in the context of acute shortage of qualified manpower in the field of education.

The present study also shows that 85 per cent of the migrant children need extra assistance to cope with their studies. Help from parents and elder siblings is almost negligible. Hence 63 per cent of them take help from private tutors. There is an acute dearth of qualified or efficient tutors in the slums given the poor culture of education in such impoverished neighbourhoods. Moreover, there are many children who cannot afford even the pedestrian coaching centres. Fettered by such serious inadequacies, their preparations falter and exam scores remain poor.

Table 7.2

Migrant Children's Requirement for Extra Help in Studies

Responses	Percentage of migrant students
Yes	85
No	15
Total	100

Fig 7.2 Need extra help in studies?

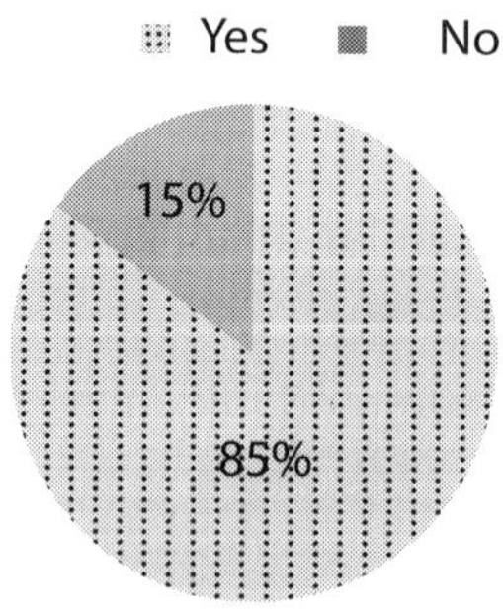

Source: Primary Data

Table 7.3

Sources of Academic Help for Migrant Children

Sources of help	% of respondents
Tuition	63
Help from parents/ Siblings	14
School gives extra coaching	09
Any other	14
Total	100

Fig 7.3 And HOW?

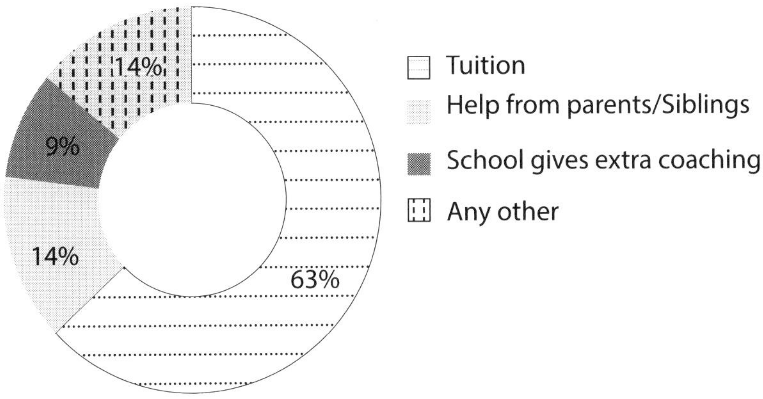

Source: Primary Data

It is possible for the government to supplement the efforts of the migrant children to perform better in exams overcoming their situations. With the participation of NGOs a programme could perhaps be launched for free study circles to support such students in the slum areas.

Besides, if the RTE proposes creation of an academic environment doing away with the need for private tuitions, the authorities should ensure that classroom teaching is adequate enough to address the needs and concerns of the first-generation literates. The level of the teachers' accountability should be linked to their promotions and increments. Heads of institutions can take up the initiative to enforce quality teaching so that the socially disadvantaged students' needs could be adequately addressed.

The teachers and principals surveyed feel that the language problem is not the only barrier to the migrants' education. They pointed to other factors as well. Of the teachers interviewed during the course of the study, 27 per cent feel that the socio-economic background is the major constraint whereas 21 per cent believe that the social gap between the migrants and non-migrants is a major issue. Only five per cent of the respondents feel that language poses a problem in learning for the migrants. But 44 per cent of the teachers think all these three factors combine to make the migrant child's learning process difficult.

Teachers' survey offered some guidelines to the challenge of integrating the distressed migrants from the slums into the mainstream. A good number of the teachers – 22 per cent – felt that the children should first be trained informally before integrating them into the mainstream. However, 63 per cent of the teachers recommended that the disadvantaged children be put directly in regular schools. The schools, they said, should take special care of the children's socio-emotional needs. A small percentage (17 per cent) of the teaching community suggested such children go to those school where pupils come from a similar background. The points need to be discussed with the other stakeholders and see if the findings can be factored into a future policy framework.

In order to popularize vocational education an initiative needs to be taken to ensure vertical growth opportunities in these areas. As suggested by many educationists, big-time employers should not look down upon the graduates from the vocational schools and polytechnics. A study can be conducted about the scope of popularizing vocational studies in school. In fact, a few organisations have already started approaching schools to run vocational courses as an outsourced programme.

A Dual Life

The social and psychological problems faced by the children from slums studying in public schools are an extremely sensitive area untouched by research so far. During the course of the present study the responses evoked from the slum children revealed a sense of humiliation because of their distressed background. A large number of them – 63 per cent – talked about nurturing an inferiority complex in the company of the children from well-off homes.

Table 7.4

Psychological Stress for Migrant Children

Feel inferior or humiliated	Percentage of migrant children
No	37
Yes, sometimes	63

Fig 7.4 Inferiority complex or humiliation?

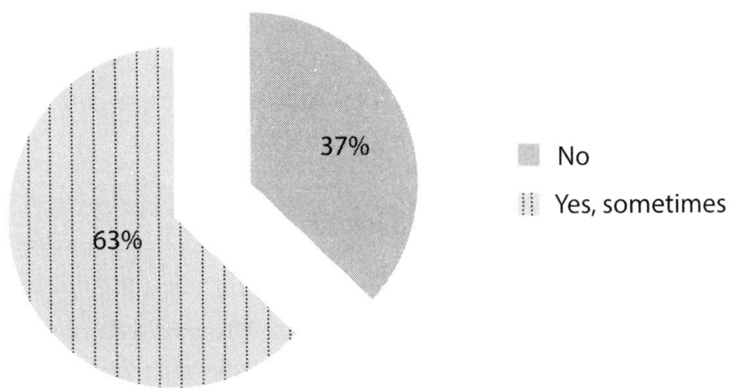

Source : Primary Data

Most of the respondents did not know how to cope with this feeling.

The author in her capacity as the principal of a school in Delhi has observed these pains and silent sufferings in children. This view was shared by the other principals interviewed by the author. After a few years in a reputed school many of these children develop an inferiority complex with respect to their parents vis-à-vis their friends'. They do not want their parents to come to the school as they feel ashamed of their status, both academic and socio-economic. It is a kind of double life that they live. Economic disparities in the two groups often lead to a kleptomaniac tendency and aggression in the underprivileged children. Most often the school authorities do not bother to orient the two socially disparate groups of children towards each other's needs and limitations. The clash of cultures traumatizes both groups and requires skillful handling on the part of the school authorities. However, in most cases the institutions are clueless about the deep-seated dichotomy. Life-skill education as introduced by the CBSE should be introduced as a way of fighting such tendencies. Teams of efficient counsellors could visit government schools regularly to assist the children. It should be mandatory for all public schools to appoint a regular counsellor for better management of children's problems.

The Task Ahead

Studies can be conducted on forced migration where people are displaced due to natural or man-made disasters or as a consequence of large-scale land acquisition for giant development projects by the government agencies. Displacement of population across international borders is a regular feature. Within a country, too, migration occurs in the aftermath of sustained violence as has been witnessed in the Kashmir Valley in the wake of the long spell of militancy, from Madurai in Tamil Nadu following caste riots. Extreme poverty and a deep sense of despondency drove thousands of people out of Bihar. As the islands in the Sundarbans delta in West Bengal are getting submerged by the rising sea as a result of climate change displaced people move to the mainland for shelter and then subsequently to Kolkata and other cities in search of livelihood. Education for the children of such internally displaced people (IDP) or internal refugees can be a major area of research. This could be an important addition to the existing volume of scholarly work to understand the phenomenon occurring across the continents.

There is scope to examine if changing social realities could make a big dent on the migrants' situation by pushing their dream for their children's education. A detailed study can be conducted about the varying responses of the cities towards the aspirations of those living in their soft underbellies.

The use of cheap and easy technology in accelerating the rate of literacy and level of education in the slums can be explored through related research. Initiatives to sensitize society to the expectations of the migrant community and their legitimate aspirations could be the subject matter of an inquiry.

The role of NGOs in taking education to shantytowns and alerting the distressed community to the possibilities and benefits of learning provides scope for a detailed study.

Future researchers can probe the scope for greater government intervention in helping the migrants climb faster up the education ladder to empowerment.

The Economist in its November 19th-25th 2011 issue wrote about the "Magic of Diasporas – How migrant business networks are reshaping the world". This can be an interesting area of research in the Indian context as a follow-up of the present study.

The problem faced by the migrant children, particularly in getting supplementary academic help, requires further investigation.

It is an imperative for the government now to take care of the education of this neglected section in a more focused manner. As the number of migrants in Delhi is rising steadily proper education and training of their children can create a vast area of trained manpower to boost the growth of the capital city. This author has observed their growing aspirations for education and better employment. Encouraged and assisted by the Government of Delhi through new initiatives, they will be able to do wonders. And returns on this investment will definitely be very high for society.

8

CONCLUSION

A deep and informed inquiry into a socio-economic development forms the basis of any future strategy and policymaking in that area. Globally a new emphasis is being laid on data collection and analysis for preparing the roadmap for every important sector. Research is now an integral part of a country's development programme. The contours of tomorrow's society are shaped by the findings of today's explorations.

This author examination over the past five years of the life of the migrant community living in the margins of Delhi society has brought out startling revelations which are very pertinent to the task of formulating the blueprint for the 21st century India. The movement of distressed households from the famished rural hinterland to the big cities at the hint of new opportunities following the economic reforms of 1991 has had many repercussions.

Living in the slums in proximity to the high-rise apartment blocks of middle-class mobility, the uprooted people realised that without skills acquired through education their children would not be able to grab the jobs made available by the opening up of many sectors of the economy hitherto protected. In the years following the New Economic Policy, literacy became a necessity for the marginalized. With their income level going up, the migrants could afford to put their children even in low-cost private schools which had English as the medium of instruction.

The present study reveals serious systemic flaws impeding and at times defeating important government initiatives. This has been acutely visible in the literacy programmes. While a successful campaign could have created enormous human resources at a cheap cost, the failure of the schooling programme only added to the dregs.

Despite such drawbacks in implementations, the stirrings on the education scene in the city's soft underbellies have raised new hope. The spinoffs of the process have far-reaching implications for the Indian economy and the nation's education scenario. Without any direct government intervention, the people who have so far been the city's faceless crowd of odd-job workers, are now a recognizable segment with definite targets and aspirations. 'A day will come,' wrote Victor Hugo, 'when there will be no battlefields but markets opening up to commerce and minds opening to ideas.' The story unfolding in the shantytowns corroborates the great French philosopher's prediction.

Surveys conducted during the course of research brought up a wealth of data suggesting a radical change in the migrant mindset about new possibilities thrown up by the structural adjustments in the economy. They began to see schooling for their children not just as something desirable but as a vehicle to ride to a better future.

An intense exploration of the social engineering process in the slums points to an exciting scenario: climbing the economic ladder to white-collar jobs and respectability, many young people in the jhuggi-jhopdi clusters subsequently merge into the city's middle-class milieu.

The picture of social mobility available through research conforms to the overall patterns of growth in the liberalised Indian economy. It also confirms the theory that churning in one part of society impacts the other segments as well. A forward movement in the social sector impacts the economy comprehensively.

'As for the future, your task is not to foresee it, but to enable it,' wrote Antoine de Saint-Exupery, the celebrated author of *Little Prince*. Those words perfectly sum up the purpose of this study.

Annexure A

Questionnaires used for the survey	page no.
Questionnaire for children	189
Questionnaire for parents	194
Questionnaire for Principals/administrators/teachers	199

Questionnaire for migrant/non-migrant children studying in classes X & XII in government/private schools to measure their educational & occupational aspirations

General Information:

1. Name: ______________________________
2. Age : ____________________ Sex : Male/Female
3. School: ______________________________
4. Class: ______________________________
5. Father's name: ______________________________
6. Occupation: ______________________________

7. Mother's name: ______________________________

8. Occupation: ______________________________

9. Monthly income of the family: ______________________________

10. Residence: ______________________________

11. Contact number (Own /PP): ______________________________

12. No. of Siblings: ______________________________

13. Year of joining the school: ______________________________

14. Previous school (if applicable): ______________________________

Specific information:

1. What is your ambition in life? (Please use the occupational aspiration checklist and rating scale) ______________________________

2. Why do you want to be this?
   a. To earn money ☐
   b. To become famous ☐
   c. To have dignity of life ☐
   d. To improve the standard of living of my family ☐

3. How have you been doing in class as far as academics are concerned
   a. Good (scoring above 60%) ☐
   b. Average (scoring between 40 & 59%) ☐
   c. Poor (scoring less than 40%) ☐

4. Do you get fee concession?
   a. Yes ☐
   b. No ☐
   c. The school provides free education to all ☐

5. How much on an average do you spend on purchase of stationery and notebooks per month?
   a. Less than Rs 100 ☐
   b. Between Rs 100 and Rs 200 ☐
   c. More than Rs 200 ☐

6. What is the medium of instruction in the school?
   a. English ☐
   b. Hindi ☐
   c. Vernacular ☐

7. Do you follow the instructions clearly in class given by the teachers?
   a. Yes, always ☐
   b. Most often ☐
   c. Sometimes ☐
   d. Never ☐

8. If not, do you think it is due to
   a. Language ☐
   b. Your family's background / cultural gap/class difference ☐
   c. Any other ☐

9. What do you expect the school to do for you in order to help you achieve your goal?
   a. To provide extra coaching after school hours ☐
   b. To explain career prospects and guide to reach it ☐
   c. To give financial assistance ☐

10. Do you need extra assistance to cope up with your studies?
    a. Yes ☐
    b. No ☐

11. If yes, how do you get it?

   a. Take tuition at home ☐
   b. Parents' help ☐
   c. School provides extra coaching ☐
   d Any other (pl. specify) ______________________________

12. Do you get enough support from your teachers?

   a. Yes ☐
   b. No ☐
   c. Sometimes ☐

13. If yes, how do they help you?

   a. By counselling ☐
   b. By taking extra care in class ☐
   c. By providing free coaching beyond school hours ☐

14. Did you ever have any feeling of humiliation/ inferiority complex/ frustration about your present situation?

   a. No ☐
   b. Yes, sometimes ☐

15. If yes, how did you overcome it?

____

____

____

16. Do your parents share your ambition?

   a. Yes ☐
   b. No ☐
   c. Can't say ☐

17. Do they meet your teachers at every PTM?

    a. Yes ☐
    b. No ☐

18. Do the teachers give necessary/actual feedback to your parents about your state of progress?

    a. Always ☐
    b. Sometimes ☐
    c. Never ☐

19. How often does the Principal meet your parents?

    a. Once in a month ☐
    b. Whenever required ☐
    c. Does not meet ☐

20. How do the school authorities respond to your parents' ambition for you?

    a. They consider it a liability for them. ☐
    b. They appreciate their concern. ☐

21. Please mention a special incident where your efforts have been appreciated by the school.

____

____

Signature of the Interviewee: ______________________

Date: __________ Place: ______________________

Questionnaire to find out the aspirations of the migrant labourers/non-migrants, how they view school education and whether they have used school education as a means to prosperity

[Note: Respondents are the parents of the children interviewed]

General Information

1. Name: ____________________ Age: ________ Sex: ___________
2. Educational qualification: ___________________________________
3. Parent of ____

   (Studying at __________________________in class_______)
4. Address:____
5. No. of members in the household: __________________________
6. No. of adults: _____M/F______ No. of children: _____M/F_________
7. Occupation: ____
8. Monthly income of the family (approx. average): ________________
9. Staying in Delhi since (year): ______________________________
10. Migrated from (State/Place): ______________________________
11. Permanent address: _______________________________________
12. Reason for migration:

    a. Prospect of better income ☐

    b. Marriage ☐

    c. Loss of property/ land ☐

    d. Natural calamity ☐

    e. Any other (specify) ☐

Specific information

1. Do you want your children/child to follow the same occupation as yours?
   - a. Yes ☐
   - b. No ☐
   - c. Can't say ☐
2. If not, then what do you think your child/children should do? (Refer to aspiration checklist):

   ____

3. Do you send them to work/take them to work along with you?
   - a. Yes ☐
   - b. No ☐
   - c. Occasionally ☐
4. Do you send your children to school?
   - a. Yes ☐
   - b. No ☐
5. What is the type of that school?
   - a. Private ☐
   - b. Government ☐

Name & address of the school: ______________________________

____

____

6. What did you consider while choosing the school?
   - a Money/ Financial cost ☐
   - b. Quality of education provided ☐
   - c. Distance ☐
   - d. Any other (specify): ______________________________

7. How do you support the educational expenses of the child?
   - a. Freeship/scholarship ☐
   - b. Can manage the fees from my income ☐
   - c. Get help from a sponsor/relative ☐
8. Up to which level do you want your child to study?
   - a. School leaving ☐
   - b Graduation ☐
   - c. Postgraduation ☐
   - d. Technical education ☐
   - e. As far as the child wants ☐
9. How long you think you can support your child's education with your own means?
   - a. Up to School level ☐
   - b. Up to college level ☐
   - c. Postgraduation level ☐
   - d. As far as the child wants to study ☐
10. Would you like your child to do some part-time odd jobs to partly support his/her educational expenses?
    - a. Yes ☐
    - b. No ☐
    - c. Only when he/she goes to high school ☐
    - d. Only when he/she passes out of school ☐
11. In what way you think the schooling of the child is essential to achieve your dream?
    - a. Education and training can change the quality of life ☐
    - b. Schooling will ensure better income for them ☐
    - c. It will open up new vistas in my child's life ☐
    - d. It is the tool to move upwards in society ☐

12. Do the school authorities cooperate with you and share your aspiration?

    a. Yes ☐ b. No ☐ c. Can't say ☐

13. If yes, how does the school help you?

    a. Gives fee concession ☐
    b. Advises correctly for child's better results ☐
    c. Provides scholarship/extra coaching ☐
    d. Does not do anything special for us ☐

14. After school where will you send your child for further studies?

    a. Formal college ☐
    b. Polytechnic schools ☐
    c. Training centres ☐

15. Have you ever thought of a non-conventional career for your child?

    a. Yes ☐
    b. No ☐

16. If yes, which area will you like your child to pursue?

    a. Sports ☐
    b. Film ☐
    c. Music ☐
    d. Any other (specify) ____________________

17. If yes what could be the reason for choosing this non-conventional career option for your child?

    a. Huge money can be earned in short time ☐
    b. Fame ☐
    c. Any other (please specify) ________________

18. Do you have any idea how much it will cost you to make your child a sportsman or a film artist or a musician?

    a. Yes ☐ b. No ☐

19. How will the family benefit from the achievements of the child?
    - a. Financially ☐
    - b. In terms of elevated social status ☐
    - c. His connections will help pull up others in the family ☐
    - d. All of the above ☐
    - e. Family does not expect anything ☐
20. Suppose the child, when starts earning, does not take care of you. How will you feel?
    - a. That is absurd ☐
    - b. I will blame my fate ☐
    - c. I am not doing things for him for any future returns ☐
    - d. I will be happy if he can lead a better life than me, no matter whether he helps the family or not ☐

Signature/ Thumb impression of the interviewee ____________________

Questionnaire for Principals/administrators/teachers to collect information with respect to educational and occupational aspirations of migrant workers in and around Delhi

The following request letter accompanied the questionnaire to teachers, Principals/ School Administrators:

Dear Administrator/ Teacher,

It has been observed that the parents from poor migrant families have been spending a significant part of their earnings on children's education in recent years, particularly after the process of economic reforms has taken roots. This survey, a part of my research project, wants to find out whether the trend is the same in Delhi and its surrounding areas.

The valuable inputs provided by you will be kept confidential and used for statistical analysis and inference only.

I thank you in anticipation for sparing your time in answering my queries.

Manimala Roy
Research scholar,
Department of Education, University of Calcutta, Kolkata
[Manimala Roy is the Principal of Basava International School, Sector 23, Dwarka, New Delhi 110 077.
Tel. 011-28051462-63, www.basavainternational.school]

General Information

Name: ____________________

Designation: ____________________

Institution (Name & address): ____________________

Total experience (no. of years) as an educationist: ____________________

Contact Numbers: ____________________

E-mail id: ____________________

Signature: ____________________

Specific information

1. Do you observe any positive change in the educational aspirations of migrant workers (semi-skilled or unskilled) in recent years?

   Yes ☐ No ☐ Can't say ☐

2. Do you receive more admission requests from this group these days as compared to requests 10 years ago?

   Yes ☐ No ☐ Can't say ☐

3. As the Head of the institution/School administrator/a teacher do you face any problem arising out of the social gap between these migrant children and the rest?

   Yes ☐ No ☐

4. What is your opinion about the effectiveness of inclusive education with respect to these children?

   a. They should be trained informally before being integrated to mainstream ☐
   b. They should be put in regular schools but special efforts to be taken to take care of their socio-emotional needs ☐
   c. It is wiser to let them study in schools where they have other children from same kind of background ☐

5. What special steps have you taken to cater to their different needs?

   a. Provide extra coaching ☐
   b. Give fee concessions and cash scholarships for brighter ones ☐
   c. Appointed a counsellor to help them settle down in school ☐
   d. Nothing very specific ☐

6. (a) Do the migrant children have any clear idea about their future course of studies/employment?

   Yes ☐ No ☐ Can't say ☐

(b) Do the non-migrant children have any clear idea about their future course of studies/employment?

Yes ☐ No ☐ Can't say ☐

7. (a) Which particular areas do the migrant students intend to pursue for future course of studies?

Science ☐ Commerce ☐ Humanities ☐
Vocational ☐

(b) Which particular area do the non-migrant students intend to pursue for future course of studies?

Science ☐ Commerce ☐ Humanities ☐
Vocational ☐

8. Do you provide vocational courses in your school? If yes, please mention the subjects: Yes ☐ No ☐

(i) Secondary level: (ii) Senior Secondary level:

9. Do you see any change in the occupational aspirations of the migrant parents for their children in recent years (after 2000)?

Yes ☐ No ☐ Can't say ☐

10. Do you think they are aware of the new types of job openings like in retail sector, call centres, travel industries and similar areas?

Yes ☐ No ☐ Can't say ☐

11. As the Head of the Institute/school administrator/teacher what do you think is the major constraint in providing education to migrants' children?

Language ☐

Their socio-economic background ☐

The social gap of these children with the rest ☐

All of the above ☐

12. Would you like to share your experience in dealing with such children in your school?

____

____

Annexure B

Scale of educational aspiration

Educational Ambition	Aspiration level	Rating scale
Eager to drop out before class X or already a drop out	Very low	1
To study up to class X	Low	2
To study up to class XII / vocational courses	Medium	3
To complete Graduation / professional degree	High	4
To complete Postgraduation	Very high	5

This educational aspiration scale was derived from the scale used by Prof. Kevin Marjoribanks of Dept. of Education, Univ. of Adelaide, Australia, in 2000 to find out the link between educational aspirations and achievements of Australian young adults (Published in International Education Journal, 2005). Educational aspirations were measured on a 5-point scale with the adolescents indicating when they planned to leave school and how much education they hoped to attain afterward.

Occupational aspiration checklist & rating scale

Kind of job aspired to	Occupational aspiration level	Rating scale
Courier service /Delivery boys	Very Low	1
Salesman/Peon/Beauty parlour job	Low	2
Travel Agency/Restaurant/ Call centres/ Lower Division Clerk / Lower level jobs in Defence/police	Medium	3
Services (Army/ Navy/Air Force officer)/Teacher	High	4
Office job in private sector/ Jobs in govt. offices/Bank/ Doctor/Engineer/Lawyer	Very high	5

Occupational checklist and rating scale was developed by Banerjee & Roy, 2010.

Annexure C

LIST OF PROMINENT NGOS WORKING FOR THE EDUCATION OF SLUM CHILDREN IN DELHI& NCR

Name	Estd	Area of operation	Mode of operation	Number of beneficiaries
Katha-Khazana	1990	Govindpuri slum	Community school	7000 children in Delhi & Arunachal Pradesh
Sankalp	1996	Gurgaon	NFE, School on wheel	More than 800 in 2010
Smile Foundation	2002	Vasant Kunj	Schools, NFE centres	244 + another 84 in queue
Deepalaya	1979	Kalkaji & Okhla	337 Educational centres including schools	50,000
Childreach International	2010	Slums of South and South West Delhi	NFE, 'My School My Voice', an interactive programme linking public school children to slum children	500
Pratham	2000	Shahdara, Karol Bagh	Interventionist approach to provide pre-school training to slum children, mobile library, remedial classes	80,000 slum children in past one decade

Name	Estd	Area of operation	Mode of operation	Number of beneficiaries
Salam Balak Trust	2002	Street children	Mobile schooling, bridge courses, shelter for homeless children	Target group: half a million street children who live in Delhi
SARD	2010	West and South West districts	PPP with MCD schools, remedial teaching	600 slum children from 20 MCD schools
NOW (New Opportunity for Women)	1990	Siddharth basti, Jeevan Nagar and Ashram slums	NFE, Adolescent girls	Currently 60 adolescent girls
Raasta	1994	East Delhi and Khora village in Ghaziabad	Remedial teaching in urban slums	7000 since its formation

Annexure D

List of pre-vocational courses offered by CBSE at secondary level (2012-13)

Trade --Code No.

1. Basic Office Procedures--- 507
2. Basic Computer Practices- --- 508
3. Basic Accountancy Procedures---------------------------------- 509
4. Fruit &Vegetable Preservation----------------------------------- 510
5. Basic Bakery--- ------------------ 511
6. Basic Confectionery-------------------------------------- ---------- 512
7. Basic Electronics-- 513
8. Airconditioning & Refrigeration--------------------------------- 514
9. Repair of Electrical Domestic Appliances---------------------- 515
10. Textile Printing Technology-------------------- ------------------ 516
11. Textile Silk Screen Printing Technology- ---------------------- 517
12. Cutting &Tailoring------------------------ ------------------------ 518
13. Skin Care & Beauty Culture--- ---------------------------------- 519
14. Automobile--- 520
15. Food Preparation & Services- ------------------------------------ 521

Source: School Curriculum, 2013, CBSE

List of vocational courses offered by CBSE at Senior Secondary level (2012-13)

Sl. No.	Name of the Course	Subject Code
1.	Office Secretary ship	
	a Office Practice and Secretary ship	604
	b Secretariat Practice & Accounting	605
	c Office Communication	606
2.	Stenography & Computer Application	
	a Typewriting (English)	607
	b Stenography (English)	608
	c Typewriting (Hindi)	609
	d Stenography (Hindi)	610
3.	Accountancy and Auditing	
	a Financial Accounting	611
	b Elements of Cost Accountancy & Auditing	612
	Additional Subject Optional	
	1. Store Accounting	
	2. Typewriting	
4.	Marketing and Salesmanship	
	a Marketing	613
	b Salesmanship	614
	c Consumer Behaviour and Protection	615
5.	Banking	
	a Cash Management and House Keeping	619
	b Lending Operations	620
	c Management of Bank Office	621

Sl. No.	Name of the Course	Subject Code
6.	Electrical Technology	
	a Engineering Science	622
	b Electrical Machines	623
	c Electrical Appliances	624
	Additional Subject Optional	
	1. Applied Physics	625
	2. Mechanical Engineering	626
7.	Automobile Technology	
	a Auto Engineering	627
	b Auto Shop Repair and Practice	628
	Additional Subject Optional	
	1. Applied Physics	625
	2. Civil Engineering	629
8.	Structure and Fabrication Technology	
	a Fabrication Technology- II	630
	b Fabrication Technology- III	631
	Additional Subject Optional	
	1. Applied Physics	625
	2. Civil Engineering	629
9.	Air Conditioning and Refrigeration Technology	
	a Air Conditioning and Refrigeration- III	632
	b Air Conditioning and Refrigeration- IV	633
	Additional Subject Optional	
	1. Applied Physics	625
	2. Civil Engineering	629

Sl. No.	Name of the Course	Subject Code
10.	Electronics Technology	
	A Electronic Devices and Circuits	634
	B Radio Engineering and Audio Systems	635
	C Television and Video Systems	636
	Additional Subject Optional	
	1. Electrical Engineering	637
	2. Civil Engineering	629
11.	Dairying	
	A Milk and Milk Products	639
	B Milk Production, Transport and Milk Cooperatives	640
	C Dairy Plant Instrumentation	641
12.	Horticulture	
	A Vegetable Culture	642
	B Floriculture	643
	C Post Harvest Technology and Preservation	644
13.	Health Care and Beauty Culture	
	A Beauty Therapy and Hair Designing - II	654
	B Cosmetic Chemistry	655
	C Yoga Anatomyand Physiology	656
14.	Ophthalmic Techniques	
	A Biology (Ophthalmic)	657
	B Optics	658
	C Ophthalmic Techniques	659
15.	Medical Laboratory Technology	
	A Laboratory Machine (Clinical Pathology, Hematology & Histopathology)	660
	B Clinical Biochemistry	661
	C Microbiology	662

Sl. No.	Name of the Course	Subject Code
16.	Auxiliary Nursing & Midwifery	
	A Fundamentals of Nursing II	663
	B Community Nursing II	664
	C Maternity & Child Health Nursing II	665
17.	X-Ray Technician	
	a Radiation Physics	666
	b Radiography I (General)	667
	c Radiography II (Special investigation, imaging and Radiography)	668
18.	Food Service & Management	
	a Advanced Food Preparation	675
	b Meal Planning & Service	676
	c Establishment & Management of Food Service Unit	677
19.	Fashion Design & Clothing Construction	
	a Textile Science	684
	b Designing & Pattern Making	685
	c Clothing Construction	686
20.	Textile Design Dyeing & Printing	
	a Textile Science	684
	b Basic Design	687
	c Dyeing & Printing	688
21.	Hotel Management and Catering Technology	
	a Food Preparation-II	690
	b Accommodation Services	691
	c Food & Beverage Service-II	692
22.	Tourism and Travel	
	a India–The Tourist Destination	693
	b Travel Trade Management	694
	c Tourism Management and Manpower Planning	695

Sl. No.	Name of the Course	Subject Code
23.	Bakery and Confectionery	
	a. Food Service & Hygiene	696
	b. Bakery Science	697
	c. Confectionery	698
24.	IT Application	
	a. IT System	699
	b. Business Data Processing	700
	c. DTP, CAD and Multimedia	701
25.	Library Management	
	a. Library Admn. & Management	702
	b. Classification and Cataloguing	703
	c. Reference Service	704
26.	Life Insurance	
	a. Principles Practice of Life Insurance	705
	b. Computer & Life Insurance Administration	706
27.	Transportation System & Management	712
28.	Poultry Farming	
	a. Poultry Nutrition & Physiology	716
	b. Poultr y Products Technology	717
	c. Poultry Diseases & theircontrol	718
29.	Financial Market Management	
	a. Accounting for Business- 1 Class XI	719
	b. Introduction to Financial Market- 1 Class XI	720
	c. Computer Applications in Financial Markets Class XI	721
	d. Accounting for Business- 2 Class XII	722
	e. Introduction to Financial Markets- 2 Class XII	723
	f. Business Process Outsourcing Skills Class XII	724

Sl. No.	Name of the Course		Subject Code
30.	Healthcare Sciences		
	a. Anatomy & Physiology	Class XI	725
	b. Health care Delivery System, Hospital Organisation and Services and Medical Equipments and Technologies	Class XI	726
	c Food Nutrition and Dietetics	Class XI	727
	d. Health Education, Communication, Public Relations and Public Health	Class XII	728
	e. Basic Concepts of Health and Disease and Medical Terminology	Class XII	729
	f. First Aid & Emergency Medical Care	Class XII	730
31.	Food Production		
	a. Food Production I	Class XI	734
	b. Food Production II	Class XI	735
	c. Food Production III	Class XII	734
	d. Food Production IV	Class XII	735
32.	Food and Beverage Services		
	a. Food Service I	Class XI	736
	b. Beverage Service I	Class XI	737
	c. Food Service II	Class XII	736
	d. Beverage Service II	Class XII	737
33.	Mass Media Studies and Media Production		
	a. Understanding the Evolution and Form of Mass Media- I	Class XI	738
	b. The Creative and Commercial Process in Mass Media- I	Class XI	739
	b. The Creative and Commercial Process in Mass Media- II	Class XII	738
	c. The Creative and Commercial Process in Mass Media- II	Class XII	739
34.	a. Geo Spatial Technology		740

Source: Senior School Curriculum, 2013, CBSE

CBSE LIST OF VOCATIONAL COURSES OFFERED FROM THE SESSION 2018-19 (CLASS IX/XI)			
Subject Code Marks distribution Theory 50 Practical 50	Name of the Vocational course under NSQF (Secondary level)		Job Roles
	CLASS (IX) (2018-19)	CLASS (X) (2019-20)	
401	Retail		Store Operations Assistant
402	Information Technology		Domestic Data Entry Operator
403	Security		Unarmed Security Guard
404	Automotive		Automotive Service Technician
405	Introduction to Financial Markets		Business Correspondent
406	Introduction to Tourism		Assistant Tour Guide
407	Beauty & Wellness		Assistant Beauty Therapist
408	Agriculture		Solanaceous Crop Cultivator
409	Food Production		Assistant Cook (reg.)
410	Front Office Operations		Front Office Executive
411	Banking & Insurance		Field Executive
412	Marketing & Sales		Marketing Assistant
413	Health Care		General Duty Assistant
414	Apparel		Hand Embroider
415	Media		Texture Artist

VOCATIONAL ELECTIVES SENIOR SECONDARY LEVEL					
S. No.	Sub Code	Course Name XI (2018-19) XII (2019-20)	Job Roles	Marks Distribution	
				Theory	Practical
1.	801	Retail	Sales Associate	60	40
2.	802	Information Technology	Domestic IT Helpdesk Assistant	60	40
3.	803	Web Application	Web Developer	60	40
4.	804	Automotive	Automotive Service Technician	60	40
5.	805	Financial Markets Management	Equity Dealer/Mutual Fund agent	60	40
6.	806	Tourism	Tour Guide	60	40
7.	807	Beauty & Wellness	Beauty Therapist	60	40
8.	808	Agriculture	Agriculture Extension worker	70	30
9.	809	Food Production	Trainee Commis	60	40
10.	810	Front Office Operations	Counter Sales Executive	60	40
11.	811	Banking	Sales Executive (Banking product)	60	40
12.	812	Marketing	Marketing Executive	60	40
13.	813	Health Care	General Duty Assistant	60	40
14.	814	Insurance	Sales Executive (Insurance)	60	40

VOCATIONAL ELECTIVES SENIOR SECONDARY LEVEL					
S.No.	**Sub Code**	**Course Name XI (2018-19) XII (2019-20)**	**Job Roles**	**Marks Distribution**	
				Theory	Practical
15.	815	X-Ray Technician	X Ray Technician	60	40
16.	816	Horticulture	Floriculturist (protected)/ Entrepreneur	60	40
17.	817	Typography & Computer Application	Executive Assistant	60	40
18.	818	Geospatial Technology	GIS operator	60	40
19.	819	Electrical Technology	Field Technician–other home	60	40
20.	820	Electronic Technology	Installation Technician	60	40
21.	821	Media	Animator	60	40
22.	822	Taxation	Assistant Tax Consultant/GST Accounts Assistant	60	40
23.	823	Cost Accounting	Jr. Accountant	60	40
24.	824	Office Procedures & Practices	Executive Assistant	60	40
25.	825	Shorthand (English)	Stenographer/Executive Assistant	60	40
26.	826	Shorthand (Hindi)	Stenographer/Executive Assistant	60	40

VOCATIONAL ELECTIVES SENIOR SECONDARY LEVEL					
S. No.	Sub Code	Course Name XI (2018-19) XII (2019-20)	Job Roles	Marks Distribution	
				Theory	Practical
27.	827	Air-conditioning & Refrigeration	Service Technician	60	40
28.	828	Medical Diagnostics	Medical Lab Technician	60	40
29.	829	Textile Design	Design Assistant (Apparel/Textile)	60	40
30.	830	Design	Assistant Designer	60	40
31.	831	Salesmanship	Sales Executive	60	40
32.	832	Music Production	Production Assistant	60	40
33.	833	Business Administration	Business Executive	70	30
34.	834	Food Nutrition & Dietetics	Assistant Dietician	70	30
35.	835	Mass Media Studies	Media Assistant	70	30
36.	836	Library & Information Science	Library Assistant	70	30
37.	837	Fashion Studies	Assistant Fashion Designer	70	30
38.	838	Applied Physics		70	30
39.	839	Applied Chemistry		70	30
40.	840	Applied Mathematics		80	20

Bibliography

Books

- Berman, Jan. *Footloose Labour: Working in India's Informal Economy*. Cambridge: Cambridge University, 1996. Best, John W. and James V. Kahn. *Research in Education*. New Delhi: PHI Learning Private Limited, 2009.
- Bhagwati, J. *India in Transition – Freeing the Economy*. Oxford: Clarendon Press, 1993.
- Bhalla, Surjeet S. (Ed.) *New Economic Policies for a new India*. Delhi: S. Chand, 2000.
- Bhaskar, Paul J. *Search of Milk and Honey*. Tamil Nadu: Peace Trust, 2002.
- Bhatnagar, Jyoti (Ed.) *Educating Immigrants*. London: Croom Helm, 1981.
- Cohen, Louis, Lawrence Manion, & Keith Morrison. *Research Methods in Education*. New York: Routledge, 2007.
- Covey, Stephen R. *The Leader in Me*, 38. UK: Simon &Schuster, 2008.

- Datt, Rudder. *India's New Economic Policy*. Delhi: S. Chand & Co, 1997.
- Dhavan, Rajeev. *Refugee Law and Policy in India*. New Delhi: PILSARC, 2004.
- Dreze, Jean and Amartya Sen. *India–Economic Development and Social Opportunity*. Delhi: Oxford University Press, 1995.
- Ferguson, George A. & Yoshio Takane. *Statistical Analysis in Psychology and Education*. New York: Mc Graw Hill, 1989.
- Friedman, Thomas, L. *The World is Flat*. USA: Farrar, Straus & Giroux, 2005.
- Garrett, Henry E. *Statistics in Psychology and Education*. Delhi: Paragon International Publishers, 2009.
- Glass, G. V. & K.D. Hopkins. *Statistical Methods in Education and Psychology*. New Jersey: Prentice Hall, 1996.
- Gopalan, S.. *Fifty Years of Indian Parliamentary Democracy: 1947-1997*. New Delhi: Lok Sabha Secretariat, 1997.
- Hicks, John, M. Mukherjee et al. *The Framework of the Indian Economy: An Introduction to Economics*. New Delhi: Oxford University Press, 1984.
- Jha, Jyotsna and Dhir Jhingran. *Elementary Education for the Poorest and other Deprived Groups*. Delhi: Manohar, 2005.
- Kamble, N.D. *Migrants in Indian Metropolis*. New Delhi: Uppal, 1982.
- Karan, A. *Politics of Population Influx and Labour Problem*. Delhi: UDH Publishers, 1986.
- Kerlinger, Fred N. and Howard B. Harcourt Publishers. Lee. *Foundations of Behavioral Research*. Fort Worth, TX : Harcourt College Publishers, 2000.
- Lipman, Pauline. *High Stakes Education: Inequality, Globalization, and Urban School Reform (Critical Social Thought)*. New York: Routledge Falmer, 2004.
- MacIver, R. M. & Charles H. Page. *Society : An Introductory Analysis*. Delhi: Macmillan India Limited, 1985.

- Madhukar, Indira (2003). *Impact of Globalisation on Education – Learning to Live Together*. Delhi: Authors' Press, 2003.
- Mangal, S. K. *Statistics in Education*. New Delhi: PHI Pvt. Ltd, 2009.
- Mehrotra, S., Panchamukhi, PR et al. *Universalizing Elementary Education in India: Uncaging the 'Tiger'*. New Delhi: Oxford University Press, 2005.
- Mehta, Arun C. *Elementary Education in India: Progress towards UEE, Analytical Report 2008-09*. New Delhi: NUEPA, 2011.
- Mishra, Lakshmi Dhar. *Anguish of the Deprived*. New Delhi: Har Anand, 1994.
- Misra, S.N. *Dynamics of Rural-Urban Migration*. Delhi: Anmol Publication, 1998.
- Myrdal, Gunnar. *Asian Drama: An Inquiry into the Poverty of Nations*. New York: Pantheon Books, 1968.
- Narasaiah, M. L. *Urbanisation and Child Labour*. New Delhi: Discovery Publishing House, 2005.
- Neetha, N. *Migration, Social Networking and Employment*. Noida: V.V. Giri National Labour Institute, 2003.
- Office of the Registrar General, India. *Handbook on Census and Vital statistics, 2011*. New Delhi: GoI, 2010.
- Pandey, V. C. (Ed.) *Education and Globalization*. Delhi: Kalpaz, 2001.
- Prashant Panijar, Smita. *Locked Homes Empty Schools: The Impact of Distress Seasonal Migration on the Rural Poor*. New Delhi: Zubaan, 2007.
- Planning Commission. *Towards Faster and More Inclusive Growth: An Approach to 11th Five Year Plan*. New Delhi: Planning Commission, GoI, 2006.
- Reddy, Adinarayan. *Project on migrant workers*. New Delhi: NHRC, 2008.
- Sami, Bernard D. *Indian migrant domestic workers*. Chennai: Migrant Forum, 2002.

- Sandbergen, L. S. *Women and Seasonal Labour Migration.* New Delhi: Sage, 1995.
- Singh, M. S. *New Trends in Education.* New Delhi: Adhyayan Publishers & Distributors, 2007.
- Singh, R. P. *Non-formal Education – An Alternate Approach.* New Delhi: Sterling Publishers Private Limited, 1987.
- Tripathi, S. N. *Migrant Child Labour in India.* New Delhi: Mohit Publications, 1997.
- Velde, Dirk William. *Globalization and Education: What do the Trade, Investment & Migration Literature tell us?* London: Overseas Development Institution, 2005.
- Weiner, Myron. *Sons of the Soil: Migration and Ethnic Conflict in India.* Delhi: Oxford University Press, 1978.

Articles, Journals & Reports

- Anderson, Kurt. 'The Protester - Cover story.' *Time,* 14 December 2011. http://content.time.com/time/specials/packages/article/0,28804,2101745_2102132_2102373,00.html
- Anonymous. 'The Unique Elementary School experience of Migrant Children: Common Difficulties that Teachers and School Administrators Perceive Migrant Children to Encounter.' 1998. Retrieved from http://www2.dickinson.edu/departments/amos/mosaic98/rinehart1.htm
- Banerjee, Manjistha. 'Provision of Basic Services in the Slums and Resettlement Colonies of Delhi.' *Institute of Social Studies Trust,* 2005.
- CBSE Secondary School Curriculum, 2011, 2012 & 2013. *CBSE.*
- CBSE Senior School Curriculum, 2011, 2012 & 2013. *CBSE.*
- Census of China, 2000.
- Census of India – Metadata and Brief Highlights on Slum Population, 2011.
- Census of India, 1991.
- Census of India, 2001, Data for Delhi.

- Census of India, 2001.
- Census of India, 2011.
- Centre for Civil society. 'Survey Report.' *Business Standard*, 8 September 2008.
- Centre for Civil Society Journals.
- Chauhan, Chetan. Article in the *Hindustan Times*, 15 January 2009.
- Chugh, Dr Sunita and Y.P. Aggarwal. 'Learning achievement of slum children in Delhi.' Occasional paper, NUEPA, 2003.
- Deepalaya News, Vol. xvii, Deepalaya Human Resource Centre.
- Department of Education, MHRD. 'National Policy on Education, 1968.' *MHRD, GoI.*
- Department of Education, MHRD. 'National Policy on Education, 1986, (Modified in 1992) Part II.' *MHRD, GoI*, 1998.
- Department of School Education and Literacy. 'Saakshar Bharat.' *MHRD, GoI*, 2009.
- Department of Women and Child Development, MHRD. 'The Indian Child: A Profile. *MHRD, GoI*, 2002.
- Devi, P. Ambiga, K.T. Geetha, and K.R. Gomathi. 'Rural out-migration: Two group discriminant analysis.' *Social Change*, Vol 39 (1), March 2009, pp. 85-101.
- Directorate of Economics and Statistics, Government of NCT of Delhi. 'NSS 64th Round, state sample, July, 2007-June, 2008.' Government of NCT of Delhi, 2010.
- Economic Survey of Delhi 2008-2009.
- Economic Survey of Delhi, 2001-02.
- Economic Survey of Delhi, 2005-06, Tables 3.4, 3.6 (1)
- Economic Survey, 1991-92.
- Economic Survey, 2000-2001.
- Economic Survey 2007-08.
- Economic Survey, 2009-10.
- Economic Survey, 2010-11.

- Fuligni, Andrew J. 'The Academic Achievement of Adolescents from Immigrant Families: The Roles of Family Background, Attitudes, and Behaviour.' *Child Development*, 68(2), 1997, pp. 351-63.
- Govinda, R. 'Putting schooling to test.' *The Indian Express,* 26 April 2011.
- Govinda, R. (Ed.) 'India Education Report,' *pp. 60-66. NUEPA*, 2002.
- Gupta, Soumya. 'Overview of School Education in Delhi. Research internship paper,' 2003, *Centre for Civil Society*. Retrieved from www.ccsindia.org .
- Herzog-Punzenberger and Angela Wroblewski. 'Country background report provided by Austria to the OECD thematic review on migrant education.' January 2009. Retrieved from http://www.oecd.org/education/educationeconomyandsociety/42485003.pdf
- Household Child Census. *MHRD*, 2009.
- Industrial Policy of Delhi, 2011-2021. Department of Industries, Government of NCT of Delhi.
- Institute of Applied Manpower Research. 'Manpower Profile: India Yearbook, 2009.' IAMR, 2009.
- Institute of Human Development, Delhi. 'A study on migrants in Delhi.' *Frontline,* Vol. 22(22), 2005.
- Jacob, Mani. 'Editorial notes on HRD Action Plan for 100 Days.' *New Frontiers in Education,* Vol. 42 (3), July-September 2009, pp. 249-60.
- Kumar, Ashok (2004). 'Socio-economic Conditions of Migrants with Special reference to Weaker Section in Delhi: A Geographical analysis.' Research Abstract, Jamia Millia Islamia, Delhi, 2004. Retrieved from http://old.jmi.ac.in/2000/Research/ab2004_geography_ashokkumar.html
- Leaders. 'India's economy: One more push.' *The Economist*, 21 July 2011.
- Marjoribanks, Kevin. 'Family background, adolescents' educational aspirations and Australian young adults' educational attainments.' *International Education Journal*, 2005, 6(1), 104-12.

- McCarthy, Kristin. 'Adaptation of Immigrant Children to the United States: A Review of the Literature,' Working paper no. 98-103, Centre for Research on Child Wellbeing, Princeton University, USA. Retrieved from www.crcw.princeton.edu.pdf
- Mehta, Arun C. 'Elementary Education in India: Where Do We Stand?' District Report Cards 2008-09, Volume II, *NUEPA*, 2011.
- Mehta, Arun C. 'Elementary Education in India: Where Do We Stand?' District Report Cards 2009-10, Volume I & Volume II, *NUEPA*, 2012.
- MHRD (1993-94). 'Development of Education in India.' *MHRD, GoI.*
- MHRD (2004-05). 'Selected Educational Statistics.' *MHRD, GoI.*
- MHRD (2010-11). 'The Annual Report, 2010-11.' *MHRD, GoI.*
- Ministry of labour and employment . '*Minimum Wages Act, 1948.*' *Delhi: GoI.*
- Ministry of Law and Justice (Legislative Department) (27 August 2009). The Gazette of India, Part II. The Right of Children to Free and Compulsory Education Act, 2009, No. 35 of 2009. *Delhi: GoI.*
- Ministry of Statistics and Programme Implementation, GoI (2007). 'NSS Report No. 534: Some characteristics of urban slums, 2008-09.' Delhi: GoI.
- Ministry of Statistics and Programme Implementation, GoI (2007). 'NSS Report No. 520: Employment and Unemployment situations in cities and towns of India, 2004-05.' Delhi: GoI.
- Ministry of Women and Child Development (2009). 'Annual Report, 2008-09.' New Delhi: GoI.
- Mishra, Pratibha J. 'A Study of Sources and mechanism leading to empowerment of women living in certain slum areas in New Delhi.' *Discovery*, Vol 4, No. 10, April 2013.
- Mukherjee, Pranab. 'Budget 2011-12: Speech of Pranab Mukherjee, Minister of Finance.' GoI.
- National Family Health Survey 3 (NFHS3), 2005-06.
- NCERT (2000). National Curriculum Framework, 2000. *NCERT.*
- NCERT (2005). National Curriculum Framework, 2005. *NCERT.*

- NCERT (2007). 'Sixth Survey of Educational Research, 1993-2000.' Volume II, pp.341-345. NCERT Publication Department.
- NESSE (2008). 'Education and Migration – Strategies for integrating migrant children in European schools and societies.' Retrieved from http://www.nesse.fr/nesse/activities/reports/activities/reports/education-and-migration-pdf
- NUEPA (2011). 'Elementary Education in India: Progress towards UEE, Flash statistics.' NUEPA.
- Pal, Ruby. 'Enlightenment through education: the care of the children of domestic helps of Kolkata.' *Journal of Social and Economic Development,* Vol 12(2), 2010, pp. 12-25.
- Petchot, Kamonwan. 'Right to Education for migrant children in Thailand.' Research paper at the Institute of Social studies, Hague, Netherlands, 2011. Retrieved from http://oaithesis.eur.nl/ir/repub/asset/10820/SB1126_RP.pdf
- Planning Commission of India (2008). *Eleventh Five Year Plan, Vol. 2.* New Delhi: OUP.
- Planning Commission, Government of India. Approach paper, 11th Five Year Plan. New Delhi : OUP.
- Priyadarshi, Manish (2008). 'Sustainability Index and Low Wage Migration – A case study of Delhi slums.' JNU research paper, 2008. Retrieved from www.young-demography.org/.../M_**Priyadarshi**_Nuremberg_20081
- R. Kumar, S. Kumar and Anurag. 'Regional Dimension in Disparities in Slum Literacy in India.' *Research and Practice in Social Sciences,* 2(2), 2007, pp. 103-123.
- 'Report of the Ninth Meeting of the High-Level Group on Education For All', 23-25 February 2010. Addis Ababa, Ethiopia. Retrieved from http://unesdoc.unesco.org/images/0019/001901/190131e.pdf
- Sagar, K. V. 'Globalisation of Education.' 23 September 2005. Retrieved from www.countercurrents.org
- Staff Reporter. 'MCD keen to replicate Tigri slum development project.' *The Hindu,* 22 April 2002.

- Sundaram, Manu. 'Education Policies for the most disadvantaged: Lessons from the Indian urban poor.' 13 August 2009. Retrieved from http://asiapacific.anu.edu.au/blogs/southasiamasala/2009/08/13/education-policies-for-the-most-disadvantaged-lessons-from-the-indian-urban-poor
- Swad, Jon and Rao, Nitya. 'A briefing for Migration DRC.' Sussex Centre for Migration Research.
- *The Indian Express*, 30 March 2011.
- The National Policy on Education, 1986.
- The National Policy on Education, 1992.
- The Planning Commission (2002). 'National Human Development Report, 2001,' p. 146, Table 2.1. Planning Commission, GoI.
- The Planning Commission. 'India Human Development Report, 2011.' Planning Commission, GoI.
- The Planning Commission. 'Tenth Five Year Plan.' Planning Commission, GoI.
- The Probe Team. 'Public Report on Basic Education in India.' Delhi: OUP, 1999.
- *The Times of India*, e-paper, 21 January 2011.
- Tilak, J.B.G. 'Approach to Education in the Twelfth Five Year Plan.' *India Education Review (http://www.indiaeducationreview.com).*
- Tooley & Nixon (2005). 'Private Education is Good for the Poor: A Study of Private Schools Serving the Poor in Low-Income Countries.' Retrieved from http://www.cato.org/pubs/wtpapers/tooley.pdf
- Tsujita, Yuko (2011). 'Migration and Child Schooling: A Study of Delhi Slum Households.' Paper presented at Global Conclave of Young Scholars of Indian Education, January 2011. New Delhi: NUEPA.
- UEE Mission (2009). 'SSA Report.' Delhi: Government of NCT of Delhi.
- UN Press release. 'UN Statistics show migration as a dynamic and diversifying force in global development.' Retrieved from https://www.un.org/migration/presskit/pressrelease12sept.pdf

- UNDP. 'Human Development Report, 1990.' Delhi: OUP.
- UNDP. 'Human Development Report, 1996.' Delhi: OUP.
- UNDP. 'Human Development Report, 2009.' New York: Palgrave Macmillan Houndmills.
- UNICEF. 'The State of the World's Children.' 2000.
- UNESCO. 'Convention agenda paper.' 11th General Conference, 1960.
- UNESCO. 'Convention Against Discrimination in Education, Agenda paper ED/2003/CONV/H/1.' page 3. Retrieved from www.unesco.org on 19 December 2010.
- UNESCO. 'Impact of Global Migration on the Education of Young Children, Policy Brief on Early Childhood.' April-September, 2008.
- UNICEF. 'Defining Quality in Education' – a UNICEF paper presented at the meeting of The International Working Group on Education. Florence, Italy, June 2000. Retrieved from http://www.unicef.org/education/files/QualityEducation.PDF on 7 June 2012.
- Watkins, Kevin. 'The Oxfam Education Report.' pp. 273-74. Oxfam GB, 2001.

Websites

- http://arpaneducation.com
- http://dda.org.in
- http://education.nic.in
- http://iej.cjb.net
- http://www.chintan-india.org
- http://www.deepalaya.org
- http://www.delhiplanning.nic.in
- http://www.ohchr.org
- www.academia.edu
- www.answers.com
- www.cbse.nic
- www.deepalaya.org

- www.education.stateuniversity.com
- www.edudel.nic.in
- www.indiaonlinepages.com
- www.jstor.org
- www.labourbureau.nic.in
- www.livemint.com (e-paper)
- www.mapsofindia.org
- www.mhrd.gov.in
- www.migrationdrc.org
- www.ministryoflabour.nic
- www.paycheck.in
- www.ssa.nic.in
- ww.thehindu.com
- www.un.org
- www.unesco.org
- www.yamunagentlyweeps.com

Acknowledgements

At the end, every journey is the sum total of support, good wishes, camaraderie, commiseration and appreciation of fellow travellers and those one has taken the road to reach out to.

Vice-Chancellor Suranjan Das and Pro-Vice-Chancellor Dhrubojyoti Chattopadhyay of the University of Calcutta extended all cooperation when I joined the University's PhD programme in 2009.

That I could complete my doctoral thesis, tough because of its challenging nature and difficult owing to my other responsibilities was solely because of the unstinted support and encouragement of Prof Mita Banerjee, my research guide and mentor, an exacting but empathetic taskmaster.

Dr P.R. Panchamukhi, Professor Emeritus and Founder Director, Centre for Multi-Disciplinary Research (CMDR), Dharwad, Prof Dulal Goldar, former principal of Delhi College of Engineering, Dr V. R. Panchamukhi, former Chairman, Indian Council of Social Science Research (ICSSR), New Delhi, and Dr Bibek Debroy, former Consultant to the Department of Economic Affairs of the Finance Ministry, Government of India, spent their valuable time going through my questionnaires for the project. I am thankful to them.

Dr D.S. Thakur of the NUEPA library dug out every document required. The library staff of the India International Centre, New Delhi, was helpful, as usual.

Dr U.N.B. Rao, Chairman, Urvi Vikram Charitable Trust, Delhi, extended his valuable support. I am also thankful to Dr. K.K. Varma of Childreach International for assistance in data collection.

I am ever grateful to Mrs Poornima Ambli, General Manager, Basava International School, New Delhi, for accommodating the exigencies of my study. She was both supportive and understanding. I am thankful to my team of teachers at Basava. Efficient and enthusiastic caregivers, they have always been my pillars of strength.

I am particularly indebted to K.P.R. Nair, MD, Konark Publishers, for his support and encouragement. I thank Mr Nair for launching me as an author. Coordinating Editor Jiza Joy and Editorial Associate Lekshmi Parameswaran at Konark were always ready to help and guide me during the process of publishing the book.

At this moment, I particularly remember my father-in-law, the late Sachchidananda De Roy. Himself a well-known education administrator, he gave me the vision for working in the field of inclusive education. Another person who believed in my work – again no longer with us – was my father Jiban Saha, himself the author of an acclaimed encyclopaedic volume on remarkable women from around the world. Both would have been very happy to see this book published. And a very special thank you to Protiti for teaching her mother APA and footnoting. Of course, I owe a lot to Bhaskar, my husband, for this book to happen. My mother, Pratima Saha, and two brothers, Apurba and Anjan, were a constant source of encouragement during the years of my work. Thanks to Naman, the latest member of our family, for keeping my spirit high with his sense of humour whenever I thought I won't be able to finish writing this book.

The greatest motivation, however, came from those slum children who seeing me in a dingy lane between two rows of rabbit-warrens would say, '*Woh madam phir aa gayi* (that lady is here again).'

Manimala Roy

Index

Aarohan 78
Absenteeism 116
Accountability 26, 68, 179
Alternative Innovative Education (AIE) centres 71, 73
Anandadaayi Kaksha 78
Anganwaris 77
Arpan 79
Aspiration(s)
  education 20, 41, 184
  educational 14, 16–17, 40, 68, 88, 92–94, 97, 104–05, 106, 112–13, 118–19, 127, 147, 161, 164–65, 167, 174–75
  migrants' 2, 68, 79, 92–93, 105, 113, 134, 164
  occupational 88, 92–94, 98, 104–05, 114–15, 119, 164–65, 174–75
  parental 108
ASSOCHAM 14

Backwardness 10
Balwaris 77
Building as Learning Aid (BaLA) 71–73
Burkina Faso 66
Business and Knowledge Process Outsourcing (BPO & KPO) 63

Cantonment Board 15
Capital
  foreign 9, 12
  human 7, 10
  investment 13
  national 1, 20, 23, 89, 100
  physical 7
Career
  choice 137
  guidance 177
Census of India 13, 23, 45, 46–49, 65, 89, 91
Central Board of Secondary Education (CBSE) 28, 38, 98, 123, 135, 139, 169, 182
Central Public Works Department (CPWD) 15
Centre for Civil Society 28–29
Centre for Global Development Research (CGDR) 16
Chalta Firta (mobile) Schools 71–73
Child/Children
  deprived 25, 68
  disadvantaged 5, 10, 26–27, 29, 36, 38, 68, 73, 118, 165, 170, 180
  educational achievements of 23

education for 2, 12, 14–15, 19, 23, 71, 79, 83–84, 87, 106, 110–11, 130, 159, 161, 164–65, 167, 173–74, 177, 183
EWS 26, 34, 122, 166
expectations 167–77
from poor migrant 23
health facilities to 76
living in slums 39, 124
marginalised 25, 40
needs of 37
never-enrolled 6
non-migrant 104
nowhere 6
of migrant labourers/workers 68, 92, 116, 134
of sex workers 68
out-of-school 6, 22–24, 26, 65–69, 71–73, 77, 111, 116–19, 123, 166
schooling 12
slum 26–27, 40, 69–70, 73–80, 116, 128, 166–67, 174, 181
street 68, 77–78
underprivileged 35, 75, 77, 116–17, 182
unschooled 22
urban 25, 68, 71
workers 6
working 68
young 14, 73

Child Reach International (CRI) 76–77
Cluster Resource Centre (CRC) 25, 71
Coaching 70, 78, 85, 140–41, 145–47, 166, 169–70, 176–79
Commonwealth education conference 7
Commonwealth Games 48–49, 63
Community Leaders' Training 71
Computer Aided Learning (CAL) 71
Computer education 70
Confederation of Indian Industry (CII) 139
Continuous and Comprehensive Evaluation (CCE) 123
Correspondence courses 70, 159
Counselling 140–41, 169–70
Credit Guarantee Fund 11
Culture 18, 27, 30, 48–49, 50, 83, 171, 178
clash 18, 27
cosmopolitan 48
public-school 49

Dakhila Abhiyan 69, 117
Data
analyses of 100–101, 119–20
migration 91, 121, 151, 172
non-availability of 121
primary 24, 100–103, 106–16, 123–24, 130–33, 135–38, 140–47, 149, 159–60, 166, 173, 177–79, 181
time series 167
unavailability of 121
Death rate 45
Decentralisation 18, 28
Deepalaya 13, 19, 76
Delhi
migrants in 90–91, 131, 151, 156–57, 166, 184
per capita income 11–12, 149
population in 15, 23, 44, 46–48, 90, 92, 94, 151
slum literacy in 127, 129
slum population in 15, 23, 48, 64
slums of 23, 40, 52, 91–92, 94, 99, 118, 161, 165
Delhi Commission of Protection of Child Rights 24
Delhi Development Authority (DDA) 15, 43, 62–63
Delhi Directorate of Education (DDE) 25–26, 28–29, 34, 40, 68–71, 73, 98, 117, 120–22, 123, 135, 166, 168
Delhi Jal Board (DJB) 15
Delhi Urban Shelter Improvement

Board (DUSIB) 14, 15, 99
Deprivation 8, 80
Developed countries 17
Developing countries 17, 28
Disadvantaged groups 4, 25, 36, 40
Discrimination 22, 36, 84, 153
District Information System for Education (DISE) 40, 61, 72, 98, 121
District Primary Education Programme (DPEP) 5
Drinking water 45, 90

Early Childhood Care and Education Centres (ECCEC) 71
Economically Weaker Section (EWS) 14, 26, 34, 40, 69, 120–22, 166
Economic
  development 4, 185
  growth 3, 7, 151, 156, 161
  liberalisation 4, 11, 17, 87, 169
  opportunities 4, 13, 80
  reforms 3–4, 8, 13, 29, 91–92, 94, 147–48, 150, 172, 185
Economic Survey(s) 9, 12, 46, 50, 54, 61, 91, 150–52
Economy 7–10, 12–13, 18–20, 29, 64–65, 88, 115, 163, 186–87
Education
  access to 16, 24, 31, 35, 39
  aspirations for 20, 41, 184
  basic 5, 8, 71
  children's 14, 19, 79, 83–84, 87, 106, 110–11, 130, 159, 164–65, 167, 173–74, 177, 183
  cost of 28, 70, 130
  dropout(s) 5–6, 67, 69, 74, 77, 117, 165
  elementary 5, 11, 31–33, 38, 67, 116
  free and compulsory 11, 26, 31–32, 65, 110, 116, 166, 173, 175
  importance of 7, 36
  inclusive 34, 177
  non-formal 65, 72–73, 117
  primary 5, 28–29
  proper 12, 184
  quality concern in 11, 15, 26–27, 36–37, 70, 164, 166
  retention 5, 38, 67
  right to 22, 65
  role of 2–5, 7
  school 8, 11, 19, 33, 164, 170
  secondary 35, 68
  sustainable 76, 83
  vocational 93, 134, 168, 180
  vocationalisaton of 35
Educational
  achievements 4, 23, 88
  aspirations 88, 97, 104, 164
  initiatives 37, 72
  planning 35–36, 72
Education for All (EFA) 6, 22, 30, 34, 66, 175
Education for All (EFA) Global Monitoring Report (EFAGMR) 66
E-governance 71
Ek Din Swadeshi 77
Employment 7, 10, 13, 16, 23, 30, 35, 52–54, 59, 63, 71, 73, 79, 88, 101, 118, 150–53, 156, 161, 172–74, 184
  growth 59, 151
  rate 5, 54, 59
  subsidiary 79, 118
Empowerment 3, 5, 60, 74, 83, 183
Enrolment 5, 24, 26, 35, 40, 61, 92–93, 120–25, 127, 134, 166–67, 175

Faridabad 44, 48, 62

GDP 7, 46, 53, 63, 156
Ghaziabad 44, 47, 62, 79
Girl(s) 16, 26, 57, 60, 66, 68, 70–71, 75–76, 78, 82, 84–85, 93, 104, 128, 159
Globalisation 9, 12, 20, 63, 87, 175

Government of Delhi 24, 29, 34, 44, 64, 68–69, 119, 184
Government of India 5–7, 10, 12, 31–32, 35, 38, 43, 60, 66–68, 153–54, 175
Government schools 19, 26–28, 37, 50, 70, 72, 82, 109, 116–17, 124–26, 134–35, 139, 166–67, 173, 182
Grant-in-aid 29, 34
Gross Enrollment Ratio (GER) 24, 57, 59
Gurgaon 44, 48, 62, 74–75

Head of the School (HOS) 117
Head teachers 32, 94, 97, 112, 138
Health/Healthcare 12, 16, 39, 158, 173
Hostel 71
Household(s)
  migrant 23, 149, 173
  poor 6, 10, 27
Housewife 102
Housing, subsidised 66
Human
  development 2–3, 17, 61
  insecurity 7–8
  -rights violations 62
Human Development Index (HDI) 3, 61, 156–57, 173
Human Development Report (HDR) 3–4, 6, 8, 10, 12, 16–17, 54, 61, 120–21, 148, 154, 156, 166
Humiliation 9, 181

In-charge of the school 32
Income 10, 156
  higher 16, 148
  per capita 11–12, 45, 46, 149
India
  economic reforms in 3, 8, 37
  population 13, 40
  rural 35, 77
India Education Report (IER) 117
Indian government 20, 65, 87
Industrial
  growth 30
  progress 29, 62
Industrialisation 48
Industrial Training Centres (ITCs) 139
Industrial Training Institutes (ITIs) 139
Industry(ies) 9, 13, 39, 51–52, 63–64, 153, 154
Infant Mortality Rate (IMR) 45–46, 54
Information and Communication Technology (ICT) 35, 76, 117, 123
Information Technology (IT) 10, 63–64
Infrastructure 7, 13, 26–27, 33, 37, 39, 62, 75, 90, 116
Internally displaced people (IDP) 183
International Centre for Women and Child 119
International Monetary Fund (IMF) 9–10
Invigorator Development Research and Action 119

Jawahar Navodaya Vidyalayas 25
Jhuggi-jhopdi (JJ) cluster/Colonies 1, 14–15, 23, 62–63, 65–66, 70, 83, 86–87, 96, 103, 186
Job(s)
  higher-paying 11, 18
  opportunities 10, 13, 50, 115, 150, 156, 159, 161
  white-collar 5, 16, 19, 84, 165, 174, 186
Juvenile delinquents 68

Kasturba Gandhi Balika Vidyalaya (KGVB) Scheme 5, 71
Katha 83
Katha Khazana 74, 83, 117
Kendriya Vidyalayas 25
Khul Ja Sim Sim 71–73

Kolkata 44, 65, 183

Labour/labourer
- affordable 65
- casual 153
- cheap 62, 65
- force 58
- market 18
- migrant 64, 92, 97
- migration/movement of 13
- skilled 102
- unskilled 102

Land & Development Office (L&DO) 15
Language 19, 49–51, 79, 131–33, 167–68, 180
- Bengali 50
- English 12, 18–19, 26–28, 49–51, 78–79, 87–88, 96, 131–32, 167, 186
- Hindi 19, 49–51, 85, 96, 131–32, 134, 167
- *Hinglish** 49
- Maithili 50
- Malayalam 50
- mother tongue 37, 49–50, 131
- Punjabi 49, 50
- Tamil 50, 89, 182

Learning centres 73, 77
Liberalisation 4, 9, 11, 17, 20, 87, 152, 169, 175
License-permit raj 8–9, 29
Life skills programme 72
Literacy
- female 53, 56, 59
- non-slum 65, 128–29
- rate 4, 45–46, 53, 56, 60, 65, 118, 127
- slum 65, 127–29, 167

Lok Jumbish 5

Market 4–5, 12, 18, 27, 74, 148, 165, 175
Master Plan of Delhi 2010 (MPD 2010) 63
Mid-Day Meal Scheme (MDMS) 5, 70
Migrant child/children
- academic help for 179
- academic performance of 123–24, 166
- course preference of 136
- expenditure on stationery by 130–31
- impoverished 124
- medium of instruction for 132
- parental support to 130
- requirement 178

Migrant(s)
- aspirations of 2, 68, 92–93, 105, 113, 164
- attitude of 15
- awareness 115–16
- children's schooling 12
- community 5, 15, 20, 24, 28, 87, 175, 183, 185
- disadvantaged 29, 38, 165, 170
- educated 147
- families 14, 33, 83, 165
- first-generation 23, 166
- flow of 90
- HDI for 61
- households 23, 149, 173
- income of households 149
- internal 17, 148
- marginalised 90–91
- poor 19, 23, 26, 39–40, 52, 94, 121
- population 17, 24, 48, 88, 92, 151
- rural 13
- seasonal 16, 17
- second-generation 23
- skilled 147
- underprivileged 62, 121, 161
- women 14
- workers 2, 10, 13, 19, 28, 59, 64–65, 68, 74, 86–87, 110, 113, 116, 129, 134, 161, 173

Migration

causes of 100–101, 163
education and 14
impact of 17
internal 88, 89, 99, 148, 175
international 88
labour/labourers 13
patterns 14, 175
phenomenon of 17
post-reform trends in 64
rural-urban 13, 19, 64
seasonal 17
Millennium Development Goals 39
Minimum Wages Act, 1948 153
Ministry of Human Resource Development (MHRD) 7, 29, 31, 60, 98, 171
Ministry of Labour 98, 153, 154
Ministry of Urban Development 43
Minority(ies) 25, 35, 70–71, 121
education 71
groups 25
Mobile
learning centres 73
schooling 75
MRTP Act 9
Multinational companies (MNCs) 19
Multi Vision Foundation 119
Mumbai 23, 44, 65
Municipal Corporation of Delhi (MCD) 15, 25, 28–29, 34, 68, 71, 76–79
Muslim(s) 50, 68, 84–85

Nai Disha 75, 119
NASDAQ Stock Market Education Award 74
National capital 1, 20, 23, 89, 100
National Capital Region (NCR) 27, 47–48, 62, 64, 68, 86, 90, 99, 117
National Capital Territory (of Delhi) (NCT) 43, 63, 80, 150
National Commission of Rural Labour (NCRL) 154
National Curriculum Framework (NCF) 36, 37, 60
National Family Health Survey (NFHS) 98, 128, 157–58, 173
National Human Development Report (NHDR) 6, 8, 12, 54, 61, 156–57
National Institute for Open Schooling (NIOS) 78
National Open School 28
National Policy on Education (NPE) 30–31, 67
National Programme of Nutritional Support to Primary Education 5
National Sample Survey (NSS) 46, 54, 150, 152–53, 173
National Sports Club of India (NSCI) 86–87, 96, 103
Natural's care 119
Nature 119
Net State Domestic Product (NSDP) 64, 148
New Delhi Municipal Corporation (NDMC) 15, 25, 28–29, 48, 68, 86–87
New Economic Policy (NEP) 8, 10–12, 19–20, 63, 87, 186
New Opportunity for Women (NOW) 75
Non-Formal Education (NFE) 73, 116–17, 165
Non-Governmental Organisations (NGOs) 18, 40, 72–79, 83, 116–19, 123, 165–66, 175, 179, 183
contributions of 116, 118
educational 73, 76, 118, 165
initiatives 40
role of 183
Non-migrants 89–90, 93–94, 96–97, 104–06, 136, 145–46, 148, 164, 168, 170, 180
Non-profit organisation 75
NPEGEL 26
NUEPA 15, 26, 40, 121
Nukkad natak 77

OBC 120–21

Occupation 98, 101–07, 112, 120
  desired 112
Organised sector 87, 152, 161, 173
Oxfam 27, 78

Parent(s)
  choosing the child's school 109
  educational qualifications 107
  illiterate 107
  literate 107, 171
  migrant 93–94, 101–02, 104, 106–11, 129, 137–38, 141–44, 159–60, 164, 166–67, 169–70
  occupational status of 102
  occupations 102
  of non-migrant children 104
  opinion on part-time odd jobs 111
Parent Teacher Meeting (PTM) 141–42, 169
Per capita
  consumption 58, 155–56
  income 11, 12, 45–46, 149
Planning Commission 5–7, 16, 35, 38, 67, 98, 150
  Eleventh Five Year Plan 5–7, 11, 23, 26, 35, 38, 67
  Tenth Five Year Plan 5–6, 11, 35, 38
  Twelfth Five Year Plan 38
Poverty 84–86, 100, 148, 174, 182
Pratham 77
Pratibha Vikas Vidyalayas 70
Pratichi Trust 8
Prayas 119
Private sector 8, 17, 29, 73, 139, 152, 161
Privatisation 9, 20, 28, 87, 152, 175
Public-private partnership 70
Public sector 152
Public Sector Undertakings (PSUs) 9
Punjab 47, 91, 151

Quality of life 7, 143–44
Quotas 9

Raasta 79
Rashtriya Madhyamik Shiksha Abhiyan (RMSA) 11, 122
Refugees 47, 49, 183
Rehabilitation 62–63, 65
Report on Access and Opening of Schools in Delhi 15
Residential Bridge Course 71, 73
Right of Children to Free and Compulsory Education Act, 2009 31
Right to
  education 12, 22, 31, 34, 65, 80
  free and compulsory education 31
  work 153
Right to Education Act (RTE Act), 2009 31–33, 65, 67–68, 80, 122, 166
R. S. Rohini Education and Charitable Society 119

Sakar Outreach 119
Sakshar Bharat programme 171
Salaam Balak Trust (SBT) 73, 77–78
Samajik Suvidha Sangam Society 24
Sampling
  method 95
  random 95–96
Samya Centre for Equity Studies 73
Sanitation 71, 90
Sankalp 74–75
SARD (Society for All Round Development) 78
Sarva Shiksha Abhiyaan (SSA) 5–6, 10–11, 15, 25–26, 38, 67, 71–72, 98, 117–18, 122
Sarvodaya Vidyalayas 29
School Audit Report 72
Schooling 6, 12, 15, 26, 29, 64–65, 67, 69–70, 72–73, 75, 77–79, 88, 101, 122, 139–40, 143–44, 169–70, 174–75, 186

benefits of 26
facilities 15, 65
formal 67, 73, 77–78, 88, 122
open 70, 78
School(s)
accessibility to 15
affordable 27
aided 25, 29, 76, 83
assessment records 123
buildings 70
composite 29
education 8, 11, 19, 33, 164, 170
English-medium 12,26,28,131,167
Hindi-medium 19, 131
infrastructure in 37
library 70
management of 71–72
MCD 25, 29, 34, 76–79
middle 7, 24
neighbourhood 31, 33, 35, 70
per capita funding of 28
primary 6, 24, 26, 28
private 18, 26–27, 29, 34, 37, 51, 61, 109, 166, 186
public 18–19, 26–29, 34, 76–77, 127, 139, 181–82
recognised 28
role of 94
types of 25
un-aided 25–26, 29, 69, 122
un-recognised 27–28
SC(s) 25, 35, 67, 120–21
Selected Educational Statistics (SES) 7
Self-employed/employment 102, 152–53
Self-esteem 77–78
Sex 45–46, 60
ratio 45, 54, 59–60
workers 68
SGDP 172
Shiksha Karmi 5
Skill 10–11, 73, 165, 172, 182
development 10–11, 73, 172
Slum Act 90
Slum children 26–27, 40, 69, 70, 73–80, 116, 128, 166–67, 174, 181
education of 26, 75
Slum clusters 24, 48
Slum dwellers 11, 24, 34, 39, 62, 65, 73, 157–58, 173–75
Slum(s)
children 26–27, 40, 69–70, 73–80, 116, 128, 166–67, 174, 181
growth of 62
list of 95
literacy 65, 127–29, 167
population 15, 23, 48, 64–65, 90, 94–95
Smile Foundation 75
Social and Rural Institutes 6
Social Enterprise Laboratory Award 74
Social
gap 145–46, 180
groups 7, 121
mobility 170, 186
responsibility 18, 78
trend 11, 147
Southasiamasala 27
South Indians 49
Special Training Centres (STCs) 117, 119, 123
Special Training Programmes 69
Standards of living 2, 20, 23, 34, 53, 88, 106, 111–12, 148, 150, 153–54, 156–57, 169, 173–75
STOP 119
ST(s) 25, 35, 68, 120–21
SUPW 70

Tamoha 119
Teacher(s) 5, 26, 32–33, 35, 37–38, 70–71, 73, 76, 82, 94, 96–97, 103, 112–16, 118, 131, 133–38, 140–42, 145–46, 165, 168–70, 176, 179–80
in-service training 71
observations 113–16, 136, 168
responses 146
support from 169

Teaching 33, 37, 53, 70, 73, 76, 78–79, 106, 116, 133, 165, 167–68, 171, 179–80
  quality of 78, 116, 171
  remedial 165
Text books 69–70, 175
The State of the World's Children, 2012: Children in an Urban World 39
Total Fertility Rate (TFR) 54, 57
Training 10, 18, 27, 32–33, 35, 40, 67, 74, 77, 88, 98, 118, 139, 143–44, 148, 165–66, 172, 184
Tuition fees 26, 29, 110, 171, 179

Unemployment 102, 150, 153
UNESCO Institute for Statistics (UIS) 66
Uniforms 69–70, 175
United Nations (UN) 3, 22, 39
  declaration of Human Rights 22
United Nations (UN) Children's Fund (UNICEF) 37, 39–40
United Nations (UN) Development Programme (UNDP) 3, 16
United Nations (UN) Educational, Scientific and Cultural Organisation (UNESCO) 22, 66
Universalisation of Elementary Education (UEE) 5–6, 15, 24, 38, 70–71, 116, 121, 174
Unorganised sectors 14, 52, 63, 65, 101, 139, 150, 152, 161, 163
Urban
  agglomeration 44, 47, 62, 89
  children 25, 68, 71
  out-of-school children 68
  poor 27, 36
Urban Resource Centres 71
Urbanisation 13, 53, 56
Urvi Vikram Charitable Trust 119
Uttar Pradesh (UP) 14, 23, 44, 49, 51–52, 61, 68, 75, 83, 85, 89, 91, 151, 154–56, 172

Vidyalaya Kalyan Samithis 72
VINYAS 73
Vocational
  courses 135, 138–40, 165, 168–69, 180
  education 93, 134, 168, 180
  guidance 70
  programmes 92, 134
  subjects 135, 139
Vote banks 62

Wage(s) 1–2, 11–12, 14, 51–52, 80, 84, 151, 153–55, 157, 163, 169, 172–75
  comparative 155
  daily 1, 11, 84, 155
  differentials 51–52, 175
  fair 153
  living 153
  minimum 11, 51, 153–54, 172
  rise in 11–12
Whole-in-the-Wall Education Ltd. 73
Women 14, 36, 53, 59–60, 65, 71, 74, 76, 83, 100–101, 117, 153, 171
  domestic helps 14, 53, 65
  empowerment 60, 74
  housemaids 14
  marginalised 76
  migrant 14
  poor 76
  urban 14
  violence against 60
  working 60
Worker(s)
  construction 52, 65, 74–75, 121
  migrant 2, 10, 13, 19, 28, 59, 64–65, 68, 74, 86–87, 110, 113, 116, 129, 134, 161, 173
  semi-skilled 5, 11, 108, 155, 163
  skilled 5, 10–11, 51–52, 65, 78, 108, 154–55, 163, 172
  unskilled 11, 51, 101, 163, 172
World Bank 7, 22, 23

YUVA 72

Zee News 23